BEYOND THE MODEL T

Henry Ford on his seventy-eighth birthday in 1941 in a wheatfield wearing a suit made of soybean fabric (188-29410).

BEYOND
THE
MODEL T

The Other Ventures of
Henry Ford

Ford R. Bryan

Wayne State University Press   Detroit   1990

94 93 92 91 90   5 4 3 2 1

Library of Congress Cataloging-in-Publication Data

Bryan, Ford R. (Ford Richardson)
    Beyond the Model T : the other ventures of Henry Ford / Ford R. Bryan.
        p. cm.
    ISBN 0-8143-2236-0.—ISBN 0-8143-2237-9 (pbk.)
    1. Ford, Henry, 1863–1947.   2. Businessmen—United States—Biography. 3. Industrialists—United States—Biography.
4. Millionaires—United States—Biography.   5. Philanthropists—United States—Biography   I. Title.
HD9710.U52F6627   1990
338.7'6292'092—dc20
[B]   89–27663
                                                              CIP

Grateful acknowledgment is made to the *Dearborn Historian* for permission to reprint "Concrete Homes for Dearborn" (vol. 24, no. 3 [1984]:87–89) as chapter 7; "Henry Ford's Experiment at Richmond Hill" (vol. 24, no. 4 [1984]:103–16) as chapter 19; and "Henry's Gasoline Rail Car" (vol. 26, no. 1 [1985]:9–11) as chapter 6.

GREAT LAKES BOOKS

Philip P. Mason, Editor
Walter P. Reuther Library, Wayne State University

Dr. Charles K. Hyde, Associate Editor
Department of History, Wayne State University

Advisory Editors

Dr. Ruth Roebke-Berens
Department of History
Northern Michigan University

Dr. Martha M. Bigelow
Director, Bureau of History
Michigan Department of State

Dr. Francis X. Blouin
Director, Bentley Historical
Library
University of Michigan

Ms. Sandra Sageser Clark
Deputy Director, Michigan
Travel Bureau
Michigan Department of Commerce

Dr. John C. Dann
Director, William L. Clements
Library
University of Michigan

Ms. Linda Downs
Curator of Education
Detroit Institute of Arts

Mr. De Witt Dykes
Department of History
Oakland University

Dr. David Halkola
Department of Sociology
Michigan Technological University

Dr. Justin L. Kestenbaum
Department of History
Michigan State University

Mr. Larry B. Massie
Allegan, Michigan

Dr. William H. Mulligan, Jr.
Mt. Pleasant, Michigan

Mr. Joseph F. Oldenburg
Assistant Director, Main Library
Detroit Public Library

Dr. Timothy J. Runyan
Department of History
Cleveland State University

Mr. Thomas Schlientz
John K. King Books
Detroit, Michigan

Dr. Stanley D. Solvick
Department of History
Wayne State University

Dr. JoEllen Vinyard
Department of History and
Philosophy
Eastern Michigan University

Mr. Arthur Woodford
St. Clair Shores Public Library
St. Clair Shores, Michigan

Dr. Barbara Woodward
Grosse Ile, Michigan

This book is dedicated to
Ford Motor Company
My employer for thirty-three years
and my benefactor for many more

CONTENTS

PREFACE

Again, as in my previous publication *The Fords of Dearborn* in 1987, a large part of the material for this book has been gathered for years from the Archives of the Henry Ford Museum and Greenfield Village at Dearborn, Michigan. These accounts were written from time to time with little thought given to combining them into a book. A few have been previously and individually published in the *Dearborn Historian*, a local Historical Commission periodical.

This volume consists of a series of articles illustrating the great diversity of enterprises pursued by Henry Ford during his long business career. Many of the projects described here were financial failures; almost all, however, were noteworthy humanitarian accomplishments. Some of the enterprises undoubt-edly helped Ford's automobile business; others could be classed as philanthropic hobbies. These projects, subsidiary to the Ford Motor Company, may more clearly express Ford's personal motives than did the Ford Motor Company itself.

This multitude of Ford exploits could not have been accomplished without the profit-making Model T automobile, which for twenty years gave Ford the means to venture as no other industrialist ever has. Almost all have been described in newspaper and magazine articles at one time or another, but it is hoped that collecting a group under one cover will show the breadth of ingenuity and the benevolent character demonstrated by Henry Ford throughout his business life.

ACKNOWLEDGMENTS

The staff of the Archives of Henry Ford Museum & Greenfield Village have made it possible for me to locate most of the information contained in this book. Without their cooperation over several years, many obscure facts would not have come to my attention. Steven K. Hamp, Director of the Archives and Library, and David L. Crippen, Curator of Research, deserve specific acknowledgment. Cynthia Read Miller, Curator of Graphics, has been especially helpful in providing photographs used in this book. Elizabeth Jordan often serves as my unofficial secretary and adviser as well as friend.

Fellow volunteers Winthrop Sears, Jr., and John W. Bennett have offered me leads to valuable materials on many occasions. And my good friend Hubert (Hub) Beudert has provided guidance on many matters pertaining to this book. Winfield Arneson, Chief Curator of the Dearborn Historical Museum, Mary MacDonald, Assistant Curator, and Donald Baut, Curator of Research, have encouraged me throughout this effort, as has my esteemed cousin Rylma I. LaChance of Dearborn, who eagerly appraises each rough draft.

I am especially grateful for the thorough editing of the manuscript by Thomas B. Seller, and for the valuable editorial advice of Anne M. G. Adamus, Managing Editor of Wayne State University Press. The steadfast encouragement of Alice Nigoghosian, Associate Director of the Press, is likewise thankfully acknowledged.

INTRODUCTION

It is said that Henry Ford was once considered a lazy farm boy who would go to great lengths to save himself from dirty, hard, physical work. He demonstrated much more initiative in this direction than the average farm boy—so much so as to vow to liberate himself, and farmers in general, from the tedium of farm work and the necessity of coping with beastly farm animals. To this end he eventually, with the encouragement of Thomas Edison, began to concentrate on the use of the gasoline engine in behalf of the farmer.

There was probably never a man more successful in meeting a preliminary goal than Henry Ford with his Model T automobile. With its success and attendant profits, Ford was in a position to launch into a multitude of projects to provide a better life for the farmer and mankind. He thus became a great demonstrator of innovative techniques that he believed would benefit humanity. He demonstrated progressive agricultural methods nearly all his adult life. He also sponsored practical educational and sociological programs from the time he could afford such costs. Some of these experimental projects were expected to be profitable; some were strictly benevolent enterprises.

Ford was wealthy enough to promote many of his avocations and hobbies on a scale where they became businesses of considerable size in themselves. Some had links with the automotive industry; some did not. The great proliferation of these activities climaxed when the Model T was at peak production and Ford was entering his sixties.

This book attempts to portray in photographs many of the personal interests of Henry Ford that are independent of or only marginal to the normal business of manufacturing automobiles. But under private ownership we find the Ford Motor Company and Henry Ford essentially one and the same. Thus the Ford Motor Company in one way or another has been involved in most of Henry Ford's major personal endeavors. Business ventures, avocations, hobbies, call them what you may—they are all demonstrations of how Henry Ford would play the game. In the end no one called him lazy.

AUTHOR'S NOTE

Several literary sources are cited repeatedly for which abbreviations or explanations are warranted. Various accessions in the Archives of the Henry Ford Museum & Greenfield Village in Dearborn, Michigan, have been used extensively for this work. In the chapter notes this archival source has been abbreviated to Archives, HMF&GV. The periodicals *Ford Times, Ford Man, Fordson Worker, Ford News,* and *D. T. & I. Railroad News* were publications of the Ford Motor Company. The frequent citations from Nevins and Hill refer to the three-volume series published by Charles Scribner's Sons in 1954, 1957, and 1962. The volume most frequently cited is the second of the series, *Ford: Expansion and Challenge—1915–1932,* abbreviated to Nevins and Hill, *Expansion and Challenge.* The generously cited book by David L. Lewis, *The Public Image of Henry Ford,* published by Wayne State University Press, is shortened to Lewis, *Public Image.*

The photographs in this book may well constitute its most valuable contribution. Unless otherwise indicated, the photographs are reproduced with the permission of Henry Ford Museum & Greenfield Village. The number after each caption identifies the picture among the more than half a million photo images in the museum's collections.

1

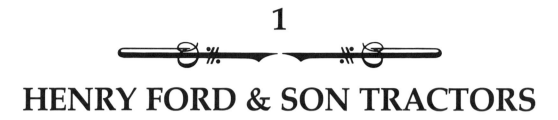

HENRY FORD & SON TRACTORS

Henry Ford is said to have been interested in farm traction engines before he was interested in motor cars. At first it was the steam traction engine that excited him in 1876 at age thirteen. However, as he grew up and planned to build engines himself, he found financial aid was more available for the building of automobiles—especially racing cars. As head of the Ford Motor Company he was experimenting with a gasoline traction engine as early as 1905,[1] and had working models built under the direction of Joseph Galamb at the Piquette plant in Detroit in 1906.[2] These he tested on the homestead property where he had grown up. But Ford Motor Company stockholders, especially the Dodge brothers, were indignant that Ford was spending company funds and workers' time on tractor experiments. As a result, Ford's tractor business became a personal endeavor, not associated with the Ford Motor Company.

By the summer of 1910 Ford had rented a large barn at 1302 Woodward Avenue at forty dollars per month, where he had six men on his payroll assembling several "traction motors" from Model T parts and special castings and wheels bought from the Russell Wheel & Foundry Company.[3] These machines he tested on his extensive Dearborn farmlands surrounding the Black farm, which he had acquired in 1909.

From 1910 to 1914 Henry and his wife, Clara, were shifting their attention from Detroit to Dearborn where they would build their new home, Fair Lane,[4] and where Henry had visions of a mammoth new engine and tractor plant on the Rouge River. To continue development of the farm tractor, a good-sized machine shop was necessary. The site chosen was in Dearborn along the south side of the Michigan Central Railroad at Elm Street. (The tall brick chimney one can now see opposite the Chicago Road House on Michigan Avenue is on that property.) This site had been the Wagner Brick Yard, and later (1923) became the Ford Engineering Laboratory. The clay dug from the earth for bricks resulted in three spring-fed ponds, two of which remain—one now a conspicuous duck refuge seen from Oakwood Boulevard.

This small parcel of land (and water) was bought from Anthony Wagner on February 8, 1913, for thirty-five hundred dollars. On the property at the time of purchase were shop buildings, some of which Ford kept intact for repairing his farm tools and implements. Many bricks in storage were used in building a 180-by-60-foot experimental machine shop. This Wagner site immediately became the center of his massive farm operations as well as tractor development.[5] At the Wagner railroad siding the

Said to be Henry Ford's first tractor, this machine powered by a 1906 Ford Model B engine carried a large water tank in place of customary radiator. This 1920 photograph was taken at the Dearborn tractor plant where Ford was accumulating historic farm machinery. (189-1131)

Henry Ford on one of his 1907 tractors with Model B engine and Model K radiator. The tank at the front holds gasoline. Note the Model K Ford in the barn in the background (13773).

stone for Fair Lane was unloaded, and a large grain elevator would soon be built.

During 1914 and the summer of 1915 experimental T-powered tractors worked the Ford lands. The Ford family moved into the Ten Eyck home at Dearborn in early 1915, and Henry supervised the experimental shop activities at the Wagner site with Jimmy Smith as an assistant. The latest Ford (Model T) tractor was demonstrated at the Michigan State Fair in September, and Ford was almost ready to move forward toward production.[6] Already the October 8, 1915, *Dearborn Independent* was announcing:

> The Ford Farm Tractor will be manufactured in Dearborn, Michigan. Large factory buildings are being erected as rapidly as possible. The factory will be completely equipped for the construction of the new tractor from the raw material to the finished product including foundry, engine rooms, and the latest in iron working machinery. The greatest activity prevails, the first of the two new buildings has been completed, and machinery is being installed.
>
> In the new tractor plant there will be no stockholders, no directors, no absentee owners, no parasites declared Henry Ford the other day in a discussion of modern industrialism. There will be no incorporation. Every man employed during the period of his employment will share in the profits of the industry.
>
> After the inauguration of this new step in the industrial development of the American people, a veritable revolution takes place in that the employes and users of the Tractor are to be Henry Ford's partners in the tractor business.[7]

Henry Ford obviously felt that business profits should be invested in expanding the business or be distributed to his employees and customers.

But Henry was not completely satisfied with his tractor yet, and it would be two full years of further development before his first mass-produced tractor

A T-powered tractor pulling a single twelve-inch plow in a field near Fair Lane on September 22, 1915. Driver is unidentified. (B-35219)

was delivered. Ford wanted a light, sturdy, inexpensive machine that most farmers could afford. By now, other good tractors were on the market, and he wanted to be certain his was the best for the money.

To manage the tractor development and prepare for production, in early October 1915 Charles Sorenson was put in charge of Dearborn operations with Eugene Farkus responsible for tractor engineering. Additional guidance was offered by Joe Galamb of Highland Park, one of the designers of the original Model T. These men had been associated with Ford in his Model T tractor development work. That fall at Dearborn, the first tractor design resembling the future Fordson was completed.[8] This was while Ford was on the Peace Mission in Europe. The tractor was on his mind in Oslo when reporters expected him to make a major pronouncement about world peace, and instead he spoke in glowing terms about his tractor in Dearborn.

No doubt at Ford's instigation, on February 3,

1916, the Ford Motor Company Board of Directors introduced a resolution to quitclaim to Henry Ford for $46,810.76 "any rights or claims it may have to the so called Tractor business including designs, patterns and experimental matter, and trade mark, copy right and patents on farm tractors, and to use the name 'Ford' in connection with the tractor business . . . *provided also that Mr. Ford use his own first name in connection with the name 'Ford' in said tractor business.*" This resolution was passed unanimously when James Couzens, who the day before had voted nay, was not at the meeting.[9]

Five or six prototype tractors were built in early 1916 at Dearborn before the design was temporarily frozen and fifty of the new models scheduled. These experimental machines, all slightly different, were used on the Ford Farms during the 1916 season. Although these new tractors had minor differences, several outstanding features were in common. These tractors had no frame. One large, hollow casting, en-

View of the Henry Ford & Son Tractor Plant looking southwest from the water tank on Michigan Avenue, October 22, 1918. (B-35742)

Loading dock at the tractor plant, May 7, 1919. This area is at the northwest corner of the plant, where a supply of rough castings and forgings is on hand. (B-35733)

closing the transmission, clutch, and differential gears, was bolted directly to the engine block to form a rigid system. Sorenson ("Cast-Iron Charlie"), an expert foundryman, made it possible.[10] Wheel spokes were also cast. The transmission was a three-speed gearshift type differing entirely from the Model T planetary transmission. The engine had a heavier crankshaft than the Model T, and the Holley carburetor was equipped with a heater to allow the engine to run on kerosene after being started on gasoline. A washed-air intake kept dust out of the carburetor. The axle was driven by a well-designed worm gear developed by Farkus. Total weight was a relatively light twenty-five hundred pounds. Ford had said, "A cat runs up the side of a tree, and it isn't its weight but its traction that makes it possible." Published specifications for the new tractor were as follows:

Engine: 4 cyl., bore 4", stroke 5", h.p. 21.4 at 1,000 rpm.
Fuel tanks: kerosene 21 gals., gasoline ½ gal.
Wheelbase: 62"
Length: 102"
Width: 61¾"
Height: 54¾"
Ground clearance: 11⅝"
Turning radius: 10½"
Driving wheels: 42" high, 12" wide.
Miles per hour: 1½, 2¾, 6¾ (plowing: 2¾).

As Sorenson prepared for production, he was hiring more workers. One man hired off the street was Mead Bricker, who became night foreman and soon superintendent. Robert Crawford, who later became Edsel Ford's private secretary, was hired at this time. Richard Kroll, who had worked in the Woodward barn, took charge of the machine shop; August Degener became head of inspection; and Jimmy Smith became chief tester. Frank McCormick, son of Ford's boyhood neighbor George McCormick, managed the assembly line. Also on the scene were some of Henry's and Clara's relatives: Roy Bryant, Ernest Kanzler, George Brubaker, Will Ford, Lewis Ford, and no doubt others. Of the relatives, Ernest Kanzler contributed the most. Kanzler established a remarkably efficient inventory and matériel flow system, which was also applied at Highland Park. Sorenson was not too pleased with the performance of some of the other relatives.[11] Will Ford, Henry's brother, was for a while in charge of personnel and later put in charge of service to customers. He was such a naturally generous man that the Service Department became unprofitable. According to Farkus, Sorenson finally put some of the problematic relatives together in a house north of the tracks, off the factory grounds, and assigned them a task of keeping some unimportant records. Lewis Ford, Will Ford's son, is pictured working hard driving a tractor on the farms. By late 1916 there were nearly three hundred men on the payroll.

In August 1916 three of the experimental tractors were demonstrated at the Nebraska State Fair with much success. On August 4 a Certificate of Co-Partnership was signed by Henry and Edsel Ford of Dearborn, Michigan:[12] "name and style of the said firm is Henry Ford and Son and the length of time for which it is to continue is indefinite, the same not being fixed by the partnership contract; that the locality of the place of business of said co-partnership is Dearborn, Michigan." This partnership also included the "Henry Ford & Son Laboratories" at Fair Lane, where "medical, botanical and chemical research" was being carried on.[13]

By early 1917 the war with Germany was at a

Machine shop on April 24, 1917, when the fifty experimental Ford tractors were being made. (B-35730)

Lewis Ford with experimental Ford tractor and twelve-inch double-bottomed plow on July 12, 1917. The tractor does not yet have the name Fordson. Lewis was son of Will Ford, Henry's brother. Lewis died on February 16, 1919, at age twenty. (B-35234)

critical stage and England found a desperate need to produce more of its own food. Percival Perry, head of Ford of Britain, was aware of Ford's tractor development in Dearborn, and in January 1917 bought land in Cork, Ireland, to manufacture tractors. At Perry's request, Sorenson and Bricker took two experimental tractors to England (shipped from Dearborn January 27, 1917) where they were demonstrated before the Royal Agricultural Society. The British were impressed, and Perry, anxious to start production, wired Edsel Ford on April 7 to send Sorenson with drawings and manufacturing procedures for approval by the British government. The request was immediately honored, for the United States had entered the war on April 6. Sorenson left in May to help Perry start the factory in Cork. In the meantime a long series of telegraphic cables provided information about matériel specifications and manufacturing methods for building tractors in Cork.[14] To build tractors in Ireland, Henry Ford & Son, Limited, was incorporated April 17, 1917, with a capital of £100,000, and shares divided equally among Henry, Edsel, and Clara Ford.[15]

But the Ford tractor, it was soon found, could not be built in Britain. British manufacturing facilities and manpower were immediately needed to build aircraft to fight the intensified German air raids. The British, in June, asked Sorenson, who was then in England, if Ford would build tractors for them at Dearborn. Letters from David Lloyd George, the Ministry of Munitions of War, and the Board of Agriculture and Fisheries all voiced the dire need for Ford's cooperation. In response, Ford offered to build six thousand tractors. Total price per tractor was not to exceed £150, and all were to be delivered to the Ministry of Munitions (M.O.M.) Tractor Assembly Factory, Manchester, England, by February 1, 1918. A down payment of £225,000 was to be made. This offer was confirmed by the British June 28, 1917.[16]

At Dearborn, Henry Ford would have preferred to have had more time before going into production, for he felt his tractor could be improved. He nevertheless had agreed to the plan to supply Britain, and production at Dearborn was pushed to the limit. On July 27, 1917, the Henry Ford & Son co-partnership was reorganized as a Michigan corporation, issuing ten thousand shares at a par value of $1,000,000, divided equally among Henry, Clara, and Edsel Ford with Henry as president.[17] The corporation was empowered to "manufacture, sell and deal in farm tractors, agricultural implements and appliances, and self-propelled vehicles and mechanisms of every description and character, and all accessories and devices appertaining or useful thereto."

A Ford Farm Tractor was on display again in September at the 1917 Michigan State Fair, and at London the Whiting-Bull challenged the M.O.M. Ford to a "ploughing" match.[18] Competing tractor manufacturers were concerned enough now to start ridiculing the alleged tendency of Ford's "kerosene burning donkey" to roll over backward pinning the driver beneath, and to kick stones from its fenderless wheels hitting the driver in the head.[19] But the event convincing Ford that he should begin shipping tractors at once was the urgent appeal by Lord Northcliffe, who, as head of the British mission to the United States, visited Dearborn in mid-October begging Ford to ship his tractors as they were, saying, "Yours are the best we can get." Production of a standard tractor, not yet named Fordson, had started in July.

By the end of 1917, 254 Ford tractors, some with radiators stenciled Fordson, had been produced.[20] The entire British order (increased to 7,000 by an order from Canada) was completed by April 1918. Production had reached 100 per day and would far exceed that figure in the months to come. The State of Michigan, through its War Preparedness Board, accepted a plan offered by Ford in march 1918 to distribute 1,000 tractors to farmers at $750 each (plus Oliver plows at about $100 each). Sales were to be

Lord Northcliffe and Henry Ford driving Fordson tractors equipped with twelve-inch, double-bottomed Oliver plows on October 16, 1917. Northcliffe wanted such tractors shipped to England immediately. Ford had been delaying shipment to make further improvements. (B-35206)

through county agricultural agents for cash, and at Henry's insistence a contract would require the buyer to plow his neighbor's fields within a reasonable radius as directed by the agents of the War Preparedness Board. It was believed the entire acreage of the state could thus be plowed, ready for the 1918 season.[21] Four other states, envious of the Michigan tractor distribution, applied for 1,000 tractors each during April. Other states followed.[22]

Production at Dearborn soared. Capital stock in Henry Ford & Son was increased to $5 million. In June 1918, 5,067 tractors were delivered. The Dearborn plant record was 399 per day, 10,248 per month.[23] The Cork, Ireland, plant went into production July 4, 1919, and produced 3,636 during 1920. The Fordson was gaining worldwide attention. Over a period of years, the Soviet Union bought at least 25,000 Fordsons, many of them shipped by way of Seattle and Vladivostok. Eventually one would see a facsimile of the Fordson built in the Soviet Union, going by the less familiar name of Krasny Putilowitz. Some of them were equipped with headlights and working twenty-four hours a day.[24] France needed about 40,000 tractors, for it had lost thousands of horses as well as men during the war. By 1920, 200,000 Fordsons were scattered all over the world.

The Fordson became such an outstanding suc-

cess that friends and relatives hurried to share in the Fordson's success. Edgar LeRoy Bryant became an early distributor in Ohio. William D. Ford was given a three-state distributorship including Michigan, and Addison Ford was allocated the retail sales district of Wayne, Monroe, and Washtenaw counties. The Dearborn Tractor Appliance Company was formed in May 1922, and capitalized at $25,000 to market a patented "hitch" for Fordsons. Officers were Clyde M. Ford, president; William D. Ford, vice president and sales manager; J. E. Miller, secretary and treasurer; and C. M. Spencer, general manager. Headquarters for this enterprise was in the Dearborn Arsenal Building.

The 1919 audit shows Henry Ford & Son with assets of $11 million, liabilities of $5 million, and profits of $4,768,120 on gross sales of $37,011,976.[25] Workers received bonuses amounting to $299,720, and a sum of $50,000 was "reserved" for Ford's salary. Ford Investment Certificates were popular with employees, and bargain prices were offered on food and clothing at the company store on the factory grounds. An office was also provided to help workers with their income taxes.[26]

In July 1919 the Ford family became sole owners of the Ford Motor Company and were rid of the stockholders who had necessitated a separate Henry Ford & Son. Beginning in December 1919 the Ford

Motor Company took over all tractor sales; many city car dealers questioned what they would do with their allotment. The new Ford Motor Company, with a capitalization of $100 million, was incorporated in Delaware because Michigan law limited corporations to $50 million. Henry Ford & Son was then merged with Ford Motor Company (May 1, 1920), with corporate power to manufacture not only automobiles and tractors but "aircraft, internal combustion engines, locomotives, railroad cars and all other manner of devices for getting from place to place."[27] Dissolution of Henry Ford & Son as a Michigan corporation was accomplished July 23, 1920, when the state recognized "Change of Attitude" papers presented by the Ford Motor Company.[28]

As the Rouge plant in Springwells took shape,

Fordson production was transferred from Dearborn to the Rouge. This move began in September 1920, affecting fifty-five hundred workers.[29] The Rouge produced its first tractor on February 23, 1921, in the B Building, where the Eagle boats had been built and where at this writing Mustangs gallop off the line. Rouge output was scheduled for one hundred per day, with additional parts manufactured for other assembly plants in Des Moines, Iowa; St Louis, Missouri; Kearny, New Jersey; and Cork, Ireland.

The Fordson tractor far outlived Henry Ford & Son of Dearborn. Fordsons continued to be built in the United States until 1928, when a total of 737,977 had been sold. Prices had ranged from $885 in September 1920 to $395 in January 1922. The Cork plant produced on a small scale immediately after creation

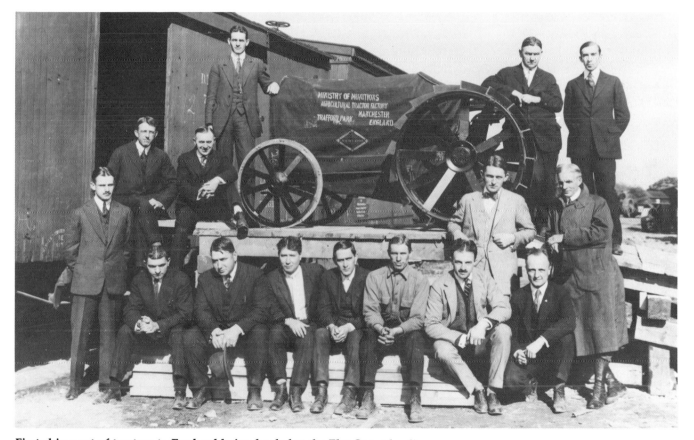

First shipment of tractors to England being loaded at the Elm Street loading dock in Dearborn in October 1917. Proud "movers" on hand, starting from upper right: E. R. (Roy) Bryant, Jack Daley, John Crawford, John Moore, George Brubaker, Bredo Berghoff, Dick Crowel, Mead Bricker, Louis Scott, Otto Rheinhart, Frank McCormick, Ernest Kanzler, Charles Sorenson, Eugene Farkas, and Henry Ford. (B-34935)

In the foreground an electromechanical cranking machine is ready to start the one hundred thousandth Fordson on February 21, 1920. Cranking just one of these tractors could tire a man. Obviously no worker volunteered to crank three hundred a day. The two hundred or so steering wheels stacked around the column would be less than a day's supply. (189-791)

of the Irish Free State in 1922, but by 1929 it had become the major producer, building 300 per day and exporting Fordsons worldwide including many back to the United States. Production finally shifted to Dagenham, England, where Fordsons were manufactured throughout World War II.[30]

Although Henry Ford had his Dearborn engineers working on improved tractor designs, including a three-wheel machine with V-8 engine built at the engineering laboratory in 1937 and a four-wheel, six-cylinder machine at Fair Lane Laboratory in 1938, he was not satisfied until Harry Ferguson, in October 1938, demonstrated a Ferguson-Brown tractor with a well-developed hydraulic linkage between tractor and implement. Thus a new era in small farm tractors

had begun, and Fordsons, which were produced far more years than the Model T, have now likewise become museum pieces.[31]

NOTES

1. Reynolds M. Wik, *Henry Ford and Grassroots America* (Ann Arbor: University of Michigan Press, 1972). According to Wik the Hart-Parr Company of Charles City, Iowa, built the first gasoline traction engine in 1902–3. Their sales manager, W. H. Williams, introduced the word *tractor* in 1907 advertising because he thought "gasoline traction engine" was too awkward an expression.
2. Nevins and Hill, *Expansion and Challenge*, p. 21.

Fordson
THE FARMERS POWER PLANT

"To make farming what it ought to be the most pleasant and profitable profession in the world."

That is Henry Ford's vision of the Fordson Tractor and what it means to the farmer. The farmers of America have done wonderful work. They have labored hard and patiently and their efforts have made prosperity commonplace for the nation.

The limitless forces of gasoline, kerosene and electricity are now ready to loose the bonds of long hours in the field, uncertain crops and shortage of labor.

The farmer's wife can now enjoy more of the beauties of life.

The tractor will make it hard to keep the boys and girls away from the farm. Conveniences now commonplace in the cities are brought to the farm and farm house by the tractor.

Mr. Ford bought thousands of acres of land, experimented for years on 62 different models of tractors at a cost of millions of dollars, before he found in the Fordson Tractor a machine he had proven a success. Mr. Ford did the experimenting with his own money. The Fordson is ready to do your work.

Ask your Fordson dealer to show you the Fordson. There are many Fordson owners near you. Ask them what their tractor has done for them.

Made By
HENRY FORD & SON, INC.
Dearborn, Mich.

A 1924 advertisement.

3. Bill of sale to Henry Ford for castings and wheels for traction motor ordered by Joseph Galamb and James Miller totaling $515.41. Bill was paid July 23, 1910. From Photo Collection Documents 560 and 561, Archives, HFM&GV.

4. Ford R. Bryan, *The Fords of Dearborn* (Detroit: Harlo, 1987), pp. 166–82.

5. Donald V. Baut, "Farming with the Fordson," *Dearborn Historian* (fall, 1967): 61–70. Activities at the Henry Ford & Son Tractor plant are described in detail, based considerably on weekly coverage in the *Dearborn Independent* for 1915–21.

6. Nationwide, newspapers claimed Henry Ford planned to build five hundred thousand of the "iron horses" the first year, and sell them at a price of about two hundred dollars. But this announcement likely referred to future plans at the Rouge location rather than Dearborn.

7. The threat of a business without stockholders, or "parasites," is thought to have been a deliberate effort to stigmatize his Ford Motor Company stockholders. On October 13, 1915, James Couzens resigned as general manager of Ford Motor Company, although he continued to hold his stock and serve on the Board of Directors for four more years.

8. Eugene J. Farkus, *Reminiscences,* Acc. 65, Archives, HFM&GV.

9. See Acc. 572, Box 32, Archives, HFM&GV.

10. Charles E. Sorenson, *Reminiscences,* Acc. 65, Archives, HFM&GV. See also Sorenson, *My Forty Years with Ford* (New York: W. W. Norton, 1956).

11. Farkus, *Reminiscences,* pp. 76–77.

12. At this date Edsel Ford was single, living at Fair Lane. He was twenty-four years old, already secretary-treasurer and a director of Ford Motor Company. Later that year (November 1, 1916) he married Eleanor Clay and moved to Grosse Pointe.

13. Henry Ford & Son Laboratories was on the third floor of the Fair Lane powerhouse. One of the projects was the distillation of alcohol from vegetable matter for use as tractor fuel. Serious consideration was being given to the purchase of a brewery for producing alcohol in quantity. See Acc. 69, Box 9, Archives, HFM&GV.

14. Telegrams between Dearborn and the British government in London during April 1917 bear the cable address Fordson. This appears to be the first use of the term *Fordson.* See Acc. 62, Box 51, Archives, HFM&GV.

15. "Memorandum in Relation to the Incorporation of Henry Ford & Son, Limited." Acc. 62, Box 51, Archives, HFM&GV.

16. See Acc. 62, Box 51, for copy of letter signed by P. Hanson, Director General of Munitions Contracts, on June 28, 1917.

17. See Acc. 329, Box 1, Archives, HFM&GV, for copy of Articles of Association of Henry Ford & Son, Incorporated. See also Lewis, *Public Image,* pp. 180–83.

18. The Whiting Bull was built by the Bull Tractor Company of Minneapolis, Minnesota. Its slogan was "Bull with a Pull" for $645.

19. Fenders became optional equipment for Fordson tractors in February 1923. Acc. 572, Box 24, Archives, HFM&GV.

20. Edsel Ford was notified January 8, 1918, that the trademark Fordson for Henry Ford & Son, Inc. had "been allowed" by the patent office. See Photo Collection, Document 552, Archives, HFM&GV.

21. "Buys 1,000 Ford Tractor," *Motor Age* 33 (March 14, 1918): 9.

22. "Iowa and Ohio Buy Fordson Tractors," *Motor Age* 33 (April 25, 1918): 13.

23. Sorenson, *Reminiscences,* Acc. 65, p. 240, Archives, HFM&GV.

24. Nevins and Hill, *Expansion and Challenge,* appendix 1, p. 676.

25. See Acc. 329, Box 1, Archives, HFM&GV for detailed audit, full year 1919.

26. *Fordson Worker* (January 1, 1920): 1.

27. *New York Tribune* (April 28, 1920).

28. See Acc. 329, Box 1, Archives, HFM&GV.

29. *Fordson Worker* (October 1, 1920): 1.

30. The shift of production from the United States to Britain is thought to have been a result of admission of "implements of agriculture" into the United States duty free. Thus "outsourcing" took jobs away from Dearborn sixty years ago.

31. Lewis, *Public Image,* pp. 287–89.

2

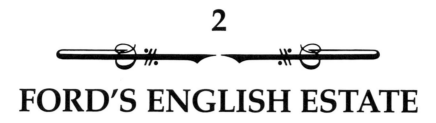

FORD'S ENGLISH ESTATE

In 1930, Mr. and Mrs. Henry Ford went to see the Oberammergau Passion Play. They returned to England by the Hook of Holland route, and whilst enjoying breakfast in the dining car from Harwich Mr. Ford availed himself of what was probably his first quiet opportunity to observe the English countryside." This quotation is from Percival Lea Dewhurst Perry's introduction to his privately published narrative, *Ten Years' Romance: An Agricultural Experiment.* Much of what follows is from this same narrative, written in 1945 and filed in the Ford Archives. Lord Perry had been associated with Henry Ford as head of British Ford operations from 1906, with a break during 1919–28, until his retirement in 1943.

As a result of this trip through southeastern England, Ford again exercised his lifelong urge to help his fellow farmer and the farming industry. Viewing the charming English landscape, he could not help noticing the dilapidated condition of the farm buildings, the obsolete farming methods employed, and the poor crops produced. He believed and hoped that these farmers could be lifted from their depressed economic state into a better life—a life at least commensurate with that of their urban counterparts.

On May 2, 1931, newspapers announced that Henry Ford had bought Lord Kenyon's Boreham House and had "joined England's landed Gentry." Ford was to acquire some two thousand acres adjoining Boreham House and eventually, through leases, control use of about five thousand acres of farmland in the historic Chelmsford district of Essex. This property was some thirty miles northeast of London.

HENRY I ENCOUNTERS HENRY VIII

Boreham Parish was midway between the coastal town of Harwich and London, a location that had been a convenient stopping place for royalty on its way to and from the European continent. Crusaders likely camped on this property after one day's march from London on their way to the Holy Land during the Middle Ages. Some buildings in this district date to the eleventh century and show signs of Roman as well as Saxon architecture. In this same parish is New Hall Manor, which came to the crown during the Wars of the Roses (1455–85), later came into the possession of Sir Thomas Boleyn, and was acquired in 1517 by King Henry VIII (Bluff King Hal). In 1713 Benjamin Hoare, a wealthy London banker, purchased New Hall estate and in 1728 built Boreham

A view of the 1728 Boreham House from the front. Photo taken July 19, 1937. (0-7204)

House on that same property. In 1737, when Benjamin Hoare disposed of New Hall, the Boreham estate retained the historic Boleyn home, home of Anne Boleyn.

The Boleyn name had been corrupted over the years to "Bullen," the Boleyn property becoming known as "Bull's Lodge Farm." In 1931, when Henry Ford bought the farm, a shepherd occupied the lodge. The shepherd, Harold Livermore, during his tenure had exposed a tunnel leading from Bull's Lodge to New Hall, about a quarter mile away. New Hall had been the summer palace of Henry VIII during his 1532–33 courtship of Anne, who was to become mother of Queen Elizabeth I. King Henry is said to have traversed the tunnel with flaming torch to meet Anne. The initials of Anne and Henry are said to still exist at the tunnel entrance into the basement of Bull's Lodge. Thus Henry Ford with Boreham House and Bull's Lodge, together with many picturesque flint-stone cottages and a hundred or more thatch-roofed farm buildings all needing repairs, was immersed in a historic project of considerable magnitude.

FORDSON ESTATES LIMITED

Henry Ford evidently had no intention of living at stately Boreham House. It is doubtful if he ever stayed there overnight. Instead, he financed a joint company known as Fordson Estates Limited consisting of several Co-Operative Societies managed by Sir Percival Perry. Thus it became an arm of Ford of Brit-

ain. Fordson Estates Limited was an agricultural experiment using modern farming methods and equipment including a generous supply of Fordson tractors. The farms were to become "demonstration" farms. Two years were spent reconditioning buildings and land, with operation of the farms under way by 1933.

At this same time, back home, Henry Ford was expanding his experimental farming by buying thousands of acres in the Tecumseh, Michigan, area where he established Ford's Cooperative Farmers Association. At Ways, Georgia, he had been buying land with the announced objective of "testing tractors." But Fordson tractor production had been moved from Dearborn to Cork, Ireland, in 1928, and moved again to Dagenham, England, in early 1933. So what better location to help his impoverished farmers and to demonstrate the merits of the Fordson tractor than just a few miles beyond Dagenham on the Boreham property now managed as Fordson Estates Limited.

The Fordson Estates land was valued at twenty pounds (ninety-four dollars)* an acre, and ten pounds per acre were alloted to put the land "into good heart," a program of land enrichment. Buying, selling, bookkeeping, and transportation operations were centralized. Cooperative farms of from 125 to 500 acres were each supplied with seed and fertilizer and tools such as tractors and cultivators, which were

---

*A value of $4.70 per pound is used as an average conversion rate for the 1933–35 period. One shilling was worth twenty-three cents. By 1944, however, the pound was worth only $2.80, and the shilling only fourteen cents.

Bull's Lodge, one-half mile from Boreham House, as it was in 1931 before restoration by Henry Ford. (0-7205)

A view of Bull's Lodge after restoration by Fordson Estates. (0-7206)

Business headquarters of Fordson Estates, about 1935. (0-7207)

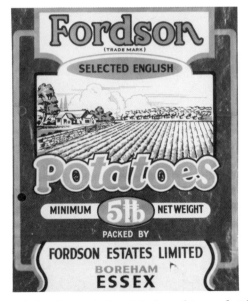

Photo of plastic potato bag label used to market Fordson Estate potatoes. (0-7221)

used almost constantly; more expensive and more specialized equipment was furnished as needed from a central depot.

Permanent employees numbered as many as two hundred, with nearly as many temporary workers employed during planting and harvesting. To participate as a cooperative member, each employee was to work two hundred days or a minimum of sixteen-hundred hours during each calendar year. Earnings were ascertained and distributed after harvest each year; but in the meantime the member received a minimum weekly "drawing" of perhaps thirty-five to forty shillings per week with the equivalent or more added to the total wages at year's end. The prevailing wage in the district during this period was thirty shillings (seven dollars) per week, and Fordson Estates aimed to pay twenty-five percent more as a minimum. One farm of 125 acres—the Danbury Co-operators Ltd.—specialized in greenhouse produce and employed twenty-seven workers. Twenty-six modern cottages had been built for the members. Weekly drawing-account wages for 1945 were seventy-five shillings—much above common farm wages. This cooperative was managed by Fordson Estates although separately financed.

Member employees were offered occupancy of one of the many well-restored and picturesque "cottages" on the estate at rents as little as three pounds per year. Some original tenants on the property, especially widows, were allowed to stay in their homes without paying rent. Livermore, the sheepherder, became a Ford employee and occupied half of Bull's Lodge after it had been converted to a duplex.

The most successful garden crops were brussels sprouts, cabbage, peas, asparagus, cucumbers, and tomatoes. This produce was trucked into London where desirable prices were obtained. Full advantage of the Fordson National Mark was taken. And as with our Sunkist oranges and Diamond walnuts, by marketing the best possible produce the Fordson name gained an excellent reputation; every marketed cucumber, for example, displayed the Fordson mark on a label like a cigar band. Other crops such as wheat, barley, potatoes, and sugar beets were grown on large acreages but with less profit.

About 135,000 apple, plum, pear, and cherry trees were planted with interplantings of soft fruits and vegetables. Nine years after planting the three-year-old stock (1941), the value of such hard fruit sold was £39,781 (perhaps $180,000). Cattle and pig farming were emphasized but poultry husbandry was omitted. Quoting Perry, "In the great orchestra of Agriculture, Nature has not only dictated the theme but insists which instruments shall play and provide the concert."[1]

HENRY FORD INSTITUTE OF AGRICULTURAL ENGINEERING

And just what was Henry Ford to do with the elaborate Boreham House? This imposing structure of twenty-four rooms was embellished with a salon attributed to John Kent and described as "one of the richest and perhaps the most perfect room, in the Italian style, in the Kingdom."[2] This mansion with thirty-two acres of surrounding parkland and a forty thousand-pound (nearly two hundred thousand dollars) cash endowment was donated in 1937 to form

One of the many "cottages" restored by Fordson Estates for occupancy by estate workers. (0-5904)

the Henry Ford Institute of Agricultural Engineering, an educational trust directed by a distinguished British Board of Trustees.

The school could accommodate forty young men in residence. The principal, recruited from Oxford University, was assisted by tutors in providing intensive short courses for farmers, farm workers, mechanics, demonstrators, and students from agricultural colleges. With the outbreak of the war in 1939, the institute provided courses in tractor driving and handling of implements for members of the Woman's Land Army. Some 150 women completed these courses. In late 1940 Henry and Edsel Ford provided scholarship money for classes of forty boys six-teen to seventeen years of age, to be taught courses in crop and animal husbandry, farm machinery, tractor engineering, farm records, and bookkeeping. The courses consisted of twenty-five percent lectures, twenty-five percent workshop instruction, and fifty percent practical fieldwork at the Fordson Estate farms, shops, and offices.

Just as Henry Ford had established the reputable Henry Ford Trade School in Detroit in 1916, he had organized a Ford Trade School at the original British Manchester factory in 1930, and the Trade School duly transferred to the new factory in Dagenham. The Trade School, however, focused on manufacturing skills rather than agriculture, and there

Main entrance to Boreham House and the Ford Institute of Agricultural Engineering. (0-6513)

A written quiz on ignition systems occupies this prewar institute group in a
Boreham House classroom. (188-26296)

was little or no association between Boreham and the factory-oriented Trade School.

Toward the end of the war, during the same period that the Ford Motor Company was liquidating its Michigan farm properties, Fordson Estates Limited passed out of Ford control. Boreham House, however, has retained its identity as a teaching institution since its 1937 establishment as Henry Ford Institute of Agricultural Engineering. The elegant Georgian mansion in a parkland setting of seventy-six acres is now the Training Center of Ford New Holland International Sales Operations, serving Ford Tractor and New Holland harvesting machinery dealers. Boreham house is now only twenty miles from

Ford's world tractor manufacturing and assembly plant at Basildon. Could Henry Ford have envisioned this? Perhaps Thomas Edison was right, saying, "Ford's foresight is so long it sags in the middle."[3]

NOTES

1. *Ten Years' Romance: An Agricultural Experiment,* self-published by Sir Percival Perry, 1945, Archives, HFM&GV, 24p.
2. Ibid.
3. *New York Tribune,* February, 11, 1914.

Women of the Women's Land Army are taught principles of gasoline engine carburetion in November 1939. (188-26304)

Plowing three long, straight, deep furrows at one time with the powerful Fordson tractor, this member of the Women's Land Army has learned her lesson well. (188-26299)

3

EAGLE'S NEST ON THE ROUGE

Negotiations for peace had failed, and now the United States, too, had declared war on Germany. Henry Ford, who had previously refused to help arm any of the belligerents, including England, now wholeheartedly offered President Wilson his full cooperation in the effort to "save the world for democracy." This was April 1917.

First there were the ambulances—2,000 Model T chassis to be supplied to the Allies in Europe. A contract for 820,000 steel helmets for the U.S. Army soon followed. Late in 1917 Ford offered to build 150,000 fighter aircraft at the same production rate as Model Ts, and at a price of twenty-five cents per pound, but this offer was not taken seriously by the War Department.[1] However, Ford was soon selected to build 5,000 of the highly sophisticated and powerful "Liberty" aircraft engines at his Highland Park plant. Just before the end of the war, the army ordered 15,000 Ford 2½-ton tanks, each powered by a pair of Model T engines. These were just nicely into production at the time of the Armistice. But by far the most spectacular of the war projects taken on by Henry Ford and the Ford Motor Company was the building of the U.S. Navy's new and experimental submarine chaser, which merited the name Eagle.[2]

German submarines were sinking Allied cargo ships at the rate of five to six thousand a year, nearly as fast as they could be built. Thinking of the need

for mass-produced merchant ships, President Wilson induced Henry Ford to serve on the United States Shipping Board. But rather than build more cargo ships to feed the submarines, the Ford people suggested a fleet of small, fast chasers to seek and kill the German U-boats. So a submarine chaser was designed by the navy specifically for manufacture by Ford. Henry Ford insisted that the hull be constructed from flat sheets of steel so that it could be assembled quickly, and that it use a steam turbine power plant, which would be much less noisy and therefore more stealthy than a ship powered by a reciprocating engine. The Edison Laboratories had developed an advanced submarine detection device that operated best in a quiet environment. The Eagle boats were designed to use this new device, which would also be manufactured by Ford.

While navy officials belabored details of the contract and the powerful Shipping Lobby tried to block Ford's entry into the shipbuilding business, Ford was preparing the site for his shipbuilding plant. About four square miles of land had been bought by Ford during 1915 in Springwells and Ecorse townships, adjacent to Dearborn. This property was south of the Village of Springwells and north of the Village of Oakwood.[3] More precisely, it was bounded on the north by the Michigan Central Railroad, on the south by the Rouge River, on the west by a Michigan Cen-

Site of the Rouge plant was a morass of mud in the early spring of 1918. The dredge *Niagara* makes its way slowly up from the river toward the future location of the B Building from which Eagles would be launched. Many men worked in hip boots all day. (833-21870)

tral connecting line extending south from the present location of Dearborn's Ternes Street, and on the east by the Pere Marquette Railroad running parallel and east of Miller Road. Bisecting this property was Roulo Creek. In 1916 a portion largely east of Roulo Creek and along Miller Road was sold by Henry Ford to the Ford Motor Company for seven hundred thousand dollars as a site for blast furnaces and foundries. The portion west of Roulo Creek was held by Henry Ford & Son for its proposed tractor plant. In the process, Maple Road and North Dearborn Road together with the many homes thereon were obliterated.

The government had offered to pay four hundred thousand dollars to widen and deepen the Rouge River from the Detroit River to the confluence of the Rouge with Roulo Creek, a distance of about three miles. There a turning basin would be formed. From the turning basin a canal 2,614 feet long, 110 feet wide, and 20 feet deep would be dredged directly north from the Rouge River to form a slip where large boats could be docked. It would be at the very end of this slip that the Ford Motor Company would launch its Eagle boats. In a sense the river was to be brought to the shipbuilding plant. William B. Mayo, Ford's chief engineer, was put in charge of plant construction, and William S. Knudsen in charge of ship production.

The vessel to be built was first conceived as a simple, bare-bones patrol boat like the British P-boat armed with a few depth charges. On such a boat men slept in the open and cooked their own meals on patrols lasting only three or four days. But Sidney Houghton, a commander in the British navy (also a furniture designer for Henry Ford) suggested a larger ship with bunks and galley suitable for forays of greater distance. As the design developed, there were also added a three-inch antiaircraft gun, two four-inch guns to sink surfaced submarines, two .50-caliber machine guns, radio apparatus, and sophisticated listening devices. The boat thus became a vessel of 615 tons displacement, 204-foot length, and 33-foot beam with a cruising radius of thirty-five hundred miles. A draft of only 8 feet was to allow torpedoes from enemy submarines to pass harmlessly underneath. A top speed close to twenty knots was said to be twice that of a submerged submarine, and a sharp steel-encased nose of solid concrete was designed to crush any submarine it could ram. The cost of each boat was estimated to be $275,000. A contract for one hundred of these vessels was accepted by the government on January 18, 1918. Henry Ford stated that once production was under way he could easily produce a boat a day, or two boats a day if necessary. The government would invest about $3.5 million in plant and waterway improvements to be sold at the end of the war to either Ford or another purchaser.

As engineering drawings for the ship were being further revised by the navy, a prototype vessel was being constructed in the craneway of the six-story Highland Park AA Building. This experimental vessel, begun February 7, 1918, and simply bolted together, was completed June 24. It was then dismantled, the parts shipped to the Rouge where it was reassembled by welding and riveting and launched as Eagle No. 7. Boilers, turbines, and reduction gearing for the twenty-five hundred-horsepower oil-fired steam turbine engine were to be manufactured at the Highland Park location. These items were soon produced in quantities beyond the number required at the Rouge.

The first major building to be constructed on the Rouge property was the Fabricating, or A, Building. This building was used primarily to cut the steel sheets into proper sizes and to punch holes into the sheets preparatory to riveting. In this building subassemblies were also fabricated by welding or riveting, and general machining work done. A Building was started February 18 and finished in twenty-four working days. B Building, the Erecting Building, was the heart of the operation. This building, also started in February and in use by mid-May, was 1,700 feet long, 306 feet wide, and 100 feet high. Inside were three assembly lines, each capable of carrying seven boats.[4]

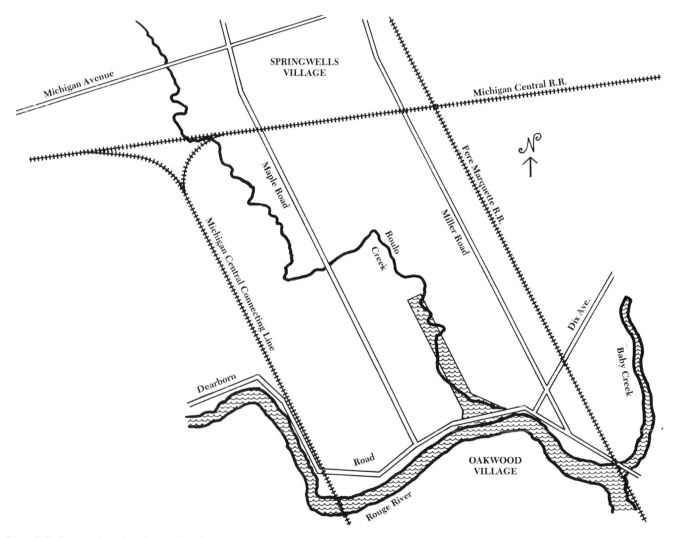

Simplified map showing boat slip dug along Roulo Creek from the Rouge River to provide a large factory site with water as well as rail transportation. (Courtesy of Dearborn Historical Museum.)

The A Building, first of the major buildings of the shipbuilding plant, finished in March 1918. Foreground shows part of the 175 carloads of cinders used to fill in the Roulo creek bed to obtain proper elevation. (833-21599)

Under William Knudsen, Frank Hada supervised construction of the hulls. Navy personnel were on hand to inspect construction and oversee final outfitting of the ships. Weekly reports of progress were issued and optimistic schedules posted despite the many difficulties that were to delay the program from the very start. In a March Report of Progress, expectations were to complete the entire one hundred ships before the shipping season closed that next November.

Report of Progress of Ships
March 19, 1918

Order received from Navy Department January 18.
Detailed specifications from Navy for hull—February 18.
Detailed specifications from Navy for power—coming in daily.
Construction started at Rouge February 20.
Progress A Building (Fabrication Shop) 100%
Progress B Building (Erection Shop)   25%
Progress Slips   15%
Progress R.R. Tracks   28%

General schedule for operation of entire plant:

Fabrication of hull parts starts April 1.
Erection of hull parts starts May 10.
First line to be filled by June 30.
Three lines to be filled by July 15.
First boat to be launched by July 1.

First boat to be completed by July 25.
100 boats to be completed by November 25.

Item likely to be barometer of progress: riveting

We have no reason to forecast any delay on the dates mentioned above.[5]

The early spring of 1918, however, had its drawbacks to high productivity. An unusually cold winter had brought on an epidemic of influenza, which lingered through the spring months causing high absenteeism. Spring floods during construction of the plant reduced the site to a quagmire. A squabble of long standing between the Detroit City Council and the Detroit United Railway delayed for months any trolley service to the shipbuilding site. And a continuing series of specification changes by the navy produced more delay. It seems that at no time was production on schedule.

Few employees at that time owned automobiles. There being no streetcar lines to the shipbuilding plant, some provision for getting workers to the site had to be provided. A transportation department using Model T trucks with trailers was organized to bring men from as far as Highland Park. As many as six thousand workers were eventually accommodated using twenty-nine trucks with trailers. Nearly all the men were unskilled workers to start, but most quickly became skilled craftsmen.

Workers quickly became skilled riveters, and many riveters also soon left the Ford six-dollar wage to take fifteen-dollar pay elsewhere. A riveter's school was operated on the premises to fill openings created as the experienced riveters left. Every two days a class of forty new riveters was taught "big riveting," "small riveting," "angle riveting," and "upside down riveting," all skills necessary in building an Eagle held together by 260,000 rivets.[6] On the job, a record 5,542 half-inch rivets were driven by one man in eight hours. One man was reported killed when hit by a flying rivet.

The riveting in the B Building is said to have produced a tremendous din. With some twenty boats in progress, the building was filled with nearly four thousand workers, there being crews of riveters, welders, erectors, pipe fitters, electricians, caulkers, and painters working simultaneously on each ship. Each keel was laid on a two-hundred-foot flatcar, which was towed down the assembly line as work on the hull progressed. When the finished hull reached the south door of the building, it was moved onto a large "transfer platform" and rolled on rails toward the west to be even with the Rouge slip. It was then rolled onto a "launching trestle" that could be hydraulically lowered below the water in the slip, leaving the boat to float. The procedure of launching required as little as forty-five minutes. With help from the dredge *Niagara* and the tug *Ruby*, boats could be launched through six inches of ice.

Along the east side of the slip was a long "out-

Construction of the B Building. This photograph from the south was taken May 11, 1918, four days after the first keel had been laid in the nearly finished north end of the same building, one-third of a mile away. (833-22074)

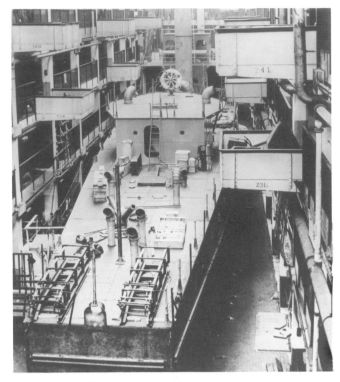

Prototype Eagle, fabricated and assembled in craneway at Highland Park between February and June of 1918. This ship was bolted together so that it could be disassembled and shipped to the Rouge shipbuilding plant. There it was reassembled by conventional welding and riveting, and launched as Eagle No. 7. (833-22503)

fitting dock" (D Building) with cranes to lower boilers and turbines into the ships. Here the ships were equipped with all the necessities including armament, navigational aids, galley, and seventy-eight bunks. A cantonment with training school and barracks capable of housing twelve hundred navy men had been built to the west of the slip. After completion, the ships were taken into the Detroit River and often to Lakes Erie or St. Clair for speed and maneuverability tests. Sometimes members of the press and Detroit notables were invited to participate to garner praise and squelch any tendency to unduly criticize the craft.[7]

In July 1918 a contract for 12 additional ships for the Italian government was accepted from Navy Secretary Franklin D. Roosevelt, but by then it became obvious that this new quota of 112 ships would not be met before the closing of the Great Lakes shipping season, usually in late November. Because Ford Mo-

tor Company owned land at Kearny, New Jersey, on seawater, plans were made to build a shipbuilding plant at Kearny almost identical with the plant at the Rouge. This new plant on Newark Bay was finally approved by the government October 7, 1918, with about $2 million allocated. But when the war ended, November 11, 1918, this supplemental contract at Kearny was short-lived; ship construction ended November 14.[8]

At the time of the Armistice, twenty-eight keels had been laid at the Rouge, twelve boats had been launched, and seven commissioned by the navy.[9] Immediately the pressure was off. No more submarine detection devices were to be installed. On November 30 the original contract was reduced to sixty ships with completion not required before November 15, 1919. During the winter of 1918–19, more than forty

Eagle No. 59 under construction in the B Building, April 1919. This hull was assembled in the record time of ten days. (833-26319)

Hull of Eagle No. 1 emerging from B Building onto the transfer platform preparatory to launching. (833-22621)

Eagles were stored at the docks at the Rouge waiting for spring delivery to New London, Connecticut, and assignment to sea duty with the U.S. Fleet.

Few if any Eagles engaged in fighting during World War I. Eagles 1, 2, and 3 did patrol duty off the Gulf of Archangel, Russia. Six were to be sent to the Philippines to replace old destroyers and gunboats, another squadron was to join the International Patrol off the coast of China, some were to be sent to the Caribbean, some to Italy, and a few were to become training ships. Eagles were also used by the government as rumrunners, for geodetic surveys, as lighthouse tenders, and by the Treasury Department for the Internal Revenue and Customs services.

Reports from the navy regarding serviceability of the Eagles were generally favorable. A navy superintendent reported of the first Eagles on their voyage into Arctic waters: "Eagles 1, 2 and 4 encountered considerable heavy weather and their behavior in a seaway has been pronounced excellent." The commanding officer of Eagle 1, from Brest, France, on August 17, 1919, stated that during the first six months of service "there were no defects in the hull, hull fittings, and equipment of this vessel." The boat had been "almost constantly underway" since April 11, 1919, serving mostly off Russia in ice-covered waters. "It speaks very well for the construction of this vessel that in bucking heavy ice, no damage was experienced to hull, frames, or bulkheads." Eagles 2 and 3 encountered the same conditions and were said to have behaved creditably.[10]

All sixty Eagles had been commissioned by October 1919. Five were almost immediately transferred to the U.S. Coast Guard under the classification of "Cruising Cutters." The remainder worked for the navy an average of fifteen years. Many were sold and "stricken" from the record during the 1930s. Four Eagles were destroyed as target vessels. But in 1941

An Eagle, one of the last to be launched, on the launching trestle being lowered into the slip. The blast furnace "high line" is visible to the far right in this photo taken August 15, 1919. (833-27534)

Jane's Fighting Ships carried eight Eagle boats in commission at that time.[11] These were pressed into submarine patrol duty inside continental waters during World War II. Some were assigned to both East and West coasts, engaging in antisubmarine warfare, as sonar training ships, and as target-towing vessels. Eagle No. 56 was sunk while on duty April 23, 1945. The remaining navy Eagles were sold after World War II, the last, No. 57, on March 5, 1947.

In September 1918, Ford had been granted government priority for matériel to construct his iron-smelting works at the Rouge. Even as shipbuilding continued, work on the blast furnace and foundry foundations was beginning. After the Armistice, as the shipbuilding contract neared completion, workers began to be transferred to blast furnace and foundry construction. There were predictions by Ford in late November that the shipbuilding plant would be used to build canal barges when the Eagle contract was finished. These barges, each with a ca-

pacity of fifteen hundred tons, some of them equipped with motors, would carry cars, tractors, and parts over Lake Erie and the inland waterways of New York State to Kearny for worldwide export.[12]

While Eagle boats were still being constructed, in July 1919 Henry Ford finally wrested control of Ford Motor Company from his minority stockholders and could proceed unimpeded with development of the Rouge. But canal barges were never built in his shipbuilding plant. The Wadsworth Manufacturing Company, a major supplier of Model T bodies, had been suffering from strikes during April and May. In mid-July 1919, before the last of the Eagles were assembled, Ford moved auto body-building machinery into B Building. Automobiles were to be its destiny. More than one riveter now became a "tack spitter."

Ten days was the minimum time in which an Eagle was built.[13] A total of sixty Eagles was constructed during the twenty-two-month contract. Construction work on the contract ended November

10, 1919—total expenditure was $46,104,042. This cost was far above the original estimates, but a Senate investigation found no deliberate wrongdoing.

Ford bought B Building, the major building of the shipbuilding plant, from the government for $180,000. Otherwise, Dearborn's history might have been different. Other shipbuilding units (buildings A, C, D, and E) were dismantled by the government in due time. Ford Motor Company had gained from dredging of the waterway and the transformation of a muddy wallow into a site suitable for its gigantic iron-smelting operations. And well before the government closed its books on the Eagle contract in August 1920, iron-making operations were well under way, Blast Furnace A having been "blown in" on May 17, 1920.

We are far from knowing the full story of each of the Eagles that left the Eagle's Nest.[14] Most were ultimately sold by the navy—some for scrap, some

for further adventure. But if each of those "Iron Aphrodites of the Sea" could tell a story, it would make much more compelling reading that you have just concluded.

NOTES

1. Nevins and Hill, *Expansion and Challenge*, p. 57n. Ford had publicly suggested use of one-man submarines to be equipped with explosives to be detonated under enemy ships. The navy scoffed at the idea. Franklin Roosevelt, then navy secretary, is quoted as saying "until he [Ford] saw a chance for publicity free of charge, thought a submarine was something to eat."
2. Ernest G. Liebold, *Reminiscences*, Acc. 65, pp. 316–39, HFM&GV. Liebold, Henry Ford's general secretary, takes credit for the name *Eagle*, having used it in an editorial for the *Washington Post* during discussions with the navy.
3. Edward F. Collins, "Dearborn's French Heritage and the Rou-

Some of the forty-two ships awaiting transfer to the East Coast in April 1919. Ships hug the outfitting docks along the east side of the slip. Visible in top center of the photo (water tank) is the cantonment where several hundred navy personnel were housed. (833-26555)

An Eagle boat with local dignitaries on a demonstration run. This would have been before the ship was turned over to the navy. (833-27883)

Eagle boats in the ice-covered entrance to the White Sea in August 1919, after a sixty-two hundred-mile voyage from the United States. These vessels helped rescue the ill-fated Polar Bears as they left Archangel at the end of World War I. Photo by J. P. Sasse. (0-4436)

leau (Roulo) Family," *Dearborn Historian* 23 (fall 1983): 109–13. This land included farms of the Rouleau and Peltier families, early French settlers along Rouleau Road (later Miller Road). Some of the property had been developed as Abbott and Beymer's Riverview Subdivision, with 180 residential lots, 70 of which fronted on the Rouge River.

4. This building, built so hurriedly in the spring of 1918, has been in constant use since that time, and as of this writing is the main assembly plant for Ford Mustangs.

5. This optimism is also reflected in accounts of shipbuilding progress reported in *Ford Man* 2–3 (1918–19).

6. According to statements of Frank Hadas in charge of hull construction.

7. Accounts of these tests have been provided by Liebold, *Reminiscences*, p. 335, and in *Ford Man* 3 (August 4, 1919): 3.

8. See Acc. 116, Box 1, Archives, HFM&GV, for papers concerning contract with the navy for a shipbuilding plant at Kearny, New Jersey.

9. *Dictionary of American Naval Fighting Ships*, vol. 6 (Washington: Department of the Navy, 1976), pp. 744–47.

10. Correspondence from Lieutenant F. C. Forster, engineering officer on USS *Eagle Two*, Murmansk, Russia, May 26, 1919. Vertical File, Archives, HFM&GV.

11. Data from C. L. Malaney, CWO, U.S. Army (Ret.), March 28, 1983. Vertical File, Archives, HFM&GV.

12. Clipping Books, Acc. 7, vols. 42–43, Archives, HFM&GV.

13. If one boat could move the length of its assembly line in ten days, production from that line would be seven boats in ten days. The three assembly lines could therefore theoretically produce twenty-one boats in ten days. Thus Ford's early estimate of two boats per day was not unreasonable.

14. See Acc. 1110, Archives, HFM&GV. A good accounting of Eagle 56, which was lost on duty during World War II, is given by Frank A. Cianflone, commanding officer. A numerical summary of all sixty Eagles is also included in this seventeen-page document.

4

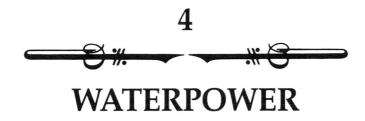

WATERPOWER

As a boy, Henry Ford was intrigued by flowing water. When he went with his father to nearby Coon's Mill on the Rouge River where their corn and wheat were ground, he observed the waterwheel furnishing the power for grinding the grain. As schoolboys, he and his friends constructed a small dam in a ditch near the school yard and ran a homemade wheel to the delight of the other children. But the boys forgot to un-dam the stream, causing a farmer's field to be flooded, for which Henry, the leader, was duly scolded.

As he grew up, Henry became busy at mechanics and building automobiles in Detroit, but as soon as he was well satisfied with his Model T in 1909, he bought property on both sides of the Rouge River near his boyhood home. At one point on the meandering fifty-foot-wide stream there had been an old mill powered by water. At this same spot, in 1910, he built his very first small but practical hydroelectric system. Only five years later the Fords built their permanent home at this site and enlarged the hydroelectric plant, which to this day supplies power to the Ford Estate now on the Dearborn campus of the University of Michigan.

When Ford bought out the stockholders of the Ford Motor Company in 1919, profits of the company no longer needed to be paid out in dividends but could be used for company expansion. It was then,

one might say, Ford jumped into his Model T and rode off in all directions. He finished building the Rouge plant objected to by the Dodge brothers. This was to become the largest manufacturing complex in the world. He purchased timberlands and iron mines in northern Michigan, coal mines in Kentucky, a railroad through Ohio, a fleet of lake and ocean ships, and began acquiring and building a series of more than thirty hydroelectric plants ranging from twenty-two to eighteen thousand horsepower (see table). Ford also tried to gain control of the gigantic Muscle Shoals operations on the Tennessee River in Alabama. But more about that later.

According to Roscoe Smith,[1] who managed the Ford hydroelectric plants for many years, Henry Ford preferred to restore old mill sites for his small plants rather than pick new sites. He wanted to preserve their historic appearance as much as possible. If there was not enough waterpower to meet his production plans at that location, he would add auxiliary steam power. Often the neat and sparkling little steam engine—always plainly visible within showcase windows—added as much charm as the waterwheel.

Two of Ford's largest hydroelectric sites were obtained from the United States government. These were dams on the Hudson River near Troy, New York, and on the Mississippi River at Minneapolis-St. Paul, both built during World War I to aid navi-

An Irving Bacon rendition of Henry Ford and friends in front of the Miller School at Dearborn where young Henry operated his homemade waterwheel. (833-80243)

gation. The power possibilities were being wasted. It is certain that Thomas Edison influenced Ford in the use of waterpower. Edison had laid the cornerstone of the hydroelectric plant at Ford's home in Dearborn in 1915. Burroughs, Edison, Ford, and Firestone—in the order of their age—carved their initials, "B E F F," in the cornerstone of the powerful Green Island, New York, hydroelectric plant in 1919.

Ford's smaller waterpower projects in south-eastern Michigan were part of his Village Industries concept, by which farmers could work in a small local factory most of the year and also care for their farms.[2] Ford did not like to see men leave the farm for better pay in the city. These village plants were noted for their high standards of craftsmanship and for their friendly, hometown atmosphere. There were about twenty of these small southeastern Michigan hydro-electric installations, each employing at most a few hundred workers. Not all of these plants can be described in this short account, but a few representative of the group are included.

NORTHVILLE

Of this southeastern Michigan group, the Northville installation is said to have been the first in production.[3] It is but a few miles up the Rouge River from Ford's home in Dearborn. The plant operated from 1920 until December 1988. For the entire period it produced valves for Ford engines.

In the early years the Fitz overshot wheel produced only twenty-two horsepower. Later it was supplemented by Detroit Edison Company power. However the waterwheel still turns, providing a picturesque setting for the present structure and a quiet millpond for resident ducks. The Northville plant had produced more than one billion valves for Ford engines since it began operating March 20, 1920. That was about seventy-five percent of Ford Motor Company requirements. At most, about 250 workers were

employed. Northville has the distinction of being the last as well as the first of the Village Industry plants to operate as a Ford Motor Company production facility. Northville was closed by Ford in December 1988.

NANKIN MILLS

This old gristmill of colonial design, supported by hand-hewn beams and finished in clapboard, was bought by Henry Ford in 1918.[4] It is located just a few miles upstream on the same river as Ford's home in Dearborn. Upon installation of a modern turbine in 1920, the system produced fifty horsepower. For about eighteen years the plant employed ten men and manufactured machine screws for assembly of Ford vehicles. The workmen lived nearby on "small farms" typically of two to five acres each, and enjoyed shop-farm security.

In 1937 it became obvious to Ford that forty horsepower was going to waste and should be used. He had estimated that, generally speaking, one

Henry Ford's first practical hydroelectric plant at his farm on the Rouge River at Dearborn. Built in 1910, it was replaced in 1915 by a larger powerhouse to serve his new residence named Fair Lane. (188-16223)

Table 1
FORD MOTOR COMPANY HYDRO-ELECTRIC POWER PLANTS
(October, 1940)

Plant name	River	Started	Max. H.P.	Head	Water wheels
Brooklyn	Raisin	1939		23	Morgan Smith
Clarkston	Clinton	1940		30	Under construction
Delhi	Huron			32	Being designed
Dundee	Raisin	1936	192	6	8 Leffels
Flat Rock	Huron	1923	1,000	7.5	2 Allis-Chalmers
Goose Creek	Goose Creek			14	Under construction
Green Island	Hudson, N.Y.	1923	8,000	14.5	4 Allis-Chalmers
Hamilton	Miami, Ohio	1920	3,275	27.5	3 Leffels
Hudson Mill	Huron			13	Under construction
Iron Mountain	Menominee	1923	10,000	30	3 Allis-Chalmers
Manchester	Raisin	1939	210	14	2 Leffels
Milan	Saline	1938	40	8	1 Leffel
Milford-Huron	Huron	1939	275	14	2 Leffels
Milford-Pettibone	Pettibone	1938	167	52	2 Leffels
Nankin Mills	Rouge	1920	52	15	1 Leffel
Newburg	Rouge	1935	36	18.5	1 Leffel
Northville	Rouge	1920	22	22	1 Overshot
Phoenix	Rouge	1922	45	19.5	1 Leffel
Plymouth	Rouge	1923	31	17	1 Allis-Chalmers
Saline	Saline	1938	88	20.6	1 Leffel
Sharron Mill	Raisin	1938	41	8	1 Leffel
Tecumseh	Raisin	1935	37	16	1 Overshot
Twin Cities	Mississippi	1924	18,000	31.5	4 Wellman Sayer Morgan
Waterford	Rouge	1925	52	23	1 Leffel
Willow Run	Willow Run	1939	20	21	2 Leffels
Ypsilanti	Huron	1932	2,500	33	2 Leffels

SITES BEING CONSIDERED

Plant name	River	Started	Max. H.P.	Head	Water wheels
Coon's Mill	Rouge		—	—	
Dexter	Mill Creek		75	13.3	
Norvel	Raisin		—	—	
Pinkney	Portage		25	15	
Southfield	Rouge		50	21	
Waterford	Clinton		30	8.6	

horsepower should employ one man. So forty more men were transferred to Nankin from the Rouge plant. These men were mostly tool-and-die makers who lived in or near Nankin Township. The plant became noted for its high-quality dies, engravings, and stencils. The trademark Ford, for example, was engraved in letters .006″ high on delicate instrument faces. And the small, inconspicuous Ford Safety Glass logo used to identify Ford automotive glass was stenciled at Nankin on rolls of motion picture film at six-inch intervals; at the Ford glass plants the identification could be sandblasted onto the glass through the stencil prepared at Nankin. For years Nankin was the sole source of dies for Ford employee badges used at Ford operations all over the world. Nankin Mills no longer belongs to the Ford Motor Company;

it was acquired in 1954 by the Wayne County Road Commission and is now maintained as part of a riverside nature center.

SALINE

One of the last of the small waterpowered mills to be renovated by Ford was at Saline, Michigan, on the Saline River at the western outskirts of the village. The site had supported a gristmill for many years before Ford's purchase in 1934. In 1938, when the mill was fully restored, the waterwheel could produce nearly ninety horsepower. The mill was to be used by the Ford Motor Company to process soybeans, which were being grown on the thousands of acres belonging to the nearby Ford Farms.[5]

Soybeans had been grown in large quantities for industrial purposes by Ford since 1932 when results of his research indicated they would greatly benefit farmers and industry alike. His working exhibits at the Chicago World's Fair in 1934 had emphasized the value of the soybean to the farmer. Ford, by 1938, was demonstrating the soybean business in the Saline area on a grand scale.

The harvested beans were cleaned, flaked, and by means of a solvent the soybean oil was extracted for use in automotive paints and plastics. The residual soybean meal was then used in Ford foundries for core making, and the surplus sold as cattle feed. The plant employed about twenty men, most of whom lived on nearby farms. If the worker did not own

Thomas Edison, John Burroughs, Henry Ford, and Harvey Firestone pose atop a waterwheel at Old Evans Mill in Leadmine, West Virginia, while on a camping trip in 1918. (833-62887)

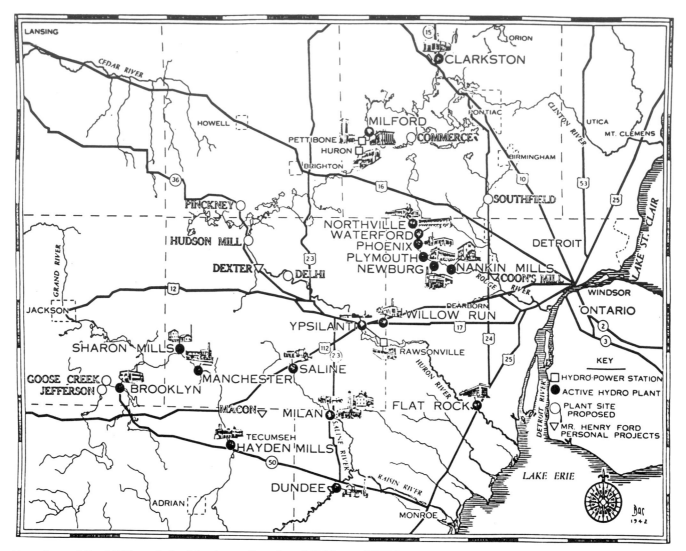

Locations of Ford Village Industries in southeastern Michigan. (77015)

land, Ford furnished him a part-time garden plot near the plant.

The Saline mill was sold by Ford in 1946, but still retains its historical appearance as an antique furniture shop. A large plastics manufacturing plant has in the meantime been built by Ford Motor Company on the opposite side of the town.

DUNDEE

Henry Ford became interested in the small hydroelectric plant at Dundee, Michigan, as early as 1922, soon after he had bought the D. T. & I. Rail-

road, a spur line of which went through the town on its way to Tecumseh. The plant was on the Raisin River and belonged to the Dundee Power Company, which produced electric power for the town of Dundee and vicinity. Assessed value of the installation at that time was $29,000.[6]

Normal head at the dam was six feet, eight inches, driving two forty-inch Trump turbines rated at seventy-seven horsepower each. Correspondence from 1922 to 1935 shows Ford's interest in the plant vacillating until October 1935, when options offering one hundred dollars per acre were obtained on farms bordering the river. Deeds were obtained in 1936. Upon acquisition, the Ford Motor Company restored the original mill structure, added a stone chimney

This old gristmill at Saline, Michigan, was used by Ford Farms for the processing of soybeans. Photo taken in May 1938. (188-23330)

The Dundee hydroelectric plant on the Raisin River specialized in the production of copper welding rods. Photo taken in July 1937. (188-21310)

and one-story wing, and considered raising the dam height by one foot. Maximum horsepower was raised to 192 by installing new Leffel turbines.

The hydroelectric plant at Dundee became a foundry and machine shop specializing in copper alloys. It employed about seventy-five workers. The chief products were welding electrodes for electric spot welding of steel. Electrodes were used by the thousands in the welding of vehicle frames and bodies—each vehicle requiring more than three thousand welds. Copper was supplied to Dundee from Ypsilanti where the production of electric motors and generators resulted in a quantity of copper scrap. A year's production at Dundee (1937) amounted to 319,656 electrodes. The City of Dundee now owns the structure, which is now undergoing re-restoration by the Old Mill Restoration Committee, a volunteer organization.

FLAT ROCK

Flat Rock, Michigan, another old gristmill site on the Huron River only fourteen miles south of the Dearborn Rouge plant, was bought by Henry Ford in 1921.[7] The purchase included power rights and six hundred acres of land. Construction was carried on through 1921 and 1922 with automotive-related production starting in 1923. Waterpower at first provided about 700 kilowatts (938 horsepower). This plant was destined to become the Ford lamp factory, making headlight, taillight, and interior light shells, reflectors, and lamp sockets. With five hundred men working two shifts the plant could produce five hundred thousand headlights a month.

In 1928 the dam was rebuilt and widened to accommodate the tracks of Ford's D. T. & I. Railroad, which had its main switching yards at Flat Rock. Auxiliary steam power is believed to have been added at this time by using a triple-expansion steam engine salvaged from one of the "199 ships" dismantled by Ford in 1927.

Employment peaked at twelve hundred in 1929. Complete lamps were assembled with wiring, bulbs, and lenses shipped in by other suppliers. These were then shipped to Ford assembly plants all over the world.

The Flat Rock plant was sold by Ford Motor Company in 1950, and operations moved to the

A view of the factory and powerhouse at Flat Rock, Michigan. The dam at far right forms a bridge over the Huron River for Ford's D. T. & I. Railroad. (833-4768)

larger Monroe, Michigan, site. The dam still serves as a railroad bridge.

YPSILANTI

The Ford plant at Ypsilanti, Michigan, has obtained its power from a hydroelectric complex on the Huron River. The manufacturing plant is in the city of Ypsilanti, but the dam and generators are four miles downriver from the plant (at Rawsonville), creating a twelve hundred-acre lake (Ford Lake) between dam and plant. The hydroelectric installation, constructed in 1932, can produce twenty-eight hundred horsepower from a thirty-three-foot water head. Two Leffel turbines generate twenty-one hundred kilowatts—the total output consumed by the Ypsilanti plant.

The plant has produced primarily automotive generators, starters, and starter switches, using about twelve-hundred workers.[8] Some seventy-five hundred generators, each made up of about five hundred parts, have been built in an eight-hour shift. Nearly one hundred needy women and perhaps twenty-five elderly men were employed at one time at light work in the plant. Boys, age eighteen to nineteen, attended Apprentice School and were paid fifty-five cents an hour during training, followed by the standard seventy-five cents.

During the Depression years of the early 1930s, the Ford Motor Company was in the business of rebuilding complete automobiles and many automotive parts. At Ypsilanti nearly fifteen percent of the total production consisted of rebuilt generators and starters.

Workers were encouraged to supplement their

income by gardening on their own land, but if they needed land there were four thousand acres of Ford land surrounding Ford Lake that the company would provide for part-time gardens. The Ypsilanti plant is still a major electrical parts supplier of Ford Motor Company.

HAMILTON

The Hamilton hydroelectric site was purchased by Henry Ford & Son in 1919, to be used as a manufacturing plant for Fordson tractor transmissions.[9] It is on the Great Miami River about fifteen miles north of Cincinnati, Ohio. The Ford Tractor Building, as it was called, was designed by Frederick G. Mueller, and built by Vaughn Building Company. The dam was designed by the Hamilton Hydraulic Company in cooperation with the Miami Conservancy District. Waterpower produced 3,000 horsepower, while a small steam plant produced steam capable of generating 250 horsepower. Most factories require some steam as well as electricity for plant use.

Production began May 13, 1920, with employment soon growing to six hundred men who were building four hundred tractor transmissions a day. At least twenty percent of the employees lived on farms. Soon, however, tractor manufacturing was concentrated at the Rouge, and by early 1922 the Hamilton plant was busy building wheels for Model T automobiles. Output of wheels was two hundred sets (eight hundred wheels) per eight-hour day, with a schedule of six hundred sets (twenty-four hundred wheels) per sixteen-hour day planned. This rate of production required the fabrication of thirty thou-

The hydroelectric plant on the Huron River just below the Ypsilanti plant of the Ford Motor Company in November 1932. (833-57216-4)

sand kiln-dried hardwood spokes daily. By April 1923 production is said to have reached seventy-five hundred wheels with ninety thousand spokes per sixteen hours. But this great number supplied less than one-quarter of total Model T requirements.

In December 1928 a report indicated that Hamilton was still building wheels, but now the entirely different all-steel Model A variety. Hamilton had passed the two million total wheel production mark, and now was fabricating the new steel wheels at the rate of fourteen thousand per day employing twenty-eight hundred people. In addition, 19,800 running boards were being produced daily. Automotive "Wheels and parts" were still being manufactured at Hamilton until World War II, when production shifted to aircraft engine parts. Ford sold the plant to the Bendix Aviation Corporation in June 1951.

GREEN ISLAND

This plant is on the Hudson River a few miles above Troy, New York.[10] It was a government facility built in 1917 consisting of the dam and 189 acres—almost one-third of the 640-acre island. An application to lease the dam and operate a power plant from the government was made in 1918 by Henry Ford & Son, not by Ford Motor Company. Henry Ford was not yet sole owner of Ford Motor Company and had organized Henry Ford & Son as a separate corporation to build tractors. Green Island was to be one of his tractor-manufacturing plants, with the distinct advantage of being on the most direct waterway between Dearborn and Atlantic ports. The license to operate was granted on March 3, 1921. After two years of powerhouse construction work, the plant was first operated on February 19, 1923, by the Ford Motor Company, which was by 1923 owned exclusively by the Ford family: Henry, Edsel, and Clara Ford.

Although 162 miles up the Hudson River from the Atlantic Ocean, the Hudson at Green Island was affected by tides of 4.5 feet, twice each twenty-four hours. The plant normally operated with a fifteen-foot head (maximum head thirty-feet), producing about ten thousand horsepower by means of four low-head turbines (then largest in the world), each providing both alternating and direct current from the same vertical shaft: 4,500 volts AC and 250 volts DC. Ford was a proponent of direct current for many years after it was usually considered inefficient. Enough power was produced at Green Island to allow the entire Ford plant to be heated by electricity rather than steam.

Employing 750–900 men, the plant first produced copper radiators. Later, leaf spring production was added. Green Island has more recently been a major supplier of aluminum heat exchangers for the Ford Motor Company. Ford Motor Company closed the Green Island plant in early 1989. On the island beside the plant, the Ford Motor Company has maintained a large public recreation grounds named Ford Park. A small pyramid of stones in Ford Park marks the spot where Burroughs, Edison, Ford and Firestone camped on their 1919 vacation trip.

IRON MOUNTAIN

Because Model T bodies were constructed with a framework of wood, Henry Ford concluded he should have his own supply of hardwood timber. The Upper Peninsula of Michigan seemed a likely area to find the supply he needed. With the help of a relative, Edward Kingsford, a tract of four hundred thousand acres was obtained during 1919, and plans for the construction of a mammoth sawmill and wood chemical plant at Iron Mountain were announced in July 1920. Power for the plant was at first generated by four huge steam boilers burning oil, wood, and refuse to provide twelve thousand horsepower.

The Green Island power plant on the Hudson River above Troy, New York. This plant was built by Henry Ford & Son in 1919. (0-7856)

Ford hydro plant on the Menominee River separating Michigan (right) from Wisconsin. Power from this plant was supplied to the Iron Mountain sawmill and chemical plant. (Photo from the John W. Bennett collection.)

Within about two miles of the sawmill the Menominee River ran, separating Michigan and Wisconsin, and consideration was given to the use of waterpower in 1922. Work was begun in 1923, but considerable time was spent in buying the property upstream that would be flooded by the dam. A head of thirty feet was to be provided. The dam was completed in 1924, and three Allis-Chalmers hydroelectric generators supplied the plant with eleven thousand maximum horsepower.

The dam extended across the river a distance of 240 feet, with a 115-foot core wall into Wisconsin and a wall of 175 feet on the Michigan side. The powerhouse and plant were in Michigan, and electricity was fed to the sawmill and chemical plant through a two-mile system of underground conduits. The wires carried 2,300 volts direct current to a substation that converted the electricity to 220 volts alternating current for plant use.

Mill and chemical plant employment peaked at eight thousand during 1925. However production of wooden station wagon bodies, "woodies," was discontinued in 1949, being displaced by all-steel bodies. During World War II the Iron Mountain plant produced thousands of wood-bodied invasion gliders used with much success in Europe and Africa. In 1945 the Ford operations were gradually closed and by 1951 Ford had sold out. The dam and generators are now being used by the Wisconsin-Michigan Electric Power Company to supply electricity to the general area.[11]

TWIN CITIES

On the upper reaches of the Mississippi River, in the lands of Hiawatha, were the sparkling falls of Minnehaha. Hiawatha no doubt enjoyed paddling his canoe down the many rapids of the great, wide Father of Waters, but the white man instead became intent on pushing his steamboats as far as possible up the Mississippi to the twin cities of Minneapolis and St. Paul, each facing the other across the legendary river.[12]

In 1912 an engineering consultant, Adolph Meyer, was commissioned by Minnesota State University to prepare a Report on Feasibility of Water-Power Development at the Mississippi High Dam by the Municipal Electric Company of the State of Minnesota. The report estimated that a peak 15,200 horsepower (10,500 kilowatts) could be produced with a yearly average of 9,000 kilowatts.[13]

The location studied, henceforth called the High Dam, became the site of a federal dam completed in 1917 for the dual purpose of flood control and a navigation aid permitting ships to reach Minneapolis docks. At the Minneapolis end of the dam were two locks that would accommodate ships 150 feet long and 50 feet wide. On the St. Paul end of the dam were foundations constructed for an eventual powerhouse.

After World War I, the Federal Power Commission was ready to permit a private or municipal developer to build and use a hydroelectric plant. It was expected that the cities of Minneapolis and St. Paul would jointly develop the project. St. Paul, however, was favoring a private investor—specifically a plan presented by Henry Ford.

Back in 1912 Ford automobiles were being sold by a distributor in Minneapolis, and in 1914 a small assembly plant had been established. Thus Henry Ford was constantly appraised of the situation about the High Dam. In the summer of 1921 Ford offered to invest $10 million to build a hydroelectric generating plant and also build a large manufacturing and assembly plant for autos and tractors—a plant to employ five thousand workers. Both cities, after two years of intense bickering, agreed to accept the Ford plan over their own municipal plans and that of another contender, Northern States Power Company. The promise of work for so many people undoubtedly influenced the decision.

The Ford hydroelectric plant and the new eleven hundred-by-six hundred-foot manufacturing plant were started in 1923 and became operational in 1925. Four huge turbines, each producing forty-five hundred horsepower, provided 80 million kilowatt hours annually—an amount equivalent to burning one hundred thousand tons of coal. The manufacturing plant, heated by steam, could assemble five hundred automobiles a day. Below the high bluff on which the new plant was built, and directly under the plant, an unexpected large quantity of pure silica sand was found. In March 1926 the manufacture of glass was started using the silica sand. This added operation could produce fifty thousand square feet of automotive glass a day.

The Twin Cities plant of Ford Motor Company was, at the time of construction, second only to the Rouge in size. It is still a major automotive assembly facility of the Ford Motor Company.

MUSCLE SHOALS

During 1921–24, while he was putting government dams to use on the Hudson and Mississippi rivers, Henry Ford had in mind a still larger waterpower

Twin Cities facilities from Minneapolis side of Mississippi River in July 1926. Hydroelectric plant is in foreground with steam power plant on river below dam. The one-story automotive assembly plant designed by Albert Kahn and once called the "most beautiful industrial plant in the world" is seen on the river bluff in background. (189-3477)

5

THE D. T. & I. RAILROAD

Henry Ford was a man who could be easily annoyed. He was a fastidious and independent perfectionist. His Model T automobile manufacturing plant at Highland Park, Michigan, was a model of efficiency, innovative beyond compare, and the envy of other manufacturers, yet Ford recognized weaknesses. His tremendous success on that fifty-six-acre site had put him in a landlocked situation where expansion was next to impossible. Another annoyance was his being solely dependent on unreliable railroad transportation to move his matériel to and from his factory. As early as 1917, six years before the Highland Park plant had reached its peak output, Henry told close relatives that what he had there was "a drop in the bucket" compared to his plans for the Rouge. He had already bought thousands of acres in the Dearborn area, and had decided that his major plants would henceforth be on navigable water.[1]

Building the Rouge was very difficult. His stockholders, especially the Dodge brothers, were dead set against it and had to be bought out at tremendous expense. The land bordering the Rouge River was swampy and the river required straightening and dredging to allow sizeable ships to navigate. About this time (1920), when work was proceeding on docks, power plant, blast furnaces, and foundries at

the Rouge, Henry foresaw other problems. He was annoyed by the likelihood that Wall Street interests might try to strangle his business by restricting his supply of raw materials. This was a period when Henry was investing heavily in forestlands, iron mines, coal mines, and was concerned about the reliability of his sources of limestone, glass sand, rubber, and lead.[2]

The Rouge waterway required the rebuilding of several bridges across the river downstream of the plant. One of these bridges belonged to the Detroit, Toledo and Ironton Railroad (D. T. & I.), a nearly defunct organization, fully mortgaged and unable to raise the $350,000 necessary to rebuild its bridge. Ford was asked by the D. T. & I. to guarantee bonds that would have to be issued to raise the money. During 1920 Ford not only advanced $521,000 toward reconstruction costs and bond-interest payments for the D. T. & I. but by July 9 had bought controlling interest in the entire system.[3] The following January a $15 million improvement program was announced, and on March 4, 1921, Henry Ford became president of the road. He had paid about $5 million for nearly all the outstanding stock except that held by two bothersome New Yorkers, and now was responsible for a complete but totally decrepit railroad system. He had bought 456 miles of badly deteriorated roadbed meandering through Ohio, 41 small railroad stations, 75 old steam locomotives, 2,800 mortgaged freight cars, and 27 vintage passenger cars. The line had been disparagingly described as "a streak of rust." Did Henry know what he was doing?[4]

The Detroit, Toledo and Ironton Railroad had started out as the old Iron Railway in 1849, and first extended only six miles from Ironton, Ohio, on the Ohio River, to Vesuvius, Ohio. But this short stretch of road into the hills included a 958-foot tunnel and a wrought-iron bridge 97 feet long, both of which may still be in service. Thus it started as a small but ambitious line. Little by little, the Iron Railway was re-fashioned through purchases, consolidations, and leases of dubious value for more than fifty years, until it became the Detroit, Toledo and Ironton in 1903 with its northern terminal at Detroit. By July 9, 1920, when Henry Ford became owner, the railroad had been through no less than twenty-six unsuccessful reorganizations. During all this time it had remained chiefly a coal-hauling line with miles of branches and sidings leading from small southern Ohio mines to its main north-south system.[5]

It turns out that Ford had not acquired the D. T. & I. blindly. He had visualized the benefits it might provide his own automotive operations. It seems that during that same July 1920 Henry Ford had also bought two coal mines, the Banner Fork properties at Wallins Creek and Tinsdale, Kentucky. Later the same year he bought a coal mine at Nuttalburg, West Virginia. These were forerunners of the Fordson Coal Company, a $15 million operation, which would more than supply the coal needs of the Ford Motor Company. The D. T. & I. would bring this coal from the coalfields directly to the Rouge.

Henry Ford could not bear to be associated for long with such a disreputable piece of property. Immediately upon his becoming president of the railroad the renovation began. Incumbent D. T. & I. officers were replaced with Ford men. E. G. Liebold became vice president and financial manager of the railroad, just as he likewise managed many other businesses for Ford. F. L. Rockelman was made vice president and operations manager. Stanley P. Ruddiman became vice president and chief engineer, and W. C. Cowling became director of traffic, all with executive offices in Dearborn.[6]

High efficiency with good wages was the keynote. Some four hundred illegal encroachments were found on D. T. & I. property. Businesses as well as

individual squatters had usurped bits of D. T. & I. territory, often having erected eyesore shacks along the right-of-way. Strict enforcement of property rights reduced these encroachments to fewer than a dozen. Railroad accounting procedures were centralized with paperwork cut in half. The Legal Department was abolished with the Claims Department absorbing that work. The backlog of freight damage claims was reduced from 1,209 to 68. The total work force was cut from 2,760 to 1,650; wages of remaining employees went from about $3.75 for eight hours to the Ford $6.00 minimum wage. Soon the average office worker was receiving $8.11, others $7.26, per day. With these increased wages, Ford was able to abrogate all existing union contracts and assign workers to any job they were capable of handling. These wages were above those prescribed by the Railway Labor Board, and high enough to receive acclaim from the Railroad Brotherhood. Before long the sixteen-hour maximum workday was reduced to twelve hours, with management forecasting an eight-hour maximum.[7]

An Employee Investment Program was inaugurated yielding ten to sixteen percent annual interest over the next several years. Coal was offered to employees at wholesale prices: "run of mine," $3 per ton; "egg," $3.25; "lump," $3.50. An employee newsletter, the D. T. & I. Railroad News, was begun in January 1923 and continued as a semimonthly until December 1927. This eight-page publication described D. T. & I. construction projects and delivered general advice to workmen. It devoted at least two pages in each issue to railroad safety, and included a practical medical page written by a staff doctor of Henry Ford Hospital.[8]

However, strict work requirements were enforced. Train crews were to be clean-shaven, in clean overalls, white cap, and goggles; and all employees were to be neat in appearance and industrious in attitude. There was to be no idleness. Of the crew of a waiting train, all but the flagman were to be either polishing the locomotive or cleaning the caboose rather than standing idle. At the end of a run, a dirty engine was immediately cleaned and polished by the engine crew before being dispatched on an-

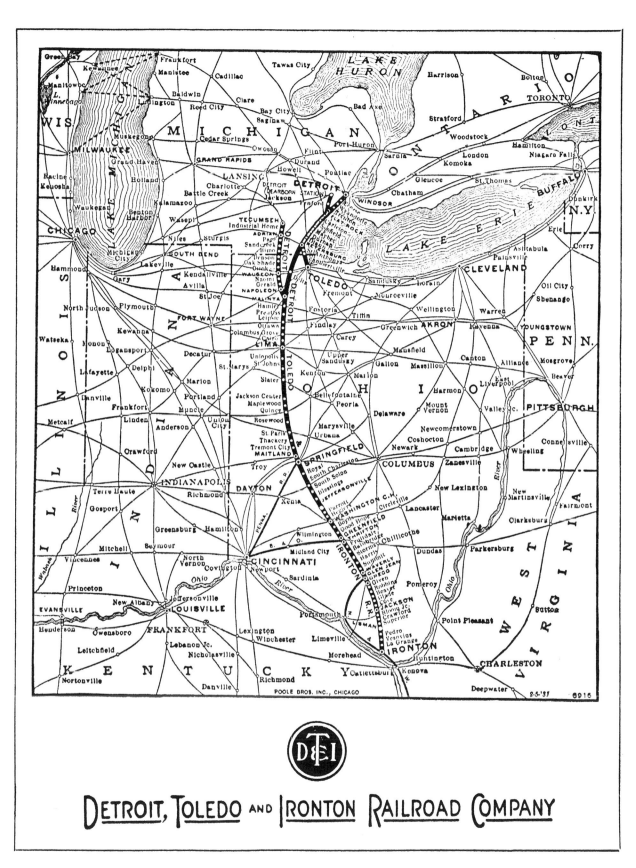

other run. An "impact recorder" hidden on the train could record the degree to which the cars had been bumped or jostled in transit, thus monitoring the performance of the engineer and reducing damage claims. Crossing guards were expected to care for a small vegetable garden or flower bed in their spare time.

This revitalized work force was to put the long neglected railroad properties in order. Miles of roadbed were reballasted with rock, gravel, and by-product slag from the Rouge furnaces. Old lightweight, sixty-pound rail was replaced with new eighty-pound rail bought from Belgium. Old rails were used as grade-crossing reinforcement. Old ties were converted to charcoal for commercial use. The Rouge concrete casting plant supplied concrete replacement fence posts for use along the rights-of-way. Bridges were rebuilt with cement shipped from Fordson. Stations and toolhouses were repaired and

repainted. Major shops and roundhouses were reequipped, and a large locomotive repair facility, which would employ 475 men, was constructed at the Rouge. Ten new steam locomotives and eight hundred freight cars were purchased in this first phase of renovation.

About 350 employees were loaned new Hamilton watches, which were periodically checked for accuracy. An electrically controlled clock system, with master in Dearborn, automatically adjusted clocks in stations the entire length of the system. New copper telegraph and telephone wires replaced the badly rusted iron wire to provide clear messages and dispatch signals throughout the system. Dispatching was done at Fordson and Springfield, Ohio. For a time, radio, with stations in Dearborn (KDEN) and Jackson and Springfield, Ohio, handled traffic messages at the rate of ten thousand per month. This was superseded by purely telephone.

Detroit, Toledo and Ironton bridge spanning the Short-Cut Canal connecting the Rouge River ship canal with the Detroit River (1923). The bridge has unique underslung counterweights. (833-34942)

Restored Locomotive No. 7 with baggage/mail car and passenger coach at
Detroit (Delray) station on West Jefferson Avenue in 1923. (U-35208)

D. T. & I. passenger train on Railroad Street in the small town of Ironton in
1923. (833-36365)

As to original rolling stock, Henry Ford had inherited seventy-five steam locomotives of which fifty could be considered serviceable. The others had been stored along the line in various states of disrepair. At least ten of these locomotives had originally been built for the Soviet Union, designed for a wide (sixty-inch) tread, and were top-heavy for our narrower

Freight and passenger station at Ironton, Ohio, in 1923. In the background are the Ohio River and Kentucky. (188-36329)

tracks.[9] These locomotives needed to be rebuilt to correct their deficiencies. The Fordson shops started a program by which eventually four locomotives a month could be rebuilt. In all, seventy-three locomotives were completely overhauled and fitted out with the characteristic nickel-plated piping and fixtures, polished and lacquered boiler sheet, and white-painted wheel rims insisted on by Ford. Upkeep of passenger and freight cars was handled at Jackson, Ohio, where elaborate erecting and machine shops could repair or rebuild all common types. New dining cars, compartment cars, work cars, and cabooses were fitted out at the Jackson facility. Besides the earlier purchase, new freight cars were added in 1927 with the acquisition of one thousand boxcars, four hundred gondolas, fifty flatcars, and forty cabooses. Titles to these new locomotives and cars were held by the Ford Transportation Company, a Ford family corporation that leased the equipment to D. T. & I.[10]

By July 1, 1922, the railroad was approaching profitability, and a request by D. T. & I. for a twenty percent reduction in freight rates was granted by the Interstate Commerce Commission despite the protests of other railroads. At that same time a major project was in the planning stage. This included:

End of the line at the Ohio River. The D. T. & I. terminated as a "cradle" designed for transferring cars to and from river barges. During Ford ownership, however, freight cars were instead transferred to and from the Chesapeake & Ohio and Norfolk & Western railroads, which owned bridges into Kentucky. Photo taken in 1923. (833-36345)

Ford with oldest D. T. & I. locomotive. One of four locomotives built in 1897, Engine No. 7 was fully restored in 1920 at the Rouge, using parts from three sister engines that had been scrapped. Number 7 served the D. T. & I. as a passenger engine for many years before being placed in the Henry Ford Museum. (0-6700)

1. Building of a new 13.5 mile double track directly connecting the Rouge plant with the D. T. & I. tracks at Flat Rock
2. Electrification of the new lines between the Rouge (Fordson) and Flat Rock
3. Employment of large steam-electric turbine generators at the Rouge powerhouse to power the electrified portion of the railroad
4. Design and construction of electric locomotives of uniquely efficient performance
5. Erection of a plant for fabrication of reinforced concrete trolley supports for the electrified system

This direct link to Flat Rock would eliminate switching charges and costly delays. Ford's intent was to move things by the shortest route to save shippers valuable shipping time and thus also reduce his own "inventory float" by \$30–40 million. This electrified system was to be separately incorporated as the Detroit and Ironton Railroad and leased to the D. T. & I. These new lines between Fordson and Flat Rock became the Detroit & Ironton Railroad; Henry, Edsel, and Clara Ford were sponsors and sole owners.

The Fordson-Flat Rock lines became major investments. Besides the new heavy-service double tracks, there were large electrified classification yards just north of Flat Rock (South Yards) and at Fordson (North Yards). Three hundred sixty-five reinforced concrete arches spanned these tracks at three hundred-foot intervals and supported the trolley wires. Power for the electrified system was generated at the Rouge powerhouse by means of 150,000-volt, 62,500-horsepower steam turbines supplying sixty-cycle alternating current. A substation phase converter near the Rouge plant reduced the voltage to

Yards at Jackson, Ohio. These shops handled most of the repairs on cars and locomotives for the entire system. (833-36491)

23,000 and frequency to twenty-five cycles, which was fed to the trolley wires. The electric locomotives were designed each with a 23,000-to-1,200 volts step-down transformer and a motor-generator to provide 600 volts direct current to the driving motors on each axle. The locomotive had eight traction motors together producing 2,300 horsepower. Two of these giant articulated electric locomotives were assembled at Highland Park shops during 1925 and 1926.[11]

There were normally four freight trains a day between Fordson and Ironton. From 1921 to 1923 car-miles and ton-miles doubled as locomotives traveled farther and hauled larger loads. The trip from Fordson to Ironton required twenty-four to twenty-six hours. On the way several connections were made through central Ohio with main east-west carriers such as New York Central, Pennsylvania, and Baltimore & Ohio. Farther south, connections were made with the Chesapeake & Ohio and Norfolk & Western, large coal carriers from Kentucky and West Virginia. At Ironton, the end of the D. T. & I. line, was a rail/river transfer point where an old "cradle" on the river's edge had been designed to roll freight cars onto and off Ohio River barges.

Passenger traffic on the D. T. & I. was practically nil. However, the Interstate Commerce Commission (ICC) forced the railroad to maintain passenger and mail service between Detroit and Springfield, Ohio, with a train each way each day. An effort to abandon the passenger trains was to no avail. In 1926 two gasoline-electric, Pullman-built cars replaced the passenger trains on the 280-mile run between Detroit and Bainbridge, Ohio. These Benzol-burning coaches were fast and economical.[12] And instead of a special steam train, flanged-wheel Model T sedans carried track inspectors over the lines in comfort.

Another major improvement in the rail system was a 56-mile cutoff between Durban, Michigan, and Malinta, Ohio. This line was built during 1926–29 as a Detroit and Ironton project, and included a 344-foot bridge over the Raisin River as well as a 1,000-foot bridge over the Maumee. During winter months concrete bridge construction was continued by using heated materials; bridge structures were protected from freezing by tight canvas enclosures filled with steam. The direct Durban-Malinta line saved 20.6 miles as well as considerable rise, fall, and curvature in the distance from Dearborn to Malinta.

Although electrification for the D. T. & I. was

completed only as far as Flat Rock, with trolley supports to Carleton, there were plans to electrify the lines as far as Springfield, Ohio. Surveys were also made for a line from near Bainbridge to Portsmouth on the Ohio River. There was serious consideration given to buying the Virginian Railroad, an electrified system that would have provided an outlet from Portsmouth to the Atlantic coast and ocean shipping. Henry Ford would have offered as much as $50 million for the Virginian, it is said. For several reasons these plans did not materialize.

From the beginning there were things about operating a railroad that nettled Ford. These things had largely to do with government regulation. The very year he purchased the D. T. & I. the Transportation

Act of 1920 read in part: "The Commission [ICC] shall as soon as practicable prepare and adopt a plan for consolidation of the railway properties of the continental United States into a limited number of systems." The D. T. & I. was by this plan to be merged with other railroads, including the Pere Marquette. Although the merger was never pressed by Pere Marquette during Ford's ownership, the realization that a merger was the aim of the government could not help dampening Ford's independent spirit.

Another restrictive government regulation concerned profits. Of any profit above six percent of "value" of the road, half was to be turned over to the ICC for distribution to other railroads. This penalized efficient management and made it difficult to mod-

Electrified "south yards" near Flat Rock in 1927. Reinforced concrete arches were cast at the Rouge plant in Fordson. (833-48757)

Electric locomotive hauling freight over Fordson-Flat Rock section. At completion, this locomotive was said to be the most powerful electric locomotive ever built. It could haul a mile and a half of loaded cars, but at relatively low speed. (833-46380)

Combination mail-baggage-passenger car, which replaced the passenger train in 1927. There were two of these gasoline-electric cars with "front wheel drive" burning high-octane Benzol fuel. Gasoline engines were placed under the floor to save space. (833-49470)

Model T "railroad sedan" used for road inspections. These operated without steering systems. Later models were fitted with pneumatic tires. (833-49469)

ernize a railroad from its own profits. The Fords were taking no dividends. All earnings were used for improvements.

The federal government had never relinquished its wartime control over freight rates, wages, hours, accounting procedures, and many other aspects of the railroad business, which left little flexibility or room for initiative without getting into trouble. In particular, Ford's interest in the use of lightweight rolling stock had been completely blocked by the ICC. In 1927, losing interest, Ford relinquished his office as president to Stanley Ruddiman. The final blow may have struck in July 1928 when Ford was slapped with a twenty thousand dollar fine for violating the Elkins Act, an act adopted by the federal government in 1903 dealing with rate discrimination. In 1928 Edsel Ford is said to have contacted the Detroit agent of the Pennsylvania Railroad saying, "My father and I have had our fun with the D. T. & I." As a result the Pennsylvania Railroad formed the Pennroad Corporation to buy the Ford railroad properties. After much negotiation and the waiving of an illegal gentlemen's agreement to favor D. T. & I. with Ford Motor Company shipments, the $36 million sale was consummated on June 27, 1929.[13]

Despite the large investments in roadbed, shops, and rolling stock, Ford's railroad was especially profitable during 1923–26. His profits had totaled about $9 million. And he sold at an advantageous time, just before the Great Depression. He had had his fling at railroading and had demonstrated how a railroad could and should be run despite contentious stockholders and repressive regulators. Now he would be content with his private railway car, the Fair Lane, riding on someone else's rails. He still had one hundred miles of track and twenty-five switch engines inside the Rouge complex should he ever want to dirty his hands.

When Ford sold his railroad properties, Stanley P. Ruddiman, who was president under Ford (1927–29), was made vice president under the new Pennsylvania management. Later, Ruddiman again became president of the D. T. & I., serving from 1933 until his retirement in 1952. The D. T. & I. had maintained its corporate identity, but was controlled by the Pennsylvania from 1929 until 1968. At that time the Pennsylvania merged with the New York Central to form the Penn-Central Corporation, a system that became bankrupt after only two years.

The D. T. & I., as such, was considered choice property, and bids were immediately offered by the Chesapeake & Ohio, the Norfolk & Western, and the Grand Trunk Western. However, the massive 1973–76 reorganization resulting in Conrail for years delayed the sale of D. T. & I., and it was a surprise when in June 1980 the Grand Trunk Western bought it for $25.8 million.

Grand Trunk now operates the D. T. & I. profitably; diesel locomotives long ago replaced steam and electric power. The giant electric locomotives were scrapped in 1937. As of this writing, the D. T. & I. now hauls primarily automobiles, auto parts, and steel. Ford business still amounts to nearly fifty percent of the total traffic. Coal, coke, and petroleum products also furnish sizeable revenues, followed closely by food and chemicals. Many of the now unused concrete arches still stand as monuments to the Ford era, as do the river bridges, the viaducts, and overpasses that still bear the D. T. & I. logo.[14]

NOTES

1. Nevins and Hill, *Expansion and Challenge*, pp. 220–25.
2. Lewis, *Public Image*, pp. 165–67.
3. The D. T. & I. was never owned by the Ford Motor Company. Apparently it was illegal for a manufacturing corporation to own stock in a railroad. Thus the D. T. & I. became a separate corporation owned by Henry, Edsel, and Clara Ford.
4. Ford R. Bryan, "Henry Ford's Excursion into Railroading," *Henry Ford Museum & Greenfield Village Herald* 15 (November 1, 1986): 38.
5. Scott D. Trostel, *The Detroit, Toledo and Ironton Railroad: Henry Ford's Railroad* (Fletcher, Ohio: Cam-Tech Publishing Co., 1988).
6. S. J. Ruddiman, "Mr. Ford's Ten Years as a Railroad Owner: A Decade of Progress," Vertical File, Archives, HFM&GV.
7. Liebold, *Reminiscences*, "Ford on Rails," Acc.65, vol. 8, pp. 640–743, Archives, HFM&GV.
8. *D. T. & I. Railroad News* 1–5 (January 1923–December 1927). Complete set on file in Archives, HFM&GV.
9. Hundreds of these locomotives were built for the Russian government before World War I. However, because of the fall of the czarist government, many were not shipped to Russia but were instead assigned to various U.S. railroads including the D. T. & I.
10. To avoid interference from the two dissident stockholders of D. T. & I., some of the investments were paid for and owned by Henry, Edsel, and Clara independently of D. T. & I.
11. W. V. Middleton, "Henry Ford and His Electric Locomotive," *Train Magazine* (September 1976): 22–26.
12. Although the cost of fuel for internal combustion engines was

relatively high, their efficiency of thirty percent was almost four times that of the typical steam locomotive.

13. Acc. 6, Box 281, D. T. & I. (Edsel Ford Files), Archives, HFM&GV.

14. "A Railroad Link between the Ohio and Detroit Rivers," *Grand Trunk Reporter* 15 (July-August 1980). Consists of a brief history of the Detroit, Toledo and Ironton.

6

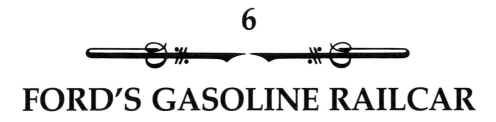

FORD'S GASOLINE RAILCAR

Detroit could truly be described as having rapid transit when the electric streetcar replaced the horsecar on Jefferson Avenue beginning August 23, 1892. Twenty years earlier the pokey horsecar system had left commuters stranded for several days when an epidemic of epizootic, the dreaded horse disease, struck Detroit and no horsecars were in service. Now with the electrics the daily ride was more sanitary, faster, and much more thrilling.

Many small horsecar lines were converted to electricity during 1892–1900. Although most of them thrived financially, riders constantly complained about service and exorbitant fares of as much as five cents. Public transportation had become a sizzling political issue with the election of Hazen S. Pingree as mayor in 1879. Pingree was a shoe manufacturer who campaigned on a three-cent maximum fare platform. There was persistent pressure on car-line management to extend lines, upgrade equipment, improve service, and lower fares or else lose their franchises.[1]

In 1901 the ambitious Cleveland-based Everett-Moore syndicate, of which Detroit Citizen's Railway was a part, formed the Detroit United Railway (D.U.R.) and took over five of the independent lines running into the city. (This same company took over the Detroit, Ann Arbor & Jackson Railway from the Hawks-Angus syndicate in 1907.) This mammoth

D.U.R. network, centered in Detroit, reached from Port Huron and Flint to Toledo, Cleveland, and Kalamazoo. Everett believed that there would be practically one solid city from Port Huron to Buffalo within a decade. But the syndicate had overextended and the entire property was soon in the hands of Canadian investors—in the hands of the "gray nuns of Montreal."

The D.U.R., operating almost all the car lines in Detroit, could not satisfy the people. Each city administration tried to analyze the problems, propose changes, and threaten operators of the lines. In 1909 the city established a Committee of Fifty to study transit needs. The committee reported, among other things, the need for a nucleus of a subway. In 1913 the voters approved a charter amendment providing for municipal ownership, and in the same year the Detroit Street Railway (D.S.R.) Commission was appointed. This three-man commission included John Dodge and James Couzens, who were engaged in the manufacture of automobiles. Over the years, automotive interests continued to be exceptionally well represented. Again in 1914 a report to the commissioners recommended the need for a subway and rerouting of several lines in the downtown area. In early 1915 the city tried to buy the D.U.R. holdings for $23,285,000; the D.U.R. refused the offer.

James Couzens, while general manager of the

Ford Motor Company, was a strong proponent of municipal operation of the city streetcar system.[2] He became involved in city affairs to the extent of Henry Ford's taking issue with the way he was spending his time. Differences over political matters resulted in Couzens's resigning from Ford Motor Company on October 13, 1915. Couzens ran for mayor of Detroit in 1918 on a platform of municipal operation of the streetcar lines. His campaign was successful, but a proposal on April 7, 1919, to buy the D.U.R. for $31.5 million was rejected by the voters. His D.S.R. commissioners, favoring a subway plan that Couzens had vetoed, resigned en masse on November 19, 1919.

Henry Ford had now entered Detroit's political picture. He placed his chief engineer, William B. Mayo, on the three-man D.S.R. Board of Commissioners. Ford was no longer an ally of Couzens. Perhaps he was jealous of Couzens's political success. (Henry Ford had lost the U.S. Senate race to Truman H. Newberry the same year Couzens had become mayor of Detroit.) Ford had decided to torpedo Couzens's plan to buy the D.U.R. by announcing that electric streetcars were obsolete. The torpedo was launched by a widely publicized speech given by Charles Sorenson, Ford's production manager, on April 11, 1919—just one week before the vote rejecting municipal ownership.[3]

Electric streetcar obsolescence was based on Ford's idea that a gasoline-powered car could be operated more economically than an electrically powered car. This premise he immediately set out to prove. Colonel Hall of the Hall-Scott Motor Car Company of California—builder of gasoline-powered railcars—was hired as a consultant. Design work, started in March 1919, was done at the Fair Lane Laboratory (powerhouse building) by Allen Horton and Harold Hicks under Hall's direction. Hicks, a graduate mechanical engineer, had prepared a cost study of gasoline versus electric operation giving a 31.04 versus 33.08 cents-per-mile advantage to gasoline. Experimental engines were built at the nearby tractor plant on Elm Street where Sorenson was boss. The all-steel car body was built by Kuhlman Car Company of Cleveland.[4]

Work on the car progressed during all of 1919, Couzens insisting that a gasoline car was not practical and Sorenson, speaking for Ford, insisting that it was. Henry remained aloof of the fray, and Edsel, the new president of Ford Motor Company, was a mere onlooker. (The project was that of Henry Ford & Son, not Ford Motor Company.) Newspapers were giving

Ford a definite edge in the publicity battle.[5] The gasoline car, it was said, would race the Wolverine, the Michigan Central flyer, to Chicago, when the car was completed. This same year, Ford obtained a twenty-year franchise to operate a car line out Detroit's Fort Street and up South Dearborn Road to his shipbuilding plant on the Rouge River and to his tractor plant in Dearborn using gasoline railcars. Hicks relates that Henry Ford told him, "You know, down at the Rouge, some day we're going to build a factory two miles long to build these streetcars."

March 1920 saw the completion of the gasoline railcar and its inspection by Couzens and the Detroit City Council. The car was about half the weight of a corresponding electric car, had a seventy-five-horsepower engine, and a seating capacity of forty-two. The engine was a four-cylinder horizontally opposed configuration with five-inch bore and seven-inch stroke (the same individual cylinder displacement as the wartime Liberty engine). Quoting Sorenson, "It is an engine, an air compressor, an electrical generator and a heating and lighting plant all in one. The power that moves the car also compresses air for the brakes and generates electric current for the lighting and signal system, while a sir-

One of the early experimental four-cylinder engines designed to compress air and generate electricity as well as drive the wheels of the railcar. (189-643)

occo fan draws air in through the housing of the engine where it is heated, then exhausted through heating pipes to warm the car." Couzens's opinion of the car was that it was designed more for interurban use than as a city streetcar, and he was suspicious of its alleged low operational costs.

In July 1920 Ford bought the Detroit, Toledo and Ironton Railroad, a steam railroad system extending from Dearborn to the Ohio River. He now owned 456 miles of track on which to test his car. He no longer needed to borrow the Michigan Central tracks and race the Wolverine to Chicago. He had other good reasons for buying the D. T. & I. besides testing his gasoline railcar. But it was now announced that Ford intended to use his gasoline railcars to provide passenger service on the D. T. & I. through Ohio.

For trials on the D. T. & I., Henry ordered a double engine of eight cylinders supplying 150 horsepower to provide a speed of eighty miles per hour. This first and only Ford gasoline railcar, aptly christened the Dearborn, was then equipped with about fourteen comfortable wicker chairs, a kitchen, and lavatory; thus it was admirably suited for use as a private car for inspecting his railroad. The only record of an inspection trip, however, tells of one of very short duration, with Jimmy Smith as motorman; after only a few miles down the line a minor mechanical problem developed, thus aborting the trip. The car returned slowly on one engine while Henry returned to Dearborn by automobile. Any further use of the gasoline railcar seems to be undocumented.

Interior of the gasoline railcar showing wicker chairs to provide flexible arrangement for private use. (189-1139)

Presumably the car was soon scrapped, its demise unpublicized.

But the project cannot be considered a complete failure—perhaps not a failure at all. In at least two aspects it was a definite success. First, the gasoline railcar was enough of a threat to D.U.R. interests to force them to lower the price of their city system to $19,850,000, thereby saving the City of Detroit millions of dollars when the system was finally bought by the city in 1922. Second, when one examines the months and months of favorable publicity given Ford for his ingenuity and his effort to serve the public, one finds the advertising value priceless—no doubt far exceeding the expense of building the car. And the project must have served Ford's original purpose of thwarting Couzens's early attempts toward municipal ownership of the Detroit streetcar system. Henry Ford in this case had no leanings toward socialism.

The completed railcar in July 1920. The gasoline engine housed in the large compartment under center of the car drove both front and rear wheels. The engine cooling fan is plainly visible. (189-1128)

NOTES

1. J. E. Schramm and W. H. Henning, *Detroit's Street Railways, 1863–1922* (Chicago: Central Electric Railways Association, 1978), pp. 9–84; Donald V. Baut, "Track 'n' Trolley," *The Dearborn Historian* 11 (winter 1971): 3–22.

2. H. Barnard, "The Battle for M.O." (municipal ownership), *Independent Man,* chapter 2 (New York: Charles Scribner's Sons, 1958), pp. 126–130.

3. Sorenson Papers, Acc. 78, Box 46, Archives, HFM&GV; Sorenson, *Reminiscences,* Acc. 65, Archives, HFM&GV.

4. Harold Hicks, *Reminiscences,* Acc. 65, Archives, HFM&GV.

5. "Ford's Street Car Pronounced Success," *Motor World* 30 (October 22, 1919): 40. For many similar pronouncements see Acc. 7, Newspaper Clipping Books (microfilm), 1919–20, Archives, HFM&GV.

7

EMPLOYEE HOUSING IN DEARBORN

Wherever Henry Ford hired people, whether for manufacturing, farming, lumbering, or mining, he was concerned about their living conditions. Housing was provided in such locations as Iron Mountain, Michigan; Glassmere, Pennsylvania; Richmond Hill, Georgia; the mining locations of Kentucky and West Virginia; and far off Fordlandia and Belterra in Brazil. If at any of his plant sites decent housing was scarce, Ford was inclined to build new houses and rent or sell them to employees at or below cost. Where housing was critically lacking or nonexistent, Ford would build a complete village with houses, schools, chapel, firehouse, hospital, and commissary.

When Ford was planning the building of the Rouge plant on the edge of Detroit (Dearborn Township) and hiring thousands of workers, he visualized the problem of insufficient housing nearby. He thought: what advantage are good wages to the employee if an unscrupulous builder overcharges for housing? In Dearborn there were three well-defined efforts to furnish housing for ordinary workers. Only the last of the three plans became a reality. (Ford's favorite executives, incidentally, were accommodated individually, often in elaborate style.)

CONCRETE HOUSES

Dearborn might well have become a city of concrete homes if Henry Ford had followed the inclinations of his close friend and mentor Thomas Edison. Edison had been in the cement-making business on a large scale since 1898. His Edison Portland Cement Company could produce one thousand barrels of cement a day. Much of the cement used in building the Rouge plant came by the trainload from this Edison company at Stewartsville, New Jersey.[1]

In 1908 Edison had patented a system of pouring concrete into cast-iron molds to produce a cement house in about six hours.[2] The object was to provide cheap housing for workmen in the form of small detached dwellings on a mass-produced basis. When the cast-iron molds were removed, after four days had been allowed for hardening, there would be a completed house in one piece, with cellar, roof, walls, stairways, doors, windows, bath, and conduits for electrical and water service. Edison is said to have put up several of these houses near West Orange, New Jersey.[3] To go with his concrete houses, Edison proposed concrete refrigerators and concrete pianos, and he did cast several concrete phonograph cabinets.[4]

It seems that early in 1913 Henry Ford asked the

manager of sales of the Edison Storage Battery Company to put him in touch with somebody who made steel forms for concrete houses; the name of F. D. Lambie, ostensibly a friend of Edison, was recommended as the one "who seems to be pushing it the hardest."

The summer of 1914 witnessed public announcements such as the following: "Henry Ford, of automobile fame, is contemplating the erection of 2000 concrete houses for his workmen. It is claimed that these indestructible five and six-room concrete houses may be built for not more than $1000 each."[5] Beginning in 1914 there seems to have been a steady stream of letters between Liebold and several firms specializing in poured-concrete housing. The American Building Corporation of New York, headed by Lambie, was especially aggressive, and must have become a nuisance to Liebold, if such a thing were possible. Lambie was apparently a friend of Edison, Westinghouse, Ingersoll, Durant, and perhaps anyone else necessary to sell Ford his technique of casting concrete houses in reusable steel forms. The cost of wooden forms, which were normally discarded after one use, was a major expense. The amount of wood necessary for forms could approach that needed to build a conventional frame house. The reusable steel forms appeared to be a distinct advantage. Edison, being a strong advocate of concrete buildings, had enthusiastically encouraged Lambie to pursue the business of poured-concrete houses, wishing him success in pouring complete two-story houses in a single casting.[6]

Lambie, in his letters to Liebold, could quote unbelievably low prices for his concrete houses. He offered either to pour the homes or lease his equipment to Ford. He sent blueprints, specifications, prices, and pictures of completed homes, and aerial views of completed subdivisions. A neat little house for $525, with basement and bath, ready to move into—"about the price of one of your automobiles"—was offered as bait. Other more spacious models were priced as high as several thousand dollars.

One house that Lambie was offering had a price of $1,025. For a professional appraisal of this house, Liebold sent the blueprints to two architects, one of whom was Albert Kahn, who handled much of Ford's architectural work. Kahn's response:

All I can say in connection with this matter is that, in my opinion, the house he has in mind

Edison's office at West Orange, New Jersey, on November 20, 1911. A model of Edison's concrete house may be seen in background. (Photo courtesy Edison National Historic Site, West Orange, New Jersey.)

cannot be built for $1025.00. I know that it will cost more nearly $1500.00, and furthermore, I doubt very much whether *here* any saving can be effected by the use of concrete over and above brick. The only way to make sure of this is to try it. I shall, of course, be glad to be shown.

Relaying this assessment to Lambie drew a most vitriolic response, Lambie pointing out that Pittsburgh Crucible Steel Company of Midland, Pennsylvania, was pouring that very model at a cost of $200 less than $1,025.

On July 3, 1915, there was more news of Ford's building plans: ANNOUNCEMENT BY HENRY FORD OF TIRE FACTORY, BLAST FURNACE, AND MOTOR PLANT ALL TO BE SURROUNDED BY A MODEL CITY FOR EMPLOYEES.[7] Lambie was quickly in touch with Liebold for further information, and Liebold replied on July 10, 1915, as follows:

Mr. Ford has purchased a large tract of land near Detroit for the purpose of building a tractor

An Edison all-concrete house completely poured in one day. Completed house is on the right. Built in Union, New Jersey, October 9, 1919. (Photo courtesy Edison National Historic Site, West Orange, New Jersey.)

plant. The property which will not be occupied by the factory is to be set aside for employees' homes, but whether or not he will be directly interested in building them has not yet been decided, but in any event there is a possibility that concrete houses may be tried out there.[8]

A letter from Lambie in October 1915 reveals the effect of the war in Europe on Lambie's thinking. He suggests to Ford a grandiose scheme of investing $100 million to build one million concrete houses for a profit of $300 million. This, he said, "would be a better investment than war loans." In a postscript he suggests that twelve apostles be sent out by American industry to stop war forever. And Ford was trying to stop the war in Europe by sponsoring a Peace Mission to Europe, hoping to end the fighting by Christmas of that same year.

The Peace Ship and many other things were to interfere with Ford's building of many concrete homes for his workers in Dearborn. World War I was diverting attention and money to other, more important ventures. Suddenly and unexpectedly, Ford and Liebold had become responsible for building Henry Ford Hospital. And because Ford Motor Company stockholders were not in agreement with the tremendous Rouge expansion plans, Ford's own money was needed to buy them out and gain control of the company.

As late as February 1918, however, Liebold re-

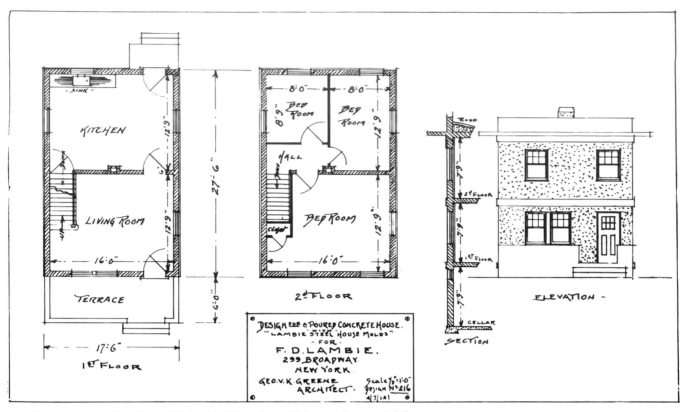

Design No. 216, offered in 1914 for $1,025, or less. This was the model that met the $1,000 price target, and was submitted to architect Albert Kahn for his appraisal. (0-6495)

ceived a letter and literature from the Lambie Concrete House Corporation. But the letter was not from Lambie, and the claims were much more modest: "These forms allow for the construction of concrete houses of any size or type which can be built at a cost less than brick houses and only slightly more than wooden ones." No concrete houses were built by Ford in Dearborn, and the problem of housing persisted.

FORDSON VILLAGE

World War I was still raging, and Ford Motor Company was building war equipment on a massive scale. At Highland Park, ambulances and Liberty motors were being produced in record numbers, and on the newly dredged Rouge River submarine-chasing Eagle boats were being launched daily. Thousands of

Fordson tractors were being shipped to Britain from the tractor plant on Elm Street in Dearborn.

But Henry Ford visualized the day when peace would reign and he could proceed with the establishment of an enormous iron and steel plant together with a much larger tractor-manufacturing plant next to his shipbuilding plant on the Rouge. He owned thousands of acres on which to develop this gigantic operation. And the Ford Motor Company had the necessary cash from record Model T profits accumulated over the previous ten years.

Envisioned as being part of this huge enterprise were homes for thousands of workers. Consideration had been given to building complete homes of poured concrete by a method patented by Thomas Edison,[9] but Edsel Ford, a man of impeccable taste, is thought to have intervened to discourage the ugly concrete approach. Edsel and Eleanor Ford then were acquainted with the exceptionally talented architect Leonard A. Willeke, who had in 1916–17 completed superb residential design work for them as well as for people such as Roscoe B. Jackson and Mrs. William Clay of Detroit in 1917–18. Willeke was also being engaged by Henry and Clara Ford to make small improvements in the Fair Lane mansion soon after it had been built.[10] Edsel Ford therefore easily obtained Henry's approval to arrange for Willeke to prepare plans for housing some thirty-five hundred workers, who would presumably be employed at the much enlarged Henry Ford & Son tractor plant on the Rouge. An expanse of about twenty-six hundred acres was available for this residential development.

The land under consideration was roughly triangular, the sides of the triangle being Michigan Avenue on the north, Greenfield Road on the east, and the Rouge River on the southwest. According to abstracts[11] of property titles, a tract "not to exceed 640 acres" was first claimed in 1805 by a John Dodemead, the claim bounded on the east by a "bois blanc" (presumably a birch tree) and on the west by "the Pattawamies Road." Other owners at later times included several well-known Dearborn families such as the Ten Eycks, Dorts, Reckingers, Clipperts, Espers, and, in 1915–16, Henry and Clara Ford. At least two early subdivisions were included, the Lorenzo D. Thomas Subdivision (1887) and Esper's Subdivision of part of Claim 312. One owner of a portion of this land in 1915 was the Detroit Zoological Society, planning a

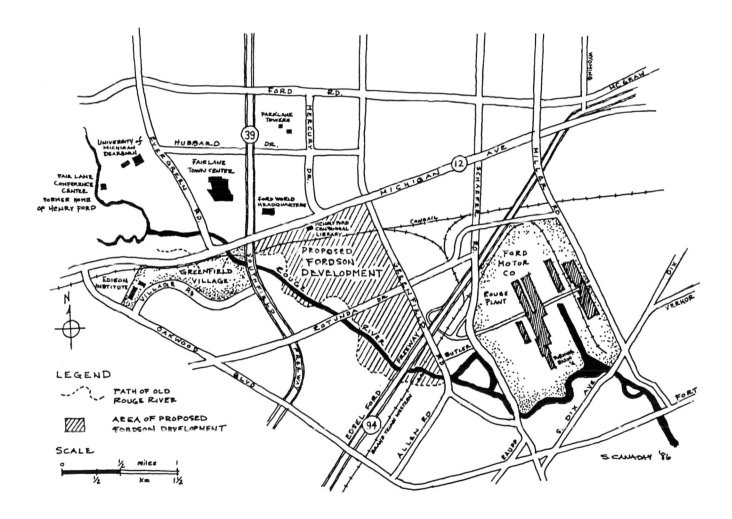

Present-day map of Dearborn showing location of proposed Fordson Village. (Courtesy of Stephen M. Canady.)

zoo in this locality. But the Fords offered so much money for the land that plans for the zoo were shifted to Detroit's Woodward Avenue.[12]

Willeke, a native of Cincinnati, had studied the latest industrial housing in Europe and Britain in 1910, and was convinced that alley-free curved streets, plentiful small parks, and a variety of residential styles were essential to an attractive, well-planned community. Besides this generalized concept, Willeke had a mastery of intricate artistic detail, having obtained architectural training in Paris, and having applied his talents on many imposing structures in Ohio and California before coming to the Detroit area. One of the many structures in California was the New Palace Hotel in San Francisco in 1906, for which Willeke was a designer.

In May 1918 Willeke was contacted by the Fords about their industrial-housing needs. In June 1918 he was sent to Youngstown, Ohio, by Edsel Ford to examine Loveland Farms, a housing development sponsored by the Youngstown Sheet & Tube Company. On August 1, 1918, Willeke was under contract to Henry Ford as "a landscape architect and designer for the purpose of preparing and submitting ideas and designs in landscape development, city planning and residential construction."[13]

While Willeke was occupied with design of the village, his surveyor, H. H. Atwell of Ann Arbor, was developing a topographical map of the area. Locations of streets, boulevards, and parks were to take advantage of existing land contours. The survey was expanded to include more land than the original estimate, and required more time than was expected largely because of a lack of men and a cold, influenza-plagued winter. But Willeke, doing all his own drafting, had completed the house designs by February 1919.

The Willeke plan incorporated seventeen hundred acres and provided housing for 3,707 families including 1,717 single homes, 758 double homes, and 1,232 four-family homes. Slightly more than half the land was devoted to homes. The Rouge River basin served as parklands and a large virgin forest area in the development was left untouched. Village centers such as the municipal center with town hall, auditorium, and stadium were connected by wide boulevards to a business center with clock tower and arcade joined by a row of shops, a bank, and a Ford dealership. An elaborate railroad station was planned with wide tree-filled greenbelts along either side of the Michigan Central right-of-way to suitably attenuate noise. Boulevards from the main entrance led south from Michigan Avenue; one of these was immediately west of the present intersection of Michigan and Greenfield roads.

Henry Ford wanted the Fordson Village plans to be kept secret during this time to avoid land speculation and profiteering by building-materials suppliers; Willeke thus did not entrust the drawings to assistants who might leak information to the public, nor did the plans bear any project title. No copies of the plans are in the Ford Archives. There is merely a folder of letters about the wages and duties of Willeke, Atwell, and an Alfred F. Nygard, an accomplished sculptor who was hired, on Willeke's recommendation, by Edsel Ford to make wax models of buildings that Willeke had designed. Ever since 1918, Fordson Village drawings have been sequestered in the office of Leonard Willeke until recognized by Thomas Brunk, a University of Detroit professor, just before the plans were going to be destroyed after the death of Willeke's wife in 1981. Leonard Willeke died in 1970.

The drawings had remained in Willeke's office because the Fordson Village project was abandoned by the Fords in favor of the much smaller Molony site.[14] The abandonment was triggered by the Dodge brothers' suit against Ford Motor Company for nonpayment of dividends. A restraining order immediately forbade the use of company money for expansion in Dearborn. The case continued until December 1917 when the Ford Motor Company was forced to pay $20 million in dividends to its stockholders. This nettled Henry Ford to the extent that he was determined to buy out all his stockholders. This was accomplished in July 1919 but at the cost of $105,820,894 to Henry Ford. The money for Fordson Village was gone.

With the impending collapse of the Fordson Village project during the spring of 1919 there was confusion as to who would be paying for Willeke's work at the "exorbitant fee" of $5.28 per hour. His time was now being divided between Fordson Village and the Molony Subdivision, the Molony project being a responsibility of the newly formed Dearborn Realty and Construction Company. In a letter to Henry Ford, Willeke states: "My time sheet . . . covers the time spent of preparing plans and specifications for 12 houses for the Dearborn Realty and Construction Co. for the Molony Subdivision from March

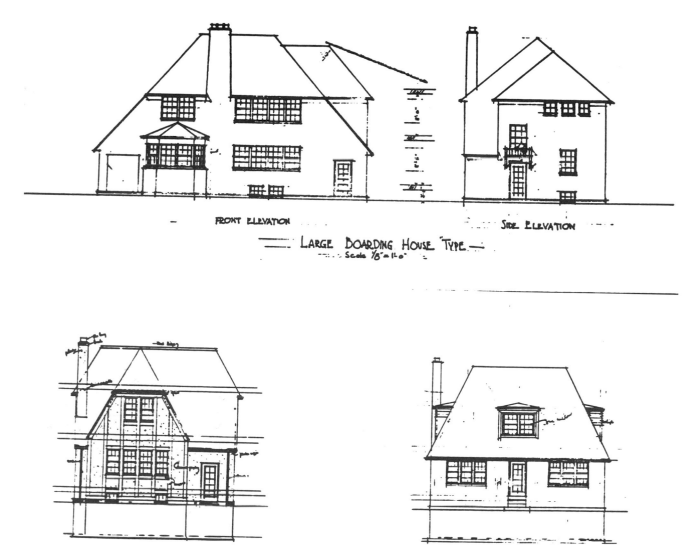

FRONT ELEVATION .... SIDE ELEVATION ....

— LARGE BOARDING HOUSE TYPE —
Scale ⅛" = 1'-0"

Typical single-family house facades designed for Fordson Village.

8th to May 5, 1919, and the number of hours was 270."[15]

Albert Wood, chief of construction for Dearborn Realty and Construction Company, after receiving Willeke's house plans, reported to E. G. Liebold (president) that Willeke's help at such a high wage was no longer needed. After April 1919 work on Fordson Village continued with wages paid by Edsel Ford. Willeke was to finish street details by that fall. By October 1919 some of the streets south of the Michigan Central tracks were physically laid out. In February 1920 Willeke recorded past work as 605 hours on Fordson Village and 570 hours on the Henry Ford Estate. Willeke worked privately for Ed-

sel and Henry Ford until February 28, 1921, but Fordson Village never materialized.[16]

Not all Willeke's time had been devoted to Fordson Village and Molony Subdivision plans. In 1918 the Fair Lane entrance gate and gate house, the log house, and service buildings were designed and built.[17] That same year he designed and built a home for himself at 39 Moss Avenue in Highland Park, and was designer of the 1919 Essex Phaeton for the Hudson Motor Car Company—for which he was paid all of seventy-five dollars.

"Fordson Village, a Model Industrial Suburb" is but a chapter in Thomas W. Brunk's account of Leonard B. Willeke. Hundreds of drawings, including those of Fordson Village, are preserved in the Leonard B. Willeke Archives now the property of Thomas W. Brunk.

THE MOLONY SUBDIVISION

Although Henry Ford and the Ford Motor Company did not proceed with Fordson Village, the Dearborn Realty and Construction Company, headed by E. G. Liebold, carried on. It was organized January 10, 1919, with Edsel Ford as vice president. One thousand shares of one hundred dollars each was held by Clara Ford (400), Edsel Ford (400), Liebold (150), and C. R. McLaughton, secretary-treasurer (50). This seems to have been a project promoted largely by Liebold. Henry Ford and the Ford Motor Company were not directly involved.[18]

Henry Ford, upset with his stockholders, had resigned as president of Ford Motor Company just eleven days earlier (December 30, 1918). Henry, Clara, and Eleanor with one-year-old Henry II had gone to California and stayed with Clara's sister, Eva, to ponder the situation. Henry soon announced from California that he would organize a new company and put Ford Motor Company out of business by building an automobile to sell for $250. So Henry at that time probably had little interest in workers' housing. Liebold was running the show.[19]

Leonard Willeke had been paid by Edsel Ford to prepare house designs for the Molony Subdivision. Willeke had worked on these plans from March 8 to May 5, 1919. Twelve house designs were submitted to Dearborn Realty and Construction Company. No doubt Willeke might have overseen construction, but Liebold had someone else in mind. This man, Albert Wood, who had been construction engineer for Liebold in building the Ford Hospital in Detroit, needed work. The hospital was now in the hands of the U.S. government as a veterans hospital (October 1918 to September 1919), and no construction work was being done. Thus Wood got the job supervising construction of the Molony Subdivision houses.

Henry Ford had owned much of the Molony property since 1910 when he had paid $20,000 for it. This land was within a few blocks of the Henry Ford & Son tractor plant, which was then employing about four hundred men but was expected soon to employ many more. Most workers did not drive an automobile in 1919, and living within walking distance of work was a distinct advantage. On April 9, 1919, the Dearborn Realty and Construction Company paid Henry $40,938 for 314 lots in the Molony Subdivision, all slated for home construction. Building began in May 1919. A total of 250 houses were built during 1919 through 1921.[20]

Homes were purchased by employees directly from Dearborn Realty and Construction Company at slightly above cost, price being determined before start of construction. Construction was extremely well organized; teams of excavators, masons, carpenters, plumbers, and electricians moved from one building to the next. Standardized windows, doors, furnaces, plumbing and lighting fixtures, and so forth saved time and cut costs. These methods were far advanced of the usual one at a time custom home–building procedures of that time. Quality of materials and workmanship was of the best, attested to by the solid condition of these homes now after nearly seventy years.

Six designs were built, with placement on lots so that no two like designs would be close to each other. Prices varied depending on model, but all were within a range of about $6,500 to $8,000 to start. These prices were $2,000 higher than predicted by Liebold.[21] With full basement, sidewalks, and paved streets, these were not inexpensive houses, and were too costly for the average production worker. During this same period many Ford workers were buying a $200-lot, erecting a $500-garagelike building on the rear of their lot, and living in the garage awaiting the time they had saved enough to build a $3–4 thousand house in the proper place in front.

During 1919 prices of a Ford home averaged about $7,000 with monthly payments perhaps $65 after a $1,000 down payment and including interest of six percent on the principal. Houses sold well during 1919. For 1920, prices were raised to cover increased costs. Prices that year reached an average of $9,000 with monthly payments correspondingly high. Sales declined.

In late 1920 Ford tractor operations were moved from Dearborn to the Rouge plant five miles away, and because of the 1921 general recession, the Ford houses became difficult to sell and plans for additional building were abandoned. But the Ford Homes were durable. People stayed in them, paid their installments, and Dearborn Realty and Construction Company over the years made a profit. When assets

Molony Subdivision houses in Dearborn's Ford Homes District as they appeared in the early 1920s. (189-479)

of $900,000 were turned over to Ford Motor Company in 1943, these profits were undoubtedly largely from interest. Liebold had once been a banker.

In 1980, when the Ford Homes were sixty years old, a Ford Homes Historic District Study Committee, headed by Joseph Oldenburg, a Ford Home resident, successfully petitioned the City of Dearborn to declare the original blocks of Ford Homes a Historic District. Residents of the area now take great pride in living in this district and intend to keep their neighborhood in fully restored condition. These streets are now included in the Dearborn Historical Museum tours of historic sights in Dearborn.

NOTES

1. Acc. 104, Box 1, Archives, HFM&GV. Correspondence between E. G. Liebold and Edison Portland Cement Company about a backlog of 2,259 carloads of cement scheduled for Rouge plant construction.
2. United States Patent No. 1,123,261, "Mold for Concrete Construction." Application filed December 29, 1908; patent granted January 5, 1915.
3. Mathew Josephson, *Edison: A Biography* (New York: McGraw-Hill, 1959), pp. 424–25.
4. Robert Conot, *A Streak of Luck* (New York: Seaview Books, 1979), p. 347.
5. *Bulletin, Universal Portland Cement Company* (July 1914), p. 1.
6. Acc. 47, Box 5, Archives, HFM&GV. Copies of correspondence between Thomas Edison and F. D. Lambie, December 1914.
7. *Detroit News*, July 3, 1915.
8. Acc. 47, Box 5, Archives, HFM&GV.
9. Ford R. Bryan, "Concrete Homes for Dearborn," *Dearborn Historian* 24 (summer 1984): 87–89.
10. Thomas W. Brunk, *Leonard B. Willeke: Excellence in Architecture and Design* (Detroit: University of Detroit Press, 1986), pp. 137–47. *Willeke* is pronounced as if were "will a key."
11. Abstract of Title, *Springwells Park Subdivision No. 1*, Dearborn Historical Museum, Dearborn, Michigan.
12. William A. Austin, *The First Fifty Years* (Detroit Zoological Society, 1974), pp. 7–8.
13. Acc. 62, Box 114, "Leonard Willeke, Architect—Fordson Village, 1918–1919," Archives, HFM&GV.
14. Joseph Oldenburg, "Ford Homes Historic District," *Dearborn Historian* 20 (spring 1980): 31–50.
15. See Acc. 62, Box 114, Archives, HFM&GV.
16. A portion of Fordson Village land was developed by the Ford Foundation as the Springwells Park Subdivision in 1939. Some of Willeke's plans are said to have been incorporated.
17. Acc. 1606, "Willeke Papers, 1916–1924," Archives, HFM&GV.
18. Acc. 47, Boxes 1–4, "Dearborn Realty and Construction Company," Archives, HFM&GV.
19. Nevins and Hill, *Expansion and Challenge*, p. 105.
20. See Acc. 47, Box 1, Archives, HFM&GV.
21. *Detroit Journal*, April 11, 1919.

8

WIRELESS TELEGRAPHY

During the 1920s, the Ford Motor Company, with Henry Ford's encouragement, pioneered several aspects of wireless communication. These ventures included a private system of wireless telegraphy, commercial radio broadcasting, and the invention of the aircraft radio beacon.

The possibility of producing electromagnetic waves suitable for communication was predicted by a Scottish physicist, James Clerk Maxwell, in 1865. Thomas Edison in 1885 applied for a patent (No. 465, 971, granted in 1891) on a means of wireless telegraphy between land stations and between ships at sea, acknowledging the curvature of the earth as a limitation. The patent was later sold to Guglielmo Marconi, an Italian. Heinrich Hertz, a German, is perhaps erroneously[1] credited with first producing electromagnetic waves in 1887, using a spark gap and inductance coil. Electromagnetic waves became popularly known as "radio" waves. Marconi first transmitted wireless messages by international Morse code in 1895, having perfected the antenna and applied the technology to limited land and sea communication in Italy and in England before establishing transoceanic connections in 1901. It is Hertz, however, who has been immortalized by the recent replacement of the term *cycle* with *hertz.* So now we have sixty-hertz house current to power our multi-megahertz microwave oven.

Wireless telegraphy became especially useful during World War I. Coded interruptions in hertzian waves allowed telegraphic messages to be transmitted without wires for several hundred miles under favorable atmospheric conditions. But by far the most beneficial development leading to the successful use of wireless telegraphy and eventually wireless telephony was the exploitation of the "Edison effect." Edison had found in 1883 that a very hot filament could emit electricity, which could be collected on a metal plate inside the evacuated lamp and measured. And he found that the current measured flowed in one direction only. Dr. J. A. Fleming of England exploited this phenomenon and is now credited with the development and application of vacuum valve, or tube, rectifiers. Edison failed to recognize fully his important discovery. Vacuum-valve technology was further extended by Dr. Lee De Forest to provide the "audion," or amplifier tube. The development of vacuum detector and amplifier tubes led to much more powerful transmitting and more sensitive receiving equipment. But it was still dot-dash language—voice and music were yet to come.

In early 1919 the Ford Motor Company telegraph department at Highland Park was handling nine hundred messages by wire every day. Henry Ford was aware of the great progress in wireless technique. He was in touch with Edison on their summer

84

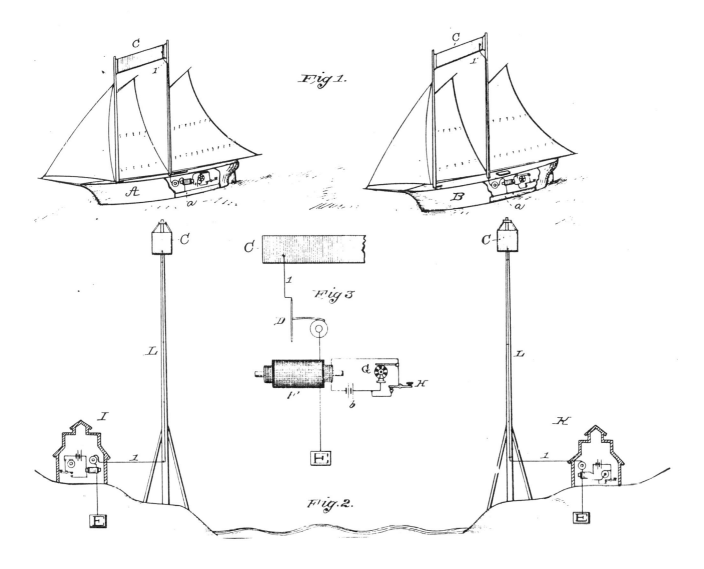

Diagrams from Edison's 1891 patent application, "Means for Transmitting Signals Electrically."

camping trips, and kept clippings of articles describing the latest accomplishments.[2] Edison was saying the Martians might well be listening in on Earth's wireless messages,[3] and Marconi believed he might be receiving signals from the planets.[4] There were glowing predictions of talking "wirelessly" from New York to San Francisco, and Marconi said, "You, from your hotel room in London, will be able to call any New York telephone number, get it inside of fifteen minutes, and then talk three minutes for five dollars." Ford was becoming enthusiastic about the general usefulness of both wireless telegraphy and tele-

phony. It would be a means of keeping in touch with his seagoing vessels, his various plants, mines, timber operations, railroad movements, his dealers, and maybe even his customers.

A wireless station, to be sure, was not a major item on Ford's 1919 agenda. He had plenty of other things on his mind. This was the year he was fighting dissident stockholders by putting Edsel in charge of Ford Motor Company and threatening to start his own company and build a new $250 car as competition. He was trying to build the Rouge plant, fight the Chicago *Tribune* in a lawsuit, launch the *Dearborn*

Henry Ford listening to early wireless. Gentlemen with him are not identified. (0-4429)

Independent, start the Ford Technical Institute, build a gasoline streetcar, plan a dirigible factory, locate timber and mining properties, take over a railroad, start a new tractor plant in Ireland, and introduce modern manufacturing methods in Japan. And the mere thought of having to borrow $100 million from the hated bankers to regain control of Ford Motor Company must have been downright discouraging. Yet wireless intrigued him.[5]

By the early fall of 1919 Ford wanted his own wireless station. Now, one would presume that Henry Ford would be smart enough to know that he should get someone trained in electrical matters to build and manage a wireless station. But Henry Ford was not that smart—he was smarter. Near the offices of the *Dearborn Independent*[6] Henry singled out his business editor, Fred L. Black, and the following conversation ensued:[7]

"Say Fred, what do you know about wireless?"

"I don't know anything, Mr. Ford. Just the stories published in the newspapers."

"Well I think it would be a dammed good time to learn. You make me one of these wireless receiving outfits."

Henry Ford is often accused of acting in willy-nilly fashion in his assignments. But in this instance it is not strange that he picked a newspaper man to develop his radio station when he had competent electrical engineers on his payroll. He was, no doubt, thinking way beyond the first electrical aspects of the station and to its end use as a public-relations medium.

With this seemingly impossible assignment, Fred Black was on the verge of quitting Ford Motor Company. But instead he decided to talk to Charlie Voorhess, head of the Henry Ford & Son power plant, about his predicament. Voorhess had just hired a young signal corps officer, Edward G. Chambers, who immediately offered to build a receiver for Fred. But because Fred Black had been personally instructed to build it, Chambers was only permitted to help. Chambers then advised Black to first see a Mr. Edwards who was in charge of the Ninth Wireless District with offices in the Federal Building in Detroit; Edwards, in turn, advised Black to take a night-school course for wireless operators at Cass Technical High School. This course, three nights a week, was designed to train operators for the lake ships.

Henry would expect immediate results with the wireless. So even before the wireless course was well under way, Black and Chambers worked on alternate evenings laying out a breadboard crystal receiving set in Chambers' bedroom at 507 Park Street, Dearborn. Meanwhile, Fred Black was still business editor of the Dearborn Publishing Company, traveling extensively to investigate the hoary details of Lincoln's assassination.[8] By late fall of 1919 Black and Chambers had also built a wireless transmitting set in Black's bedroom at 448 Nona, using a Ford battery for power. This might be considered Henry Ford's first transmitting station. The transmitter employed Morse code and had a range of four or five miles.

To be sure, a wireless transmitter in Fred Black's bedroom was not exactly what Henry Ford had in mind. The next location for a transmitter was the unoccupied twelve-by-twelve-foot valve building next to the waterworks on Michigan Avenue.[9] There the 158-foot high water tank served as an antenna support, new twenty-watt De Forest equipment was installed, and the station licensed "limited commercial" as KDEN. A successful trial message was sent from the Dearborn station to Inter-City Radio Company of Cleveland on March 22, 1920.[10] The first transmission of company business was from Dearborn to the

Ford's wireless station at the waterworks on Michigan Avenue in October 1920. Small pump house, left foreground, housed wireless equipment. (189-1250)

Northville plant in April 1920 by Morse code. This same telegraphic communication system was improved and expanded in the next few years to include stations at Fordson, Highland Park, Phoenix, Flat Rock, Iron Mountain, and L'Anse, Michigan, as well as Springfield, Jackson, and Ironton, Ohio, on the D. T. & I. Railroad. The Ford Motor Company is believed to have had the first industrial interplant wireless system, and the first railroad interstation wireless.

Wireless telephone was added to telegraph on June 28, 1920, and the term *radiophone* applied.[11] In October 1920 "duplex wireless telephony," a system developed in the Ford laboratory at the tractor plant on Elm Street, allowed two stations to converse as they would on a telephone. Before this the receiving operator had to wait until the entire message had been received before he could answer. In November 1920 the Ford station was one of the first to broadcast election returns (Harding versus Cox) with radio, and in January 1922 Ford is said to have addressed his tractor dealers in Cleveland by radiophone announcing a thirty-seven percent price reduction.[12]

By late 1920 long high antennas, or aerials, had begun to appear above homes in Dearborn, and little inexpensive crystal receivers requiring no batteries were being built. Often a tuner was formed by winding copper wire around an empty oatmeal box to

Interior of wireless station in April 1922. William O. Gassett is at right typing incoming messages. (0-1694)

A Detroit, Toledo and Ironton Railroad dispatch office where wireless, telegraph, and telephone were all used. (0-6699)

form an inductance coil, and a galena crystal with "catwhisker" served as detector, or rectifier. The signal, if any could be found, was barely strong enough to be heard on earphones. As soon as a station was heard, the earphones would be passed gingerly from one listener to another before the sound disappeared—the catwhisker having perhaps become dislodged. But it was a great thrill to hear anything understandable, and to think of it as coming out of thin air. A few persons were erroneously convinced that a filling in one of their teeth acted as a detector and they could hear faint music with no further equipment!

Both wireless telegraphy and telephony were handled side by side in the little waterworks valve building. But because of often garbled speech, telegraphy was found to be more reliable than telephony. The long wavelengths employed by wireless in those days were extremely subject to static and fading because of variable atmospheric conditions. Radiophone was tried along the D. T. & I. Railroad with only moderate success during 1922–25 when copper telegraph lines were being built for permanent use. The big volume of messages was being relayed in dot-dash fashion by wireless telegraphy; three operators were busy at Dearborn on each of two shifts handling calls to and from the various manufacturing plants and the D. T. & I. stations. Public announcements predicted that all Ford branches throughout the world would soon be connected by wireless.

Edward Chambers left Ford in late 1921 to become chief engineer of WCX, the Detroit *Free Press* station (now WJR), and Charles W. Thomas, a De Forest development engineer, took Chambers's place in February 1922 as head technical man at the Ford operations.[13] William O. Gassett, a U.S. Navy radioman, also joined Ford in the spring of 1922. Gassett, not completely satisfied with the water plant antenna system, was quickly taught the Ford method:

[Ford:] "Why don't you hook the wires to the railroad track and use it for an antenna?"
[Gassett:] "Suppose that wouldn't work?"
[Ford:] "How do you know that wouldn't work? Have you ever tried it?"[14]

In May 1923 William J. Kryden, an experienced radio operator from the Dutch navy, joined the Ford team, working with Bill Gassett for many years. Charlie Thomas, Bill Gassett, Kryden, and helpers built and maintained all the equipment needed for Dearborn and outlying receiving and transmitting purposes.

During 1923, when the new Ford Engineering Laboratory on Oakwood Boulevard was under construction, just behind the laboratory a new wireless station was being built that would allow much improved performance for both telegraphy and commercial radio. Station KDEN, the telegraphic operation, would now have a total output capacity of fifteen hundred watts, divided between two separate sending equipments of one thousand and five hundred watts. Message capacity was approaching two thousand per eight hours.[15] This station, with its three 165-foot antenna towers on the corners of East Lake (see photos in the following chapter) became capable of reaching not only the Ford Great Lakes Fleet but under favorable weather conditions could contact Ford oceangoing ships such as the *East Indian* and *Onoda* on oceans half-way around the world. The ore carriers *Henry Ford* and *Benson Ford* were equipped with wireless radio compasses in 1924 when radio fog signals became standard equipment in lighthouses on the Great Lakes. In 1926, when Ford Motor Company purchased 199 obsolete ocean-type merchants ships to be scrapped, much radio gear was salvaged.

Several of the ship hulls were converted to barges and propelled by tugs. Both tugs and barges were equipped for wireless communication.

In 1927 Ford had two distinct types of private-use systems for wireless telegraphy. Long-wave equipment operated as WAV, and the equally powerful short-wave equipment as WBO. Both systems were achieving amazing results; WAV was heard on a vessel off the coast of Japan, and WBO was reported heard in Siberia.[16] At times the two frequencies were used interchangeably to get messages through during atmospheric disturbance. Ford had been using wireless on his yacht, *Sialia,* since 1922; now much later (1928) the Ford rubber plantations in Brazil used high-frequency sending and receiving apparatus to keep in touch with the Dearborn station using coded wireless telegraphy. This new wireless station at Dearborn was touted by newspapers as being perhaps the largest radio station in the world.[17]

Private facilities for wireless telegraphy were used extensively by Ford to conduct company business until 1929. But as with so many of his attempts at innovation, continued use of interplant and marine wireless was being hampered by federal legislation because of lobbying pressure in Washington. Ford and other private businesses were eventually forced to turn over their wireless messages to giant common carriers such as Western Union and Radio Corporation of America, which were in the communication business for profit. Even the Brazilian government followed suit, authorizing its own communication industry to take over the Ford wireless

Police Ford, in 1921, equipped with wireless, ready for immediate communication with headquarters. (0-7062)

communications, offering only much greater delay and much greater cost to Ford.

In April 1929 a move was made to create a Ford Communications Company to enable Ford Motor Company messages to be transmitted legally. But when it was found that such an organization would be required by law to accept and transmit messages for non-Ford businesses as well, the idea was abandoned. The licenses of WAV and WBO were not renewed, and Henry Ford then turned to common carriers for wireless telegraphy.

NOTES

1. Thomas Edison is reported to have demonstrated, using a buzzer, the transmission of electrical power a short distance through air at the 1881 Paris Exposition where Hertz was an onlooker.
2. Acc. 67, Clipping Books, 1919–20 (vol. 15), Archives, HFM&GV.
3. *Bay City Tribune*, February 3, 1920.
4. *Cedar Springs Liberal*, March 24, 1920.
5. In 1896, the year he built his first automobile, Henry Ford had enrolled in a class offered by the National School of Electric- ity, but he did not attend classes and asked for cancellation of tuition payments.
6. The *Dearborn Independent* was first published in January 1919 and dubbed "the greatest publication ever to be published in a tractor plant."
7. Lewis, *Public Image*, p. 178.
8. Henry Ford was being publicly criticized for his remark at the *Tribune* trial that "history is bunk." Thus Ford was looking for an example to support his contention. A book, *The Escape and Suicide of John Wilkes Booth*, by Finis Bates claimed that Booth had lived until 1903, finally committing suicide in Enid, Oklahoma. Fred Black had been assigned the job of finding Bates, getting the facts, and proving history was indeed "bunk."
9. Ford R. Bryan, "Dearborn's Chemical Park—Part II: Henry Ford's Waterworks," *Dearborn Historian* 23 (summer 1983): 40–49.
10. "Wireless Flashes Ford Messages," *Ford Man* 4 (May 3, 1920): 1.
11. "Dearborn and Northville Connected by Radiophone," *Fordson Worker* 1 (July 1, 1920): 1.
12. "Mr. Ford Makes Price Cut by Wireless," *Ford News* 2 (February 1, 1922): 1, 5.
13. Charles Voorhess, *Reminiscences*, Acc. 65, pp. 79–80, Archives, HFM&GV.
14. William O. Gassett, *Reminiscences*, p. 12, Acc. 65, Archives, HFM&GV.
15. "New Radio Installation Adds to Communication Facilities," *D. T. & I. Railroad News* 2 (March 1, 1924): 1–2.
16. *Ford News* 6 (July 22, 1927): 1, 3.
17. "Ford May Have World's Biggest Radio Station," *New York Times*, July 1, 1923.

9

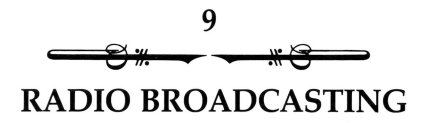

RADIO BROADCASTING

As soon as the Dearborn wireless pioneers Fred Black and Edward Chambers had developed their radiophone at the tractor plant and had it operating in the waterworks valve building in June 1920, there were many uses for it. Licensed for "limited commercial" and "experimental," the radiophone was first directed toward interplant, marine, and railroad communication but with only limited success. Wireless telegraphy was better for that purpose. In the meantime Ford's operators tuned their receiver to Arlington, Virginia, at noon and 10:00 P.M. to obtain accurate naval observatory time. They experienced the sound of "canned music" coming from the Western Electric experimental radio station in New Jersey, and in September 1920 listened to the first broadcast of baseball's World Series between Cleveland and Brooklyn.

The first broadcasting station to feature entertainment came on the air in 1920: KDKA was the Western Electric & Manufacturing Company of East Pittsburgh. The first in Michigan was 8MK (WWJ), the *Detroit News*, August 20, 1920. Ford Motor Company needed better equipment and a 'broadcast' license to address the public likewise. Henry Ford favored such a move because he not only was anxious to control the expression of his ideas on many issues but also wanted to broadcast old-time music and possibly advertise Ford cars.[1]

Shortly after Charlie Thomas and Bill Gassett arrived in early 1922 the Ford station was ready to broadcast on a regular schedule. With the call letters WWI, the station began entertaining early in May of that year, broadcasting at 250 watts, on about 360 meters, every Wednesday evening from 10:00 until 11:00 P.M. A small studio was provided in the upper portion of the tractor building.[2] Fred Black was still general manager, Ben Donaldson was program planner and announcer, and many other employees with special talents participated in the programs. Thomas and Gassett were busy building and maintaining equipment for KDEN and its associated wireless stations as well as experimenting with the operation of the new WWI broadcast equipment. Thomas recalls that WWI broadcasts were often deliberately changed in frequency or power or both frequency and power from Wednesday to Wednesday to find the most favorable operating conditions for reaching a maximum audience. "I don't suppose we ever went on the air twice with the same system," he admits. Ford dealers were urged to listen for the program and respond by mail to the station. The geographical scope of the returned mail determined whether the change was an improvement or not. Ford must have been pleased with WWI because in October 1922 he announced plans to build a chain of four hundred such stations in as many cities.[3]

By November 1922 Michigan had twelve broadcasters including WWJ, the *Detroit News;* WWI, Ford Motor Company; KOP, the Detroit police department; WKAR, Michigan Agricultural College; and WCX, the *Detroit Free Press.* Dearborn's WWI was apparently the second station to broadcast in the state. Ford programs were published in detail and with glowing commentary in the *Ford News* beginning in June 1922. Station listings giving broadcast wavelengths (rather than frequencies) were published in the Detroit newspapers. The Ford public broadcast wavelength was shorter (360 meters) than the wavelength used for interplant wireless (1,713 meters).

The early Ford public broadcasts used talent largely from the ranks of Ford employees. The Ford Motor Company Highland Park Orchestra, the River Rouge Orchestra, and the Ford Hungarian Gypsy Orchestra were used extensively. The Highland Park Temple Pipe Band, the J. L. Hudson Ladies Quartet, and the Sacred Heart High School Orchestra of Dearborn offered their services. Entertainers received very little pay if any. Just being on radio was reward enough, it seems. Talented Dearborn people were

The new radio station, which began operations in February 1924, handled public broadcasts of WWI as well as interplant, marine, and railroad messages. This view is looking northwest toward Michigan Avenue and Elm Street. The neat little limestone building with tile roof is still in use. The towers are gone. (189-2490)

Interior of the new wireless station in February 1924. Operators relayed messages by phone and wireless between Ford plants, the railroad, and ships on the lakes and oceans. This same station, with studios in the engineering laboratory, broadcast the Wednesday evening programs of WWI. (189-2162)

given a chance. Sam Eggleston played his Jew's harp. Gosta Hagelthorn, on the harmonica, played selections from *La Traviata* and from *Boccaccia*, adding several Swedish folk songs. Gene Farkus played a flute, emitting such clear, sharp notes that the modulation of the transmitter was completely upset.

Later there were entertainers from afar. The Ford Hawaiians and the Ford Dixie Eight were popular with audiences and were undoubtedly paid handsomely. The California Bird Man whistled bird voices obligato while his wife accompanied him on her harp. And besides a great variety of tenor, soprano, baritone, contralto, violin, cello, piano, and concertina solos, there was always the health talk by a Henry Ford Hospital physician. "Prevention of Scarlet Fever," "Prevention of Rheumatism," "Indigestion," "Significance of Hoarseness," and "The Lost Art of Walking" were some of the topics. The first political talk was given in November 1922 by Senator-elect Ferris of Michigan, who spoke on "Good Citizenship." Henry Ford joined the speakers on November 31, 1923, when as a feature of International Radio Week he directed his voice to England, speaking on the internationalization of the English language—"The Language of Peace." This was a long speech for Ford—139 words. But he was never told that the equipment was not operating properly and that his spirited message may not have traveled much beyond the Rouge River.[4]

Beginning May 16, 1923, the time for the Wednesday evening program was changed from 10:00 P.M. to 8:00 P.M., and the wavelength changed from 360 meters to 273 meters in accordance with the new United States Radio Commission regulations. The programs continued to feature classical, popular, and folk music, old-time dance tunes, and talks on such topics as traffic safety, health, and advances in medicine.

The new engineering laboratory was being built on the site of the tractor plant during 1923. Just behind this large laboratory was also built a new radio station, which during its construction was declared perhaps the largest in the world.[5] Some were certain that the station was to be used by Ford to gain the presidency of the United States. The station began broadcasts in February 1924; the three 165-foot high aerial towers, 450 feet apart and straddling the East Lake, were indeed impressive. The transmitter building, 34-by-28 feet, handled both KDEN and WWI activities with five transmitters in operation. The power of WWI had now been increased from its orig-

inal 250 watts to 1,000 watts; normal broadcast range was about 750 miles. In the southwest corner of the large new laboratory building a new broadcasting studio was readied and connected by remote control wires to the transmitting building. As many as thirteen men were at one time working on radio equipment. For a year or so, a man from Eitel-McCullough was hired specifically to construct radio tubes. Henry had remarked, "Why should we pay so much money for these high-priced tubes?"[6]

But even with this great effort being put into the new station, it was soon found that the thousand-watt power of WWI was not enough to keep pace with local competition. Listeners began to complain that WWI was being drowned out by the *News* and *Free Press* stations. Estimates were that $250,000 would be required to close the gap.

Also it seems that Radio Corporation of America (RCA) was in a preferred patent position making it possible for them to control licensing of all oscillating circuits, and to a great extent vacuum-tube circuits in general.[7] This centralized control of the radio industry began to be reflected in federal legislation that gradually restricted private radio communication and eventually made it illegal for Ford Motor Company to use radio solely for its own private busi-

Mr. and Mrs. C. B. Hutchins, the "California Bird Man" and his wife, broadcasting over station WWI in January 1923. (189-1833)

The "Ford Hawaiians," a popular musical group that performed over station WWI during 1923–25. (189–1836)

ness. Ford was expected to join a chain such as RCA's National Broadcasting Company (NBC) network or the Columbia Broadcasting System (CBS), and thus provide broadcast facilities presumably more "in the public interest." This would mean that Ford would have to accept programs and advertising from other establishments perhaps not to his taste. He believed there might be programs broadcast from his station that would damage the reputation of the Ford Motor Company. Henry had no intention of giving up radio as a means of reaching the multitudes, but he would have to handle it differently.

Programs of the public broadcast station WWI abruptly disappeared from the *Ford News* in January 1926, and it was assumed that the broadcast license was in trouble. The next two years saw emphasis devoted to development of radio between tugs and barges, engines and cabooses, aircraft and ground, and invention of the remarkable radio range beacon (to be described in the next chapter). But for oppor-

tunities in public radio broadcasting, Henry Ford became completely disillusioned when the Federal Radio Commission (forerunner of the FCC) insisted on enforcement of a myriad of federal regulations. Ford did not like regulation from Washington.

An attempt was made on April 22, 1929, to establish a separate Ford Communication Company, Ford's asking the Michigan Utilities Commission for approval of a one hundred thousand dollar-stock issue. This organization was to be owned by Henry and Edsel Ford, not the Ford Motor Company, and was to include radio stations at Dearborn, Fordson, Chicago, L'Anse, equipment on several boats, and the three aircraft beacon stations. But this organization never functioned. It would also have been subject to the same restrictions, resulting in lack of private control over operations.

Then, according to Thomas, Henry Ford walked in one morning and said, "Well, I think we'll just drop the station." Thus Ford was, in a way, forced out of public broadcasting by federal legislation, thus becoming a customer of the big networks. Application for renewal of the license was withdrawn in September 1929, and the October 1929 Lights Golden Jubilee Banquet honoring Thomas Edison and featuring President Hoover as speaker was broadcast over WWJ and the NBC network. In January 1934 Fred Waring's Orchestra was playing over eighty CBS stations, the programs sponsored by seventy-five hundred Ford dealers. The 1934 World Series was carried over both NBC and CBS stations, sponsored by Ford Motor Company. Without federal interference, Henry Ford might have been using his own system of four hundred stations as he had predicted in 1922.

The monstrous station at Dearborn is shown on blueprints as property of the Edison Institute in 1930, and Bill Gassett was using it as a superamateur station for his Edison Institute Radio Club (W-8N2S). When the Piccards made their historic balloon ascent from Ford Air Port in 1934, Bill Gassett built two lightweight (ten pound) radios with which the Piccards could communicate with the ground. These high-frequency (fifty-six megahertz) instruments provided successful transmission and reception at 57,979 feet—an altitude record then for radio. Students working at world fairs in New York and San Francisco in 1939 could talk with their parents in Dearborn by way of Edison Institute radio. The massive towers of the station came down in 1942 when

the steel was needed as wartime scrap for the Rouge open hearths. The transmitting building was then stripped of its radio equipment and converted to an office for the Edison Institute.

Bill Gassett left Ford in 1941, but Charlie Thomas continued to do experimental work on automotive and aircraft systems. Experimental radios were installed in 1930 Model A cars, and as early as 1932 a steering column radio receiver had become an "authorized" accessory on a Ford car. In 1935 Henry Ford had a two-way radiotelephone in his personal car. Henry Ford I was not interested in the manufacture of radios as a business. They were not mechanical and he did not understand them. But much later, when the publicly owned Ford Motor Company was expanding in 1961, Henry Ford II did not hesitate to acquire the well-established name of Philco and build electronic equipment not only for his company but for the marketplace.

A rare photo of Henry Ford wearing glasses. Here he is reading the Hoover testimonial. Although Ford in his sixties used reading glasses, he preferred not to be seen wearing them. (0-376)

Henry Ford, in a posed photograph, on the occasion of his speaking out in favor of Herbert Hoover during the fall 1932 presidential election campaign. (0-7061)

Dearborn's radio-equipped Lincoln police cruiser in 1932, with (left to right) Police Chief Carl Brooks, Laverne (Bill) Ford in front seat, Mrs. Clyde M. Ford, Judge Lila Neuenfelt, and Mayor Clyde M. Ford. (Courtesy of Rylma [Ford] LaChance.)

NOTES

1. Not happy with the way newspapers had treated his views, Ford began publication of his own paper, the *Dearborn Independent*, in 1919 to have an independent means of expression. Ford dealers were assigned quotas to boost circulation.
2. Lewis, *Public Image*, pp. 178–79; C. W. Thomas recollections.
3. This announcement created a rash of newspaper publicity in October 23, 1922, editions all across the country. See Clipping Books, Acc. 7, vol. 30, Archives, HFM&GV.
4. Based on statements of William J. Krynen and William O. Gassett, radio operators.
5. *New York Times*, July 1, 1923, as an example.
6. As related by William O. Gassett, in his *Reminiscences*, p. 12, Acc. 65, Archives, HFM&GV.
7. Ibid., p. 23.

10

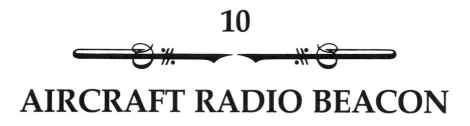

AIRCRAFT RADIO BEACON

At one time Henry Ford felt that Detroit could become the commercial aircraft center of the world, just as it had become the automotive center, and for a time in the late 1920s and early 1930s it was.[1] He and Edsel became leaders in this new industry. In 1924 they joined with William B. Stout, constructed an airport (now the Ford Motor Company Dearborn Proving Grounds), built a factory, and started production of all-metal airplanes. In addition, by 1925 they had pioneered a flying service with inaugural flights to Chicago followed quickly by daily services to Cleveland with mail and cargo. Ford became well acquainted with some of his pilots and was concerned about their safety. After several instances of a pilot's losing his way and being forced to land in unknown territory because of bad weather, a concerted effort was begun in 1926 to develop a flying aid that would help pilots determine their location and get them home despite bad weather conditions.[2] The United States Bureau of Standards in Washington and the Army Air Service Wright Field Laboratories at Dayton, Ohio, were conducting experiments to apply radio as an air-navigational aid. The bureau was developing a two-way telephony system designed to display a light on the aircraft instrument board; the air service experimented with spark-gap telegraphy. Neither laboratory had perfected a device. Ford men visited Wright Field and the bureau, examined their work, and found that the bureau in particular was looking for someone with the finances to continue such work. Next, a civilian, Eugene S. Donovan, from the Wright Field experimental group was hired by Henry Ford in 1926 to come to Dearborn and work with Charlie Thomas on such a device. Together, combining their knowledge and experience, a successful system based on more advanced vacuum-tube telegraphy was devised.[3]

The Ford system incorporated an ingenious transmitter, which could radiate signals in specific selected directions rather than in all directions at once, which was the normal fashion. The Ford radio beacon guided the plane by sending out signals alternately on two sending loops set at predetermined angles. From one loop the letter A (dot-dash) and from the other loop the letter N (dash-dot) were transmitted continuously in Morse code. Each loop was known as a beam leg. The loops were so constructed that they were together at one end (the sending station), spreading out at a thirty-degree angle for miles from the station. Signals from the two loops were sent out in rapid succession, the dot of the A signal being sent just as the dash of the N signal was completed. When the pilot was within this thirty-degree wedge of airspace, he heard a steady

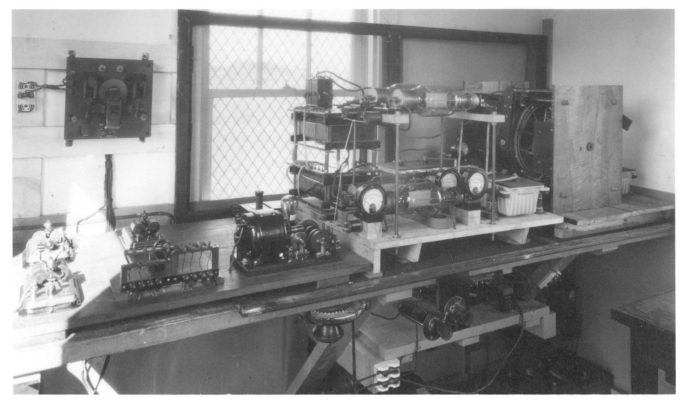

The dual transmitters with matched frequencies but variable power, which delivered the *A* and *N* signals to their respective antennas through the goniometer directional control. Photo taken September 10, 1926. (189-13682)

hum caused by the merging of the *A* and *N* signals. Outside the wedge he would hear only an *A* or an *N* depending on which side he was off course. This interlocking signal approach to the problem was novel. There were other important technical aspects of the system such as the "three-dot vertical marker beacon" and the means of "bending the beam," which are best described in the *Ford News*,[4] an article by James Barbier,[5] and the Donovan patent.[6]

This five hundred-watt radio beacon was first used in cooperation with Wright Field on February 16, 1927, when a Ford plane piloted by Harry Brooks flew from Dearborn to McCook Field at Dayton, Ohio, in a heavy snowstorm using a Ford-designed radio beam at Dayton for guidance. On the return trip the Dearborn beacon was used. Tests were made using the device on flights between Dearborn and Cleveland—sometimes across Lake Erie, sometimes around the lake. Bill Gassett was transferred to airport operations about this time, where he took charge of the beacon and broadcast weather reports

every hour on the hour to Ford planes and any other planes equipped to listen. Although the Ford Airlines, flying four daily flights between Dearborn and Cleveland as well as two daily flights between Dearborn and Chicago, had a nearly perfect reliability record, the advent of the radio beacon was considered a godsend to the pilots who had until now been forced to fly "by the seat of their pants."

The Dearborn beacon was in the southwest corner of the Ford Air Port, close to the present intersection of Oakwood and Rotunda, and nearly a half-mile southeast of the terminal on Oakwood from which the beacon was controlled. The little ten-by-ten-foot wooden beacon sending cubicle was unmanned, could operate automatically twenty-four hours a day, and required but a few hours maintenance a week. This remote control feature permitted installation of radio beacons along a flight path with all controls at major terminals. Beacon stations operating under experimental licenses W8XZ, W8XC, and W9XH were owned by Ford Airlines at Cleveland, Chicago (Lan-

Inside the transmitting cubicle the heart of the apparatus was the circular goniometer used to control direction of the beam. Above the goniometer were the meters, the fixed coupling condensers, and leads through the wall to the outside aerial loops. (189–3688)

sing, Illinois), and Buffalo. The Dearborn station usually had active loops aimed at Chicago (west), Cincinnati (south), Buffalo (east), and a fourth pointed due north.

In June 1927 a Ford trimotor participating in the Third National Air Tour was equipped with a radio beam receiving set to guide the plane over about thirteen hundred miles of the four thousand-mile course. Arrangements had been made to have beacon sta-

tions of Ford design in operation by the army station at Dayton, the General Electric station at Schenectady, and the Bureau of Standards station at College Park near Baltimore.[7]

On May 2, 1928, the Ford Motor Company finally applied for a patent on a device "especially adapted for use in connection with the piloting of airplanes and other aircraft . . . which will send out a signal in a predetermined direction so that a pilot may fly on that signal and may be kept on his course by following the signal." The patent was not granted until December 5, 1933, but the Ford radio beacon is acknowledged as the first successful radio beacon. Ford was happy to see the device used freely, never accepting any royalty payments. On February 26, 1928, Harry Brooks, perhaps Henry Ford's favorite test pilot, lost his life in an accident off the coast of Melbourne, Florida, while endurance-testing Ford's Flivver plane. This tragedy is thought to have hastened the work on the radio beacon.

Ford Motor Company was exceptionally generous with assistance in helping other airports build beacons, and their use quickly spread across the United States. Then, suddenly, because the value of the beacon had become obvious, the government decided that all radio ranges should be operated by the government. The Ford Motor Company soon received a letter requesting appearance before the Federal Communication's Commission to explain why the company was operating beacons and why it wished to continue to operate them. Gassett appeared before the commission and was told emphatically that all radio beacons, lighthouses, and so on, were a function of the government and should be operated by the government. Ford Motor Company thereupon lost its case and its licenses.

Gassett, returning to Dearborn fully disgusted, suggested to Ford that he charge the government a patent fee for each of the government-operated beacons; Ford's comment was that he was in the automobile business and not the radio business.

In 1933 this first successful radio beacon station, which had operated so well at Ford Air Port, was moved into the Ford Museum of the Edison Institute where the little station building is now on display, although it has been gutted of much of its equipment. To summarize, in William Gassett's words, "The number of lives and the amount of property the radio range has saved will never be known. The radio range was a very great contribution to aviation."

Radio beacon transmitting station and antennas at Ford Air Port in 1926. Aerial wires, barely visible in original photograph, have been drawn in to show their arrangement. Dirigible mast appears at far right. This view was looking east from the Oakwood side of the airport. (189-3684)

NOTES

1. Richard Hagelthorn, "Dearborn's Spruce Goose," *Dearborn Historian,* 22 (summer 1982): 71–82.
2. The following anecdote was told to the writer by Walter (Don) Spain, a trimotor crew member: On a flight to Buffalo, a Ford crew caught in a heavy rainstorm flew far off course and was forced to land in a farmer's cornfield. They phoned Dearborn to report that they were stuck in the mud in Ontario and would have to wait a day or so for the ground to dry out to take off again. The three young, single fellows were invited to stay at the home of the farmer who, incidentally, had three attractive daughters. The daughters were proud to have these young aviators escort them to the local dance hall where fun was had by all. After three days and nights of this rural brand of socializing, an urgent message came from Dearborn: "Get that plane back here! We flew over it today and the field is not at all wet. We expect you out of that field first thing in the morning."
3. Charles Voorhess, *Reminiscences,* Acc. 65, pp. 77–79, Archives, HFM&GV.
4. "Guiding Aerial Flight by Radio Beacon," *Ford News* 6 (April 8, 1927): 4–5; "The Radio Beam," *Ford News* 20 (November 1940): 247.
5. James Barbier, "Radio Beacon," *Herald* 13 (June 15, 1940): 291–97.
6. Patent no. 1,937,876 Radio Beacon, Eugene S. Donovan, Dearborn, Michigan, assignor to Ford Motor Company, Highland Park, Michigan, a corporation of Delaware. Application May 2, 1928, serial no. 274,397.
7. "Ford Plane with Tour Is Winged Laboratory," *Ford News* 7 (July 1, 1927): 1–6.

11

THE *DEARBORN INDEPENDENT*

Over the years, Ford Motor Company published a great variety of pamphlets and periodicals for customers, employees, and dealers.[1] None became as troublesome as the *Dearborn Independent*, which was Henry Ford's personal publication.[2]

During World War I, and particularly at the time of his venture to Europe on the Peace Ship, Ford believed the press had treated him unfairly. Again in 1918, during his candidacy for the United States Senate against Truman H. Newberry (Republican), it was Ford's belief that the "capitalistic" press caused him to lose. Because he believed the press could not be trusted to tell the truth as he saw it, he would publish his own paper.

Dearborn supported a typical small-town weekly, the *Dearborn Independent*, established in 1901, a paper Henry Ford had read for many years. This financially wavering newspaper was bought by Ford in November 1918. Ford liked the name *Independent*, but discarded the worn-out printing press. In its place he bought a superior machine from Sprague Publications in Detroit, the concern that had been publishing the *American Boy*. Certainly this printing press had a wholesome reputation.[3]

Ford immediately formed the Dearborn Publishing Company. He became president; Clara Ford, vice president; Edsel Ford, secretary-treasurer, and

E. G. Pipp, editor. Pipp, who had been with the *Detroit News*, brought others with him including William J. Cameron, of whom we shall hear later. Printing equipment and editorial room were housed in the tractor plant of Henry Ford & Son in Dearborn. Almost three hundred Fordson tractors were also being built daily here. The first issue of the *Dearborn Independent* appeared in January 1919.[4]

The *Dearborn Independent* carried the subtitles "The Ford International Weekly" and "Chronicler of the Neglected Truth." The paper was tabloid size consisting of sixteen pages selling for five cents a copy, or $1.50 per year. At the start and for several years there was no commercial advertising. Henry Ford believed that advertisers often controlled the content of newspapers. Later the price per copy was raised to ten cents and advertising slowly crept in: Firestone and Goodyear tires, tire-patching kits, railroad excursion trips, Kaffee Hag—nothing "harmful" or "competitive." By 1925, however, a full-page advertisement for the Ford automobile had appeared.

Ford's newspaper was thoughtful to say the least. Such a strong stance was taken on so many controversial issues that Pipp, the editor, is thought to have felt uneasy. He is not listed as editor in November 1920—he had left the Dearborn Publishing Company. His assistant, William Cameron, became

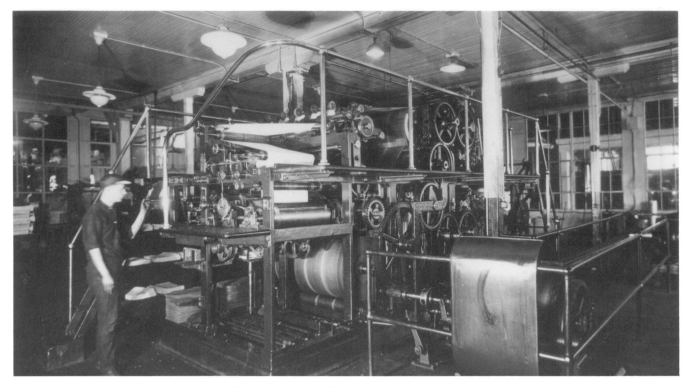

The circa-1890 printing press bought by Henry Ford from the publishers of the *American Boy.* Here the press is shown printing the *Dearborn Independent* in the Henry Ford & Son tractor plant on April 27, 1923. This press is now on display in the Henry Ford Museum. (189-1963)

editor in January 1921. Cameron and Ford seemed to get along well. Cameron could almost read Henry Ford's mind, a talent that was to serve him well.

In each issue of the *Independent* was an editorial page written by Cameron, and a "Mr. Ford's Own Page," probably also written by Cameron. The ideas on Ford's page presumably reflected Ford's thinking.[5] Subjects on Ford's page covered the gamut of philosophical topics. A random sampling finds categories such as opportunity, education, idleness, individuality, cleanliness, employment, wages, profit sharing, labor, capital, bankers, poverty, war, peace, human relations, right and wrong, privilege, and prohibition. Sometimes his page was devoted to one subject; sometimes several subjects were treated on the page. There was never more than one page of "Ford's Own."

Most of the articles in the *Dearborn Independent* were written by guest writers, many on subjects of worldwide interest. At first the *Independent* was entirely nonfiction, educational, and presumably factual. Together, these guest writings also covered a great breadth of serious subjects, each providing a definite viewpoint. There was little compromise presented. Early issues repeatedly praised the work of Woodrow Wilson and the League of Nations. To lighten this heavy menu, writers of fiction such as Hugh Walpole, Robert Frost, and Booth Tarkington began to be introduced. Cartoons were plentiful, each depicting a serious problem, however. Photographs were generously used to illustrate articles about travel and foreign countries.

The subtitle "Chronicler of the Neglected Truth" appealed to a host of free-lance writers, many of whom could be classed as crackpots. Cameron and Liebold made the selections.[6] It is doubtful whether Ford reviewed these contributed articles, but it is said Cameron sometimes prepared several rough drafts of "Mr. Ford's Own Page" before final acceptance by Ford. Cameron's editorial page treated subjects much like Ford's page, for example: "The Right Way Is the Only Way," "Success Is Doing," "Prohibition Is Not a Failure." Cameron was a genius at interpreting and amplifying Ford's thoughts. An off-hand cryptic remark by Ford would be expanded into a full-page editorial by Cameron, whereas the average reporter would likely ask, "What in the world did the old man mean by that?"

Feature pages appearing in each issue included "I Read in the Papers," "Chats with Office Callers," "Briefly Told," and "Can You Tell Me?" The items on these pages were also saturated with moral advice. Could it be that Henry Ford was publishing an adult version of his beloved McGuffey Readers?

The *Dearborn Independent* was distributed primarily through Ford dealers, the dealers pressured into being responsible for selling (or buying) large quotas of subscriptions. Dealers rebelled, but pressure continued, sometimes using "lead pipe" methods. Distribution through newsstands was far short of meeting the one-million circulation desired by Ford. Salesmen were hired to canvas door to door at high Ford wages to meet circulation goals. During the first year, with a circulation of 72,000, Ford lost $284,000. It is doubtful the paper ever turned a profit. By 1924, however, circulation had reached 650,000, and by 1925–26 it had grown to 900,000.[7]

But from the very beginning Ford's *Dearborn In-*

Working at Linotype machines in the tractor plant during April 1923. (189-1939)

dependent was heading for trouble. To most readers the tone of its articles seems to have been acceptable, but to some it was vicious. This was primarily because of articles blaming Jews for many of the problems of the world. Not only guest writers contributed to the attack; the slurs became apparent in Cameron's editorials. The extent Henry Ford was aware of the content of his newspaper is not certain. As president of Dearborn Publishing Company he at least allowed the defamation and may have been an instigator. Though Cameron became uneasy in the assignment, he did not refuse to continue. There are some who attributed the attack on the Jews to Liebold's influence.[8] In any case this tendency by the *Dearborn Independent* meant serious trouble. Perhaps as a consequence of threatened legal action against the *Independent,* during September 1923 the names of Clara and Edsel Ford disappeared from the masthead. Only the names of Henry Ford and William Cameron remained.[9]

The first article deploring the "international Jew" appeared in the May 20, 1920, issue. These accusations appeared in one form or another for more than two years. More than one lawsuit was filed against Ford and his paper. After 1922, having received private advice from President Harding and several Jewish friends of Ford, the paper moderated. But in April 1924 there was trouble again. A series of three articles by Robert Morgan (a guest writer) entitled "Exploiting Farm Organizations" brought instant response from the subject of the attack, Aaron Sapiro, a prominent Chicago attorney. Sapiro sued Ford for $1 million for libel. Sapiro had been organizing farm cooperatives throughout the United States and, according to Morgan, had been collecting excessive fees for his work. Morgan insisted Sapiro had been exploiting the farmer rather than helping him.

By May 1925 the press facilities had been moved out of the tractor plant and into the new engineering building on the same site. A different masthead for the *Independent* appeared that month. Henry Ford remained president, E. G. Liebold became vice president and treasurer (he had been general manager), and Ford's legal counsel, Clifford B. Longley, became secretary. Cameron continued as editor. Under these officers the *Independent* adopted a smaller, more modern format; touches of color were added, advertising became more prominent, and the price returned to five cents.

The trial with Sapiro in March 1927 at Detroit's

Front page of the April 12, 1924, issue of the *Dearborn Independent.*

Federal District Court gained spectacular newspaper coverage. Even the *Dearborn Independent,* in its April 2, 1927, issue, printed verbatim transcriptions. Ford and Cameron were called as witnesses. Cameron protected Ford by taking the rap and admitting he was to blame. Ford did not appear as a defendant but managed to settle out of court, agreeing to make a public apology and pay court costs of $140,000. The apology was made public by a statement on July 7, 1927.

The long legal proceedings had been wearisome to Henry Ford. During the month of the trial, April 1927, he gave instructions to the paper's business manager, Fred Black, to plan to stop the paper in "reasonable time." It was to die with dignity. During the rest of 1927, its last year of publication by Ford, the paper, still selling at five cents a copy, was featuring full-page promotions of *Good Morning*, a dance instruction book published by the Ford School of (old-fashioned) Dancing.[10] The Ford book of 169 pages sold for seventy-five cents. A volume of 452 pages, containing ninety-eight *Independent* articles, entitled *Ford Ideals*, was also offered for one dollar postpaid.

It is difficult to assess the damage the *Dearborn Independent* may have caused Ford. Even though the publication greatly upset some of the population during this period, circulation of the paper steadily grew, as did Ford automobile sales. The general population seems not to have been greatly disturbed. The situation tended to verify the adage that, whether good or bad, publicity is helpful to business. Henry was tired of it, however, and was glad in 1927 to switch his attention to the "new Ford," the Model A, which was being readied for introduction. It is un-

likely he was aware he had spent $4,795,000 on the *Dearborn Independent*.[11]

Cameron continued in Ford's employ, in a few years becoming well known for his inspiring radio lectures on the Ford Sunday Evening Hour during the 1930s. The old R. Roe & Company rotary printing press, based on patents between 1881 and 1899 and kept in immaculate condition by Ford, was retired after it turned out its December 31, 1927, issue. The press is now on display in the Henry Ford Museum in Dearborn.

NOTES

1. In 1924 the Ford Motor Company was publishing seven major publications, with a total circulation of more than ten million. The earliest had been the *Ford Times*, inaugurated April 13, 1908, and now in its 81st year.
2. "The Why and Wherefore of the Dearborn Independent," *Ford News* 4 (October 1, 1924): 3.

Composing room at the new location of the Dearborn Publishing Company in the engineering laboratory of Ford Motor Company, August 1925. (189-2969)

3. Nevins and Hill, *Expansion and Challenge*, p. 124.
4. *Dearborn Independent*, 1–9 (January 1919–December 1927), Archives, HFM&GV.
5. Fred L. Black, *Reminiscences*, pp. 21–22; E. G. Liebold, *Reminiscences*, p. 442, Archives, HFM&GV.
6. W. J. Cameron Files, Acc. 44, Boxes 3–7, Archives, HFM&GV.
7. Circulation Reports, Dearborn Publishing Company, Acc. 62–2, Box 52, HFM&GV.
8. Lewis, *Public Image*, p. 138.
9. *Dearborn Independent*, September 15, 1923.
10. Eva O'Neal Twork, *Henry Ford and Benjamin Lovette: The Dancing Billionaire and the Dancing Master* (Detroit: Harlo Press, 1982), 267 pp.
11. Nevins and Hill, *Expansion and Challenge*, p. 311.

12

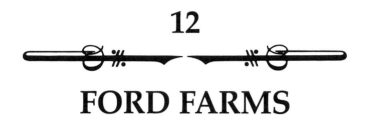

FORD FARMS

Henry Ford was perhaps first and foremost a farmer, though with a well-recognized mechanical talent. His ancestors had been eking out an existence on a small patch of leased stony earth in Southern Ireland for generations. So Henry's father, as might be expected, soon after reaching America as a young man, exhibited a strong land-hungry appetite—accumulating more than two hundred acres of rich Dearborn soil in his own name within a span of about ten years.[1] Those were the days when land in combination with a good supply of healthy, pliant children spelled security. Henry had two younger brothers and two sisters who lived to adulthood, both brothers becoming farmers to an extent. For a time, when Henry was about twenty-eight (1891), he seemed to be giving up the farm completely and for good. He moved with his wife, Clara, to Detroit and concentrated on steam, electrical, and gasoline engines. His father must have been for a time disappointed in him. But in 1902, three years before his father died, Henry had bought the homestead property and evidenced his continuing interest in agriculture.

Henry turned out to be infinitely more land-hungry than his father. The amount of land he accumulated from automotive profits is almost inestimable. Over the years he acquired 26,000 acres of farm and hydroelectric property in southern Michi-

gan; 75,000 acres of timber and rice land at Richmond Hill, Georgia; 400,000 acres of timber and iron-mining land in northern Michigan; and 2.5 million acres of tropical forest in Brazil for the production of rubber. And this does not include farmlands in Florida,[2] New England,[3] as well as Old England,[4] nor his coal, dolomite, lead, and railroad properties, and many worldwide factory sites. The total acreage must have reached more than 3 million, the equivalent of 4,700 square miles, or roughly the size of Connecticut.

Near Dearborn were the fabulous Henry Ford Farms of southeastern Michigan, which were under the daily direction of Henry Ford through such alter egos as Ray Dahlinger and Fred "Big Fritz" Loskowski.[5] It has been told that Ford owned so much farmland in southeastern Michigan that he could walk from Tecumseh (fifty miles away) to Dearborn without stepping off his property. But that seems a bit improbable unless he walked along his D. T. & I. Railroad.[6] He did, however, own so much land that Fred Gregory, his buying agent, frequently had to remind Ford, when Ford proposed buying a piece of property, that he already owned it.

The farmland in southeastern Michigan is of particular interest because it was managed in detail by Ford himself. His foremen received instructions almost daily about what to plant, where to plant, and

Pupils of Henry Ford School are taken for a sleigh ride on a cold February day in Dearborn (1926). This school was on Ford Farm land and twelve years later, after a new and much larger school had been built, this building was converted to a tomato-canning factory. (0-1610)

when to plant, as well as when and how to harvest. And Ford was often there to see how it was done. He had been experimenting with farm crops from the time he had started to experiment with farm tractors—about 1906.[7]

The large tract of land bought by Ford in Dearborn Township near his boyhood home in 1909 was managed by Clara Ford's brother, Marvin Bryant; his son Edgar LeRoy Bryant acted as bookkeeper. Later, about 1915, farm management was turned over to Ray Dahlinger as general superintendent of the official entity, Henry Ford Farms; Dahlinger's wife acted as treasurer. The Dahlingers were thus to become Ford's landscape gardeners on a grandiose scale.

By 1915 Henry Ford had already bought 2,843 acres in the Dearborn area costing $3,754,054. He paid generously for the land but refused to pay exorbitant prices. In 1921 he is said to have had 7,000 acres worked almost entirely by tractors rather than horses. By January 1931, just before he bought the Quirk Farms,[8] he owned 8,486 acres in southeastern Michigan. Quirk Farms was a corporation holding a tract of 1,748 acres southeast of the city of Ypsilanti for which Ford paid $300,000. This corporation, under Henry Ford, was to gain title to some two hundred additional properties of about 12,500 acres in

the townships of Clinton, Macon, Milan, Raisin, Saline, Superior, Tecumseh, and Van Buren as well as Ypsilanti. By 1947 Ford had close to 26,000 acres for which he had paid about $14 million,[9] almost all of which was used for agriculture. These farms were in Wayne, Washtenaw, Monroe, and Lenawee counties, largely southwest within fifty miles of Dearborn, the headquarters for the Ford Farms. This area was known to agriculturalists as having some of the richest farmland in Michigan.

Acquisition of the Henry Ford Farms took place principally during two periods: 1909–19 in the Dearborn area and 1931–34 in the Tecumseh area. During the first fifteen years or so, Ford's experiments focused on application of tractors to farming. Later the experiments focused on the use of farm crops in industry. Until the great farm depression of 1921–23, the emphasis had been entirely on greater farm efficiency and productivity. During and after that depression the emphasis was on using the overabundance of farm crops.

Ford's giant land holdings were made up of hundreds of small, family-sized farms—many with livable house and usable barns. These buildings, if in fair condition, were repaired and modernized to the highest of rural standards. At least a hundred such premises were thus restored and were easily recognizable by their pristine white exteriors and neatly garaged implements. Sometimes the farmer stayed and worked the same land as an employee of Henry Ford Farms. If he did so, he followed some precise rules pertaining to his behavior and that of his family.[10] Most often, however, Ford selected his farm families as he would his seed corn—a healthy, vigorous variety; he paid them well and expected maximum output.

Wherever Henry Ford owned most of the land in a community he became not only a responsible citizen but a liberal benefactor. He made certain that his lands were well fenced, the roads in good repair, and schools for the farm children were the best possible. Many schools were enlarged, modernized, equipped for an expanded curriculum, and taught by well-paid teachers—all at Ford's expense. He often gave money for religious structures (but not a preacher), and gave land and money for community buildings such as a town hall, fire station, commissary, and post office (but not a bank).

More important, with the efficiency of the Fordson tractor and associated implementation, Ford was convinced that the farmer could now complete his yearly work on the farm in less than a month's time.[11] He therefore proceeded to find other work for the farmer. Near most of these agricultural communities

he found waterpower and set up small manufacturing plants to employ farmers during their off seasons. The Village Industries at Saline, Milan, Dundee, Tecumseh, Manchester, Brooklyn, and Sharon Mills were examples of these rural industries in the Macon area. There were at least twenty such plants in rural southern Michigan, with seven on the Rouge River upstream from Dearborn employing twenty-four hundred part-time farmers.[12]

From the Ford grainfields where Fordson tractors powered the vibrating separators, Ford trucks carried the grain directly to the Dearborn Elevator & Grain Mill. The elevator had been built by S. J. McQueen & Company of Fort William, Ontario, for $74,448, by an agreement signed by Henry Ford on October 13, 1917.[13] Located on the Michigan Central Railroad at Oakwood Boulevard in Dearborn, the elevator had fifteen sixty-five-foot-high circular bins with a conveyor to handle 2,000 bushels per hour and an elevator capacity of 99,800 bushels.

Carrying the grain processing a step further, a four-story flour mill was attached to the elevator during March and April 1920 by an agreement of March 2 between Henry Ford and his Dearborn Construction Company. The building alone cost about $48,000, and together with the milling machinery bought from the Nordyke & Harmon Company of Indianapolis brought the total cost of the mill to

These nineteen Fordsons are leaving the field after making quick work of plowing this old cornfield on a damp, cold day in 1927. (188-6442)

Henry Ford Farms Elevator and Grain Mill. The mill is the four-story building to the right of the elevator. The long, low building in the foreground is the barn housing the Fair Lane, the private railroad car used by the Fords. (Courtesy of the Dearborn Historical Museum.)

Artichokes	Oats
Asparagus	Parsley
Beans—Soy	Peanuts
Beans—Navy	Peas—Green
Beans—Green	Peas—Field
Barley	Peppers
Beets	Potatoes
Buckwheat	Pumpkins
Cabbage	Radish
Carrots	Rye
Cauliflower	Rutabagas
Cantaloupe	Sunflower
Celery	Spinach
Corn—Field	Strawberries
Corn—Sweet	Squash
Cucumbers	Tomatoes
Egg Plant	Turnips
Flax	Wheat
Onions	Watermelons

$120,117.58. The mill, with a dozen white-frocked employees and Ralph Shackleton as mill superintendent, could produce one hundred barrels of flour in a twenty-four-hour day. Flour from the mill was sold to Ford commissaries, to Henry Ford Hospital, and retailed in Dearborn grocery stores.[14]

But also during 1924 an analysis revealed a loss of $1.40 for every barrel of flour produced. (The mill and elevator were sold to Ford Motor Company in 1944 for $133,068.75 and torn down in 1957.)

The variety of crops grown on the Ford Farms seemed almost endless. Following is a list from which Ford was asked by Dahlinger to choose planting acreage in January 1932.[15]

Of these crops, wheat, oats, barley, rye, and soybeans constituted large acreages, as did apple and peach orchards and hay fields. Garden crops were distributed much more widely; many gardens were in villages and cities as well as the countryside.

Employed on the farms and gardens during the active season were from five hundred to a thousand men and boys, under the guidance of Raymond C. Dahlinger and his foremen. During peak periods men were "borrowed" from Ford Motor Company. Although farm work usually paid about a dollar a day less than the factory, many preferred to work outside.[16] Many minors were employed for farm work. State approval of occupation of minors permitted males age sixteen to seventeen to work eight hours per day, forty-eight hours per week, at wages of fifty to sixty cents per hour. Males age fourteen to fifteen could work after school and during vacations, eight

FLOUR MILL OUTPUT (SALES RECORDS—1924)[17]

	Pounds			Aver. Price		
Bread & Pastry	2,499,925	12,499	Bbls.	$6.48	Bbls.	$80,585.08
Low Grade	168,200	841	"	3.58	"	3,014.14
Bran	715,053	357.52	Tons	29.40	Tons	10,511.09
Middlings	331,255	165.62	"	32.63	"	5,404.18
Whole Wheat	65,660	328.3	Bbls.	5.64	Bbls.	1,851.95
Screenings	415,632	278.01	Tons	29.19	Tons	8,115.11
Total	4,195,725					$109,480.55

PASTRY
5 POUNDS NET WEIGHT
WHEN PACKED

Ford Flour

HENRY FORD FARMS
DEARBORN
MICH.

The popular five-pound sack of flour sold through Ford commissaries and local grocery stores. (Courtesy of the Dearborn Historical Museum.)

hours a day and sixteen hours per week with wages of two to four dollars per day. In the Dearborn canning factory, for example, thirty boys worked along with six men during September 1938 canning 52,505 cans of tomatoes in a three-week period.[18] Another forty to fifty boys were busy picking the eighty acres of tomatoes. Hundreds of boys were employed hoeing weeds from the soybean fields in the Macon area.

Dearborn Fordson High School horticultural students managed garden plots on Ford Farms along Greenfield near William Ford School. Edison Institute students, both boys and girls, raised vegetables on Ford land and sold their produce at a roadside stand on Village Road near Southfield. Artisan Cooperative Industries, consisting of a group of boys living in a house owned by Henry Ford at 1034 Brady Street in Dearborn, raised vegetables on the Ford land along Michigan Avenue during 1933, selling their produce to the Dearborn Inn, the Wardell Hotel in Detroit, and to Ford Motor Company commissaries. Income from their vegetable sales paid for food and clothing bought from the commissaries.

During the Depression years of the 1930s, Ford Farms accepted the responsibility of furnishing garden land and seed to almost anyone seeking a vegetable garden. These were referred to as "welfare gardens." A fleet of forty tractors was kept busy plowing an estimated fifteen hundred acres of tiny gardens—from Flat Rock on the south to Birmingham on the north. Henry Ford encouraged all his factory employees to have gardens. Records were kept of the size and condition of employee gardens, for a large well-kept garden (or ideally a farm) indicated loyalty to Ford principles.

And Ford Farms was also in the gardening business on a large scale, selling produce on the open market at unbelievably low prices, much to the annoyance of local truck gardeners.[19] And Clara Ford, as president of the Woman's National Farm and Garden Association, was involved in promotion of roadside marketing of flowers, baked goods, and home-canned fruits and vegetables, having elegant architectural models made of roadside stands and observing the operation of Ford Farms–sponsored roadside markets in Dearborn. Clara Ford also provided lists of people and institutions deserving free fruit and vegetables from the Ford Farms. The Dearborn City Welfare Department, during the Depression, benefited from gifts of crops such as four hundred acres of carrots, one hundred acres of onions, and sixty acres of peas.[20] Almost any capable man out of work and living in Dearborn or neighboring Inkster was offered work on the Ford Farms. Mayor Clyde M. Ford or Police Chief Carl Brooks could arrange it.

During World War II "victory gardens" were

Clara Ford with a model roadside market displayed at a New York convention of the Womans National Farm and Garden Association. (0-7145)

popular. Again Ford Farms sent crews with tractors, plows, and disc harrows to prepare garden plots far and wide. And even as late as 1986 a vestige of the same spirit remained as Ford Tractor Operations promoted Farm-A-Lot, encouraging Detroiters to maintain gardens on city-owned vacant lots, private lots, and backyards by providing soil preparation, free seeds, and technical assistance. Ford tractors and rotary tillers prepared the soil for some one hundred thousand Detroiters, it is said.[21]

On the Ford Farms, about 1930, Dearbornites witnessed the harvesting of fields of dandelion seeds by means of small vacuum cleaners, and a trial field of marijuana was found to have little value as an in-

dustrially useful crop. In 1931 an experiment applying coal and coke dust as fertilizers for Irish cobbler potatoes revealed that coke dust performed better than coal, but neither produced a yield equivalent to standard N-P-K fertilizers.

Beginning in 1932 Ford chose soybeans as the ideal crop for combined farm and industrial use. Thus he did not invent a crop but instead adopted a plant introduced into the United States in 1804 and known in China for nearly five thousand years. During 1932–33 he is said to have spent about $1,225,000 on soybean experiments involving three hundred varieties. Nearly seventy-four hundred acres were planted to soybeans on his farms in Lenawee County yielding more than one hundred thousand bushels. Varieties there included itosan, manchu, early brown, and black eyebrow. A ton of dry beans would yield four hundred pounds of oil and sixteen hundred pounds of meal—the latter containing forty-five percent protein and the remainder carbohydrates. The soybean vine provided about one ton of cattle forage per acre, and the nodular roots of this legume added needed fixed nitrogen to the soil. Soybeans were indeed a most valuable plant.

At the Chicago World Fair in 1934, Henry Ford demonstrated the "industrialized American barn"[22] where soybeans were processed into oil and soybean meal. The oil was further used in the manufacture of paints in place of linseed oil, and the meal used in industrial plastics formulations as well as cattle feed. The demonstration was meant to convince farmers that they could become industrialists on a small scale, processing beans into useful articles and by-products. Nearly everyone has had his hands on one of those soybean gearshift knobs, horn buttons, or light switches.

Dearborn, in May 1935, had the distinction of being the site of the first "chemurgy" conference in the nation. Meeting at the Dearborn Inn at the invitation of Henry Ford, this Joint Conference of Representatives of Agriculture, Industry and Science, a group of three hundred prominent Americans, resolved to:

1. Promote the gradual absorption of much of the domestic Farm Surplus by domestic industry
2. Put idle acres to work profitably
3. Increase the purchasing power of the American farmer on a stable and more permanent basis, and thereby
4. Increase the demand for manufactured products, thus
5. Creating new work for idle hands to do; reviving American industry; restoring American labor to productive enterprise; and relieving the economic distress of the Nation.[23]

On the first day of the two-day conference Henry and Edsel Ford hosted a luncheon (Henry Ford seated with Irénée du Pont) after which the group took buses to the Edison Institute Museum where, under the replica of Independence Hall, a Declaration of Dependence upon the Soil and of the Rights of Self-Maintenance was signed in a setting of antiques related to Lincoln and Jefferson. The group then visited the Greenfield Village Laboratory of R. A. Boyer where the soybean oil extraction unit

The Greenfield Village School Market and the Dearborn Pantry Shelf operated during the Depression on Village Road at Southfield, on Greenfield Village property. (Photo courtesy Dearborn Historical Museum.)

Early fall sale of Ford Farms produce—melons, peaches, apples—at one of the Dearborn locations in 1931. (0-7146)

was demonstrated; and at one of the technical sessions at the inn, R. H. McCarroll, chief chemist of Ford Motor Company, spoke on "Increasing the Use of Agricultural Products in the Automotive Industry." The second "chemurgy" conference (1936) was again held at the Dearborn Inn; George Washington Carver was an honored guest with whom Henry Ford then established a lifelong friendship.[24]

A look at the "Dearborn" Farms in June 1939, involving about six thousand acres, including the Greenfield Village grounds where Dahlinger's wife reigned supreme, reveals the following inventory.[25]

Employees:	Farm	488	Dairy Farm	16
	Village	40	Boys Garden Farm	31
	Residence	20	Boys Brushing	35
	Orchards	12	Camp Legion	67

Livestock included 12 carriage horses, 11 saddle horses, 6 ponies, but no draft horses. There were a total of 135 cows (80 fresh, 20 dry) and 35 young cattle. Ten ducks, 50 chickens, 15 goats, and 90 beehives finished the livestock list. More than 600 farm implements of 96 types are listed, among them 71 tractors, 95 plows, 48 harrows, 3 steam-threshing engines with separators, 8 combines, 12 binders, 15 tractor cultivators, 25 hand cultivators, 11 hay mowers, 57 power lawn mowers, and 24 hand mowers. There were 79 trucks of various types, tree lifters, orchard sprayers, potato diggers, grain drills, ditchers, road graders, street sweepers, and snowplows—whatever was needed.

Perry Hayden, a Quaker miller of Tecumseh, who sold his small picturesque grain mill to Henry Ford in 1934, induced Ford to participate in a project known as Dynamic Kernels.[26] Starting with one cubic inch of wheat (360 kernels) planted in the fall of 1940, the program was to harvest and give to the Friends Church of Tecumseh a tithe of one-tenth of the crop each year for six years. This project was inspired by the Bible:

> Six years thou shalt sow thy field, and six years thou shalt prune thy vineyard, and gather in the fruit thereof; but in the seventh year shall be a sabbath of rest unto the land, a sabbath for the Lord. (Lev. 25:3–4)

Hayden furnished the starting handful of Bald Rock wheat, and Ford furnished the land, a four-by-twelve-foot plot. The wheat was ceremoniously sown and ceremoniously harvested; Hayden, the Friends Church congregation, and Ford with his farm crew participated each year. With annual increases in yield ranging from thirtyfold to fiftyfold, the program flourished and the publicity spewed forth.

The plot of wheat grew to 1,440 square feet the second year, to one acre the third, and in 1944 the fourteen-acre plot was harvested using old-fashioned

equipment Henry used as a boy. While Henry Ford operated the large 1880 steam thresher, Henry Ford II operated the miniature thresher built for the grandchildren in the 1920s. The 1945 crop of 330 acres was harvested by Ford employees using twenty combines powered by Ford tractors. Eight Ford trucks carried the 4,868 bushels of grain to the granaries, the entire cutting completed in one afternoon. However, Ford, being quite ill, could not be there in 1945, and Hayden announced the dissociation of Ford from Dynamic Kernels.

But Hayden carried on.[27] Because no one farm could furnish the twenty-six hundred acres to be planted that fall, seed was divided among 267 small farmers in Michigan, Ohio, Indiana, Wisconsin, and Tennessee; tithing was pledged to churches of twenty-seven denominations. This was handled through the cooperation of the Lenawee County 4-H clubs. The final harvest in 1946 was 66,500 bushels yielding more than $100,000. A ten-acre patch of wheat in the center of the Adrian fairground racetrack served as ceremonial center for the sixth and final harvest.

Farming was a satisfying but costly philanthropy for Ford. The southeastern Michigan farms alone show operating losses of $13,524,477 for 1913 through 1944.[28] Farms in two other localities (Georgia, 1925–47, and Massachusetts, 1923–45) together lost another $5,575,915. Besides these strictly "farm" losses, "schools" associated with the farms cost another $1,435,707 between 1927 and 1947. According

The "chemical laboratory" at Greenfield Village in 1930. Research at this laboratory under Robert Boyer revealed the adaptability of the soybean to a multitude of uses. (0-6212)

Combines harvest soybeans near Tecumseh in 1939. (188-17641)

to Liebold,[29] the Internal Revenue Service refused to believe a working business could repeatedly lose $800,000 to $1 million a year, and consequently limited Ford's allowable farm loss deductions to $25,000.

Edsel Ford died in 1943, and although Henry was not in the best of health (age eighty) he again became president of Ford Motor Company. But others in the family, including Henry Ford II, began to lend a helping hand. Farm losses were just one of the many loss operations that needed to be eliminated. Ford Farms, including Quirk Farms, were transferred to Ford Motor Company on July 3, 1944, some of the acreage being immediately resold to the Defense Plant Corporation site of the Willow Run bomber plant. Over the next few years the extensive farmlands in Lenawee and adjoining counties were liquidated.[30]

Over the years Henry and Clara Ford and the Ford Motor Company donated many parcels of former Ford Farms land to organizations for public use. Following is a partial Dearborn list; often the gift included new buildings as well as land:

Edison School
William B. Stout School
William Ford School
Bryant Library
Centennial Library
University of Michigan—Dearborn
Henry Ford Community College
The Edison Institute
Oakwood Hospital
Veterans Hospital
Christ Episcopal Church
Dearborn Community Center
Ford Field
Ford Woods Park
Southfield Interchanges
I-94 Interchanges

As late as September 1971 Ford Motor Company, through its Corporate Contributions Office, executed a "deed of gift" involving 123 acres of Lenawee County land to Boysville of Michigan, Inc.

Yet Ford Farms still linger with us in Dearborn, accounting for our large midcity greenbelt and an occasional soybean field administered by Ford Land Development Corporation, a subsidiary of Ford Motor Company. Would it not be fitting if a small soybean patch could be perpetually maintained circling the Ford Homestead Memorial on Ford Road near Greenfield? After all, wasn't Henry Ford really a farmer at heart?

NOTES

1. Ford R. Bryan, *The Fords of Dearborn* (Detroit: Harlo Press, 1987): 93–112.
2. Ford's Florida acreage, bought in 1924, was east of his home in Fort Myers in the counties of Glades, Hendry, and Lee. The 7,290 acres of mainly pastureland were along the Caloosatchee River and in the townsites of Goodno and LaBelle. The property was sold at substantial loss in 1941. See Acc. 844, Box 1, Archives HFM&GV.
3. In the Framingham, Marlborough, and Sudbury districts of Massachusetts, Henry Ford, between 1923 and 1928, bought eighty-eight parcels of land totaling 2,667 acres. Included in these properties was the Wayside Inn. Losses for the inn, farms, and schools for the years 1923–45 totaled $2,848,187. See Acc. 384, Box 1, Archives HFM&GV.
4. A tract of two thousand acres purchased in 1931 at Boreham, Essex, was devoted to the instruction of young men and women in the use and maintenance of farm equipment. (See chap. 2.)
5. F. W. Loskowski, *Reminiscences*, Acc. 65, pp. 1–122, Archives, HFM&GV.
6. Ford R. Bryan, "Henry Ford's Excursion into Railroading," *Herald* 15 (November 1, 1986): 38–47.
7. See chap. 1.
8. From records of L. J. Thompson, Acc. 844, Box 1, Archives, HFM&GV. In January 1931 Ford bought all the stock of Quirk Farms. After disposition in 1945, the corporation was dissolved.
9. Reynold W. Wik, *Henry Ford and Grassroots America* (Ann Arbor: University of Michigan Press, 1972), pp. 1–259.
10. "Constitution and By-Laws of Ford's Cooperative Farmers Association," Acc. 572, Index No. 3862, Farming 9.12, Archives, HFM&GV.
11. Nevins and Hill, *Expansion and Challenge*, p. 227.
12. R. H. McCarroll, "Increasing the Use of Agricultural Products in the Automotive Industry," *Proceedings of the First Dearborn Conference of Agriculture, Industry, and Science* (Dearborn: May 7–8, 1935), 235 pp.
13. A copy of this agreement is in Acc. 47, Box 1, Archives, HFM&GV. The agreement had but one signatory, L. G. Liebold, acting as attorney for Ford and president of Dearborn Construction Company.
14. "Modern Milling Methods Exemplified in Ford Flour Mill; Superior Product," *Ford News* 3 (March 15, 1923): 3, 8.
15. Of ten thousand acres, about fifteen hundred were already planted to winter wheat and rye. Acc. 23, Box 10, Archives, HFM&GV.
16. Raymond Newman, *Reminiscences*, Acc. 65. pp. 4, 5, Archives, HFM&GV.
17. Acc. 572, Box 3826, Archives, HFM&GV.
18. "Tomato Production and Cost Report, 1938," Acc. 445, Box 6, Archives, HFM&GV.

19. At Detroit's Eastern Market, for example, truck gardeners from Utica and Warren, Michigan, selling cabbage at two cents a pound were upset one day when Ford Farms dumped several truckloads on the market asking only one cent.

20. Loskowski, *Reminiscences*, Acc. 65, pp. 60–67, Archives, HFM&GV.

21. *Automotive News*, 60 (May 12, 1986): 52.

22. Lewis, *Public Image*, pp. 282–86; "A Bushel in Every Car," *Ford Life* (May–June 1972): James Sweinhart, *The Industrialized American Barn* (Chicago World's Fair pamphlet, Ford Motor Company, 1933), Acc. 931, Box 25, Archives, HFM&GV.

23. *Proceedings—First Dearborn Conference*, Joint Conference of Representatives of Agriculture, Industry, and Science, held at Dearborn Inn, Dearborn, Michigan on May 7 and 8, 1935, p. 181. Printed and distributed by the Chemical Foundation Incorporated, 654 Madison Avenue, New York.

24. Ford R. Bryan, "A Prized Friendship," *Herald* (November 2, 1983): 90–95.

25. Acc. 587, Box 185, Folder 1151, Archives, HFM&GV.

26. Collection of newspaper clippings under heading Dynamic Kernels, Vertical File, Archives, HFM&GV.

27. Letter from Perry Hayden to Fred Smith, superintendent of Edison Institute, dated July 24, 1944. Acc. 23, Box 10, Archives, HFM&GV.

28. See Acc. 844, Box 1, Archives, HFM&GV.

29. E. G. Liebold, *Reminiscences*, Acc. 65, p. 61, Archives, HFM&GV.

30. Departmental communication dated July 3, 1944, about "Transfer and Operation of Henry Ford Farms as a department of the Ford Motor Company," Acc. 445, Box 1, Archives, HFM&GV. Wayside Inn properties valued at $1,617,000 were donated to a nonprofit corporation on October 17, 1944. Georgia properties at Richmond Hill were sold by the Ford Foundation to Southern Kraft Timberland Corporation on November 28, 1951.

13

NORTHERN MICHIGAN LUMBER

Henry Ford had barely wrested control of the Ford Motor Company from his minor stockholders when he began to acquire his own supplies of raw materials such as coal, limestone, silica sand, iron, and timber. On these ventures it is certain Ford wanted his source of supply primarily for reliability rather than for profit. Most of these ventures were losing operations, but benefited his automobile business by providing an uninterrupted supply at a reasonable cost.

For timber, Ford had in mind the Upper Peninsula of Michigan, which still consisted largely of virgin hardwood forest—about sixty percent birch, maple, and elm. The pine had been ravished years before by the greedy lumber barons. When Ford was building automobiles in 1919, hardwood was used extensively for body framework, floorboards, and wheels—250 board feet in each Model T. Much wood was also used for shipping containers, railroad ties, boxcars, storage bins, wood paving blocks, and so forth.

At Iron Mountain, Michigan, the authorized Ford dealer was E. G. Kingsford, husband of Mary Flaherty, a first cousin of Henry Ford. Kingsford was invited by Ford to join the Ford, Edison, Burroughs, and Firestone group (the Vagabonds) on their annual vacation trip, this time to New York (Green Island)

and New England. On this trip Ford discussed Upper Peninsula timber possibilities with Kingsford.[1]

By that same fall of 1919 Kingsford had located forest tracts amounting to 313,447 acres costing about $3 million. Kingsford together with Ford's secretary, Ernest Liebold, handled the buying. Not until the summer of 1920 did Ford see any of what he had bought. He took Edsel, Liebold, Mayo, and Clarence W. Avery to Iron Mountain where Avery was to take charge of northern Michigan operations with Kingsford as vice president, lawyer, and real estate adviser. On a 2,000-acre area at the edge of Iron Mountain, a tremendous sawmill and wood-chemical plant were to be built. Timberlands as far as a hundred miles away were to feed logs to the Iron Mountain complex. Smaller, remote milling sites were to be later established at L'Anse, Pequaming, Alberta, Big Bay, and Munising.

By 1923 Ford had bought more land to total nearly 400,000 acres mainly in the four counties of Baraga, Marquette, Iron, and Dickinson. In Baraga County particularly, Ford's property taxes paid nearly all county expenses. Besides the timber acreage, about another 200,000 acres of mineral rights, flowage rights, and miscellaneous properties were finally acquired, making a total of about 550,000 acres. Kingsford estimated these properties to have a total

This load of logs is on its way from the Upper Peninsula of Michigan to the 1893 Chicago World's Fair. Northern Michigan forests have supplied vast quantities of timber for decades.

value of $12,769,610.[2] These Upper Peninsula properties, which included iron mines as well as the timberlands, were incorporated as a subsidiary of Ford Motor Company under the name of Michigan Iron, Land & Lumber Company.

Lumbering started in 1920 at Sidnaw, sixty-five miles northwest of Iron Mountain.[3] There in the deep forests Ford built a camp the likes of which no sober lumberjack had ever dreamed. With electric lights, steam heat, showers, and clean private bunks, a lumberjack never had it so good. Deducted from their five-dollars-a-day pay was the cost of sending clothing to the laundry, thus assuring that workers wore clean clothes. Wholesome, well-cooked food served in a large, clean dining hall, a recreation room, and movies—this did not conform one bit to the typical dirty, louse-infested lumber camp. The lumberjacks of Sidnaw were known locally as the "lumberladies." Sidnaw was of such pride to Ford that in 1924 he took the Edisons, the Firestones, and the Edsel Fords on a pleasure visit there.

The harvesting of mature trees on Ford property was carried out with forest conservation in mind. In the beginning, at Sidnaw, trunks of trees were cut at only six inches from the ground rather than the usual twenty to twenty-five inches. Limbs and underbrush were removed and used for making charcoal. This manner of harvesting not only conserved materials but also provided better growth conditions for new trees and limited forest fires. Logs were shipped from Sidnaw on the Chicago, Milwaukee and St. Paul Railroad directly to Iron Mountain for sawing, planing, drying, and fabrication into useful automotive parts. The sawmill and chemical-processing plant were just outside Iron Mountain, between the city and the Ford hydroelectric plant being built on the Menominee River. The area encompassing the new plants was incorporated as the Village of Kingsford in 1923. This Ford complex is still the largest industrial enterprise ever undertaken in the Upper Peninsula of Michigan.[4]

The sawmill, powered by the eleven thousand-horsepower hydroelectric plant, could produce 215,000 board feet of lumber per day. A battery of fifty-two huge dry kilns, large enough to hold 6.5 million board feet of lumber, could release 400,000 board feet of dehydrated wood in twenty-four hours. Finished wood parts were shipped from Iron Mountain as knockdown frames to body builders such as Mengle Products in Louisville, Kentucky, or to Murray Body Company in Detroit, who together could supply Ford with as many as nine thousand assembled bodies per day for Model T, Model A, and V-8s until 1937 when all-steel bodies prevailed. Iron Mountain then produced Ford station wagon bodies (woodies) complete and ready for final drop on the assembly line. By 1951 wood had almost vanished from the automotive scene, giving way to simulated wood trim.[5]

Wood wastes from the Iron Mountain sawing operations were used not only to produce steam; hardwood chips were charred, ground, mixed with starch, and compressed to form nearly a hundred tons per day of the well-known Ford charcoal bri-

Locations of Ford's lumbering operations in the Upper Peninsula of Michigan. (Courtesy of James Porter.)

Steam heated housing for lumberjacks at Sidnaw, Michigan, Ford's most remote lumbering camp, 1926. (Photo from the John W. Bennett collection.)

quettes sold by Ford dealers all over the United States. These pillow-shaped briquettes are still manufactured by Kingsford Products Company of Oakland, California, and sold by the name of Kingsford.

The adjacent five-story chemical plant, completed in 1924, used softwoods and hardwood chips,

and by destructive distillation in huge retorts produced large quantities of such chemicals as methanol, ethyl acetate, methyl acetate, methyl acetone, allyl alcohol, and a residue of wood tar. Methyl alcohol was marketed as antifreeze, the ketones were used in paints, and ethyl acetate for artificial leather. Less-than-perfect hardwood logs were designated "chemical logs" and sent directly through chipping machines to be fed into the chemical retorts.

The dry kilns and chemical plant operated twenty-four hours a day, and the lumber mill normally two shifts. By 1925 employment in Kingsford had peaked at seventy-six hundred workers. Hundreds of houses on Ford land were leased to employees at reasonable rates, and at least 150 additional modern homes were constructed. The relatively high wages, reaching six dollars per day, went a long way at the Ford commissary, which sold food and clothing at little above cost.

L'ANSE

Eighty miles directly north of Iron Mountain, on Keweenaw Bay of Lake Superior, another lumber mill was acquired by Ford at L'Anse in Baraga County in 1922.[6] This plant at L'Anse was complete with sawmill, dry kilns, planing mill, and powerhouse. Adjoining the L'Anse plant were thirty thousand acres of prime hardwood forest. Total employment at the mill and in the woods was about one thousand. At the L'Anse plant as many as 180,000 board feet of finished lumber could be produced daily to be shipped to Iron Mountain and made into auto parts. The yards at L'Anse, as large as any known, held 36 million board feet—23 million of cut lumber and the remainder decked logs. Railroad and derrick facilities together with dockage for lake freighters provided efficient transportation. Steam tugs were on hand to assist lake ships. Although located on the shore of Lake Superior, L'Anse is only ten miles from Mount Curwood, which at 1,980 feet is the highest point in Michigan. A large, modern high school was financed by Ford at L'Anse; children were brought by bus from nearby Pequaming and Alberta, mill towns owned by Ford.

A 1942 aerial view of the Iron Mountain (Kingsford) plant, looking southeast. (Photo from the John W. Bennett collection.)

Steam cranes handle logs like matchsticks at Iron Mountain. (Photo from the
John W. Bennett collection.)

PEQUAMING

A few miles north of L'Anse was the beautiful little town of Pequaming[7] overlooking Keweenaw Bay and backed by forty thousand acres of hardwood extending across the five-mile Abbaye Peninsula to Huron Bay. Pequaming was already a picturesque lumbering town when Henry Ford bought it lock, stock, and barrel for $2,850,000 in 1923. The town had been built in 1870–80 by the wealthy Charles Hebard, who had overseen it for almost fifty years. Ford bought the town complete with three churches, schools, a town hall, a hotel, eighty-five houses, a powerhouse, sawmill, docks, tugs, and barges. The sawmill could cut sixty thousand board feet per day. Ford, with three hundred workers, was virtually the only employer and taxpayer in the village.

ALBERTA

Nine miles south of L'Anse, on U.S.-41, Ford built a model sawmill and village in 1935.[8] The mill and houses were in full view of passing motorists, demonstrating how a lumber mill operation should be managed. The project was named Alberta after the daughter of F. G. Johnson who was then in charge of the Ford Upper Peninsula operations. Signs along the road for miles made it clear that the village and surrounding forests were the property of Ford Motor Company. Visitors were welcome to picnic on the neatly mowed grounds beside the millpond and visit the immaculately clean mill in operation. The residence area, with twelve homes and two school buildings, was in plain view of tourists, and neat as a pin.

The Alberta site was of little consequence in the total production of lumber, but it did provide another example of Henry Ford's idealistic rendition of rural life. The little mill could cut sixteen thousand board feet of lumber daily with twenty-two workers, twelve of them family men living in company houses. Mill workers living at Alberta were each allowed two acres of farmland for summer planting, but this effort failed because of deer from the forest feeding on the crops.

The Alberta mill operated until 1954, after which it was donated with seventeen hundred acres of land to the School of Forestry and Wood Products of Michigan Technological University at Houghton, Michigan, and is now known as the Ford Forestry Center. Alberta was intended to be a model of self-sufficiency, which it was not. But as a public-relations ploy, both during Ford ownership and to this day and beyond, Alberta can be classed as an outstanding success.

HURON MOUNTAIN CLUB

Henry Ford seemed enamored with the northern Michigan woods. For added privacy, even in the Upper Peninsula, in 1930 he built a "cabin" at the exclusive and well-guarded Huron Mountain Club near Big Bay on Lake Superior, about thirty miles northwest of Marquette. In these woods he constructed a two-story log home using logs from his Pequaming

Vertical band saw cuts off a board as log moves forward on carriage. This is one of the two high-speed saws operated at Iron Mountain in 1946. (Photo from the John W. Bennett collection.)

View of one battery of dry kilns showing method of piling lumber to go into kilns. (Photo from the John W. Bennett collection.)

View of wood distillation building in 1927. (Photo from the John W. Bennett collection.)

View of lumber operations at L'Anse, looking toward Keweenaw Bay. (Photo from the John W. Bennett collection.)

Pequaming lumber mill looking east from Keweenaw Bay in 1946. (Photo from the John W. Bennett collection.)

The "bungalow" at Pequaming. Although occupied by the Fords for a few days in the summer, this building was used for childrens' household arts training during the school year. (Photo from the John W. Bennett collection.)

The Alberta mill, a model of neatness. (Photo from the John W. Bennett collection.)

Alberta homes backed up against an almost endless forest. (Photo from the John W. Bennett collection.)

forests. This was a true summer retreat for the Fords. Cruising north on one of their large ore carriers plying between Dearborn and Duluth, the Fords would disembark at Marquette and drive to their refuge in the deep forest of the Huron Mountains. The many photographs showing deer from the surrounding woods at the door of the cabin being fed by household servants proves the Huron Mountain summer home of the Fords was indeed secluded.

BIG BAY

A few miles from the Huron Mountain Club, on the shore of Lake Superior, is the small town of Big Bay.[9] Henry was eighty years old (1943) when he bought the large sawmill, power plant, and almost everything else in Big Bay as a personal project. He is said to have bought Big Bay as a sort of summer plaything on which he spent several million dollars. The town's fifty-two houses were bought for his employees at the mill, and an inn costing five hundred thousand dollars to renovate was used as a summer

Living room of the "cabin" belonging to the Fords at the Huron Mountain Club, about 1945. (0-8543)

Lumber mill at Big Bay with Lake Independence at right. (Photo from the John W. Bennett collection.)

The Ford Hotel on the hill overlooking the town of Big Bay. Henry and Clara occasionally occupied their private suite, but the building more often served vacationing friends of Ford Motor Company officials. (Photo from the John W. Bennett collection.)

hotel for Ford executives and friends. A trip to Big Bay became a vacation bonus for those in the good graces of the powerful at Ford Motor Company. Big Bay became another of Ford's model towns—pretty but unprofitable.

Although the town was abandoned by the Ford family in 1951, after the deaths of Henry and Clara, a hundred or so people still live in Big Bay; it is a delightful summer spot. Henry's picturesque hotel on the hill overlooking the shoreline was used in 1959 as a setting for the movie *Anatomy of a Murder*. The author of the book on which the movie was based was Robert Traver, who lived in nearby Ishpeming.

MUNISING

In 1944 Henry Ford spotted a steam engine for sale in an abandoned sawmill at Munising, Michigan. He not only liked the engine but was also impressed by the site of the mill directly on Lake Superior. He bought the mill and the entire mill property including the steam engine. Work on renovation began at once and was carried on during the following year, but the mill never became operational. Ford's health was deteriorating to the point where he was losing interest. The use of wood in automobiles was diminishing, and the supply of forest logs in the Munising vicinity would no longer have been adequate for a mill that size. The mill was abandoned and within a few years sold along with other Ford holdings in the Upper Peninsula.[10]

During the more than thirty years Henry Ford operated lumber mills in the Upper Peninsula of Michigan, there were major changes brought about by economic reasons. Some of the conservation practices begun by Ford, such as cutting tree trunks close to the ground and clearing remaining brush, were found to be too expensive. By 1923 the Ford Motor Company had found that lumber cutting and hauling could be contracted out at much lower cost. Gradually, contractors handled almost all the Ford forest work. In 1935 Ford disposed of large holdings of mostly softwoods to the federal government for the Ottawa National Forest. The cost of shipment of for-

Station wagon bodies on Iron Mountain assembly line, about 1946. (Photo from the John W. Bennett collection.)

est products the five hundred miles or more to Dearborn became a greater economic burden. And with unionization of Ford labor after 1941, profits from Upper Peninsula operations became marginal at best. The amount of wood needed for the manufacture of postwar automobiles was minimal. For many years before closing, the Iron Mountain plant was selling most of its lumber products commercially through the Dearborn by-products office.

Ford at one time was employing as many as ten thousand workers in his lumber operations. One of his goals was to keep as many employed at five dollars a day, or more, as practicable. Older people in the Upper Peninsula in particular eagerly express their appreciation for Ford's distinct contribution to the development of that extensive area.

NOTES

1. Nevins and Hill, *Expansion and Challenge,* pp. 217–19.
2. M. E. Willmott, "History of Michigan Iron, Land and Lumber Company," unbound manuscript, Acc. 654, Archives, HFM&GV.
3. "Iron Mountain Is Busy Scene," *Ford News* 1 (November 1, 1920): 1.
4. Walter G. Nelson, *Reminiscences,* Acc. 65, pp. 3–79, Archives, HFM&GV.

5. Conversations with John W. Bennett, former supervisor in the Iron Mountain plant.
6. David L. Lewis, "The Rise and Fall of Old Henry's Northern Empire," part 1, *Cars and Parts* 16 (December 1973): 90–97.; part 2, *Cars and Parts* 17 (January 1974): 100–105.
7. Albert Olsen, *Reminiscences,* Acc. 65, pp. 1–16, Archives, HFM&GV.
8. John Tobin, "A Northwoods Novelty: Henry Ford's Village of Alberta, Michigan." Vertical File, Archives, HFM&GV.
9. Lewis, *Public Image,* p. 487.
10. "Ford to Drop Farming: Starts Program to Dispose of Its Sideline Activities," *New York Times,* March 28, 1946.

14

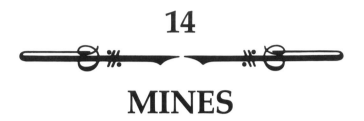

MINES

When the Michigan Iron, Land and Lumber Company was organized in 1920, a considerable portion of its holdings was classified as "undeveloped mineral lands." These were primarily iron-bearing lands located in Marquette, Iron, and Baraga counties. Workable mines included the Imperial, estimated to contain 3.5 million tons of ore; the Oliver, estimated at 2.5 million tons; and the Richards, estimated at 4 million tons. The Imperial was near Michigamme, Michigan, the Oliver at Iron Mountain, and the Richards at Crystal River. Eleven other iron mines on the Ford property had at one time been producers but were not reactivated by Ford. Value of the ores from the three mines varied from twenty cents a ton (Oliver), to forty cents a ton (Richards), to fifty cents a ton (Imperial). Together, the estimated value of the total ore available was $3,750,000.[1]

Of the three mines, the Imperial on the Marquette Range became Ford's largest producer of ore. It too had been abandoned for several years by Cleveland Cliffs, and Ford was required to undertake an extensive rebuilding program to get it into operation. Temporary shelter was provided for workers before permanent homes were built. The powerhouse, shafthouse, skiphoist, drying lockers, and shower rooms for miners all needed refurbishing. Other buildings required were a dormitory for single men, a blacksmith shop, a first-aid station, and a general store. For families of about two hundred employees, a well-equipped school building was provided, serving also as a community center.

Iron miners did not work as deep as Michigan copper miners, nor in as dusty conditions as West Virginia coal miners. But iron miners found underground conditions often wet and sticky. The Imperial had horizontal levels as low as six hundred feet below the surface, reached by a forty-degree inclined main shaft. An extensive pumping system cleared low points of seepage, and steam heating aided in drying and warming passages. Electricity from the powerhouse provided lighting to main passages in the mine and power for the rail trams moving the ore.

The mine operated all year on two shifts, produced as much as nine hundred tons per day.[2] Ore was carried by means of the Duluth, South Shore & Atlantic Railroad the forty miles to Marquette on Lake Superior where it was dropped into the holds of Ford ore carriers to be taken to the Rouge plant in Dearborn. Ore was first taken from the Imperial by Ford in October 1921.[3] This ore was stored at the mine site during winter when ships were not sailing the lakes. The Rouge received a steady supply of Imperial ore during the shipping season of 1922. Although good quality for Michigan ore, blast furnace operators at the Rouge were not completely happy

Shaft house at Imperial mine in 1924. During winter months ore was piled at surface to be taken to ship docks in spring. Building at left contained drying and shower rooms where miners changed from wet working clothe to dry ones. (833-37017)

One miner shovels iron ore into tramcar while the other drills holes with compressed-air drill for insertion of powder to loosen ore. Powder was ignited as workers left for lunch or at end of shift so that fumes could dissipate while they were away. (833-37027)

with this high-sulfur, forty-five to fifty percent limonite ore, and mixed it with a better grade from other sources.

During the depth of the Depression (1933) the Imperial became inactive.[4] World War II, however, generated renewed interest in raw materials, and beneficiation was applied to these limonite ores to raise the iron content before shipment. Beneficiation together with "pelletizing" kept the Imperial area near Michigamme commercially viable until the end of the war. But the Imperial had not been profitable to Ford. His higher wages, superior housing, schools, and other community benefits produced costs greater than the income from ore.

Records of Oliver and Richards mines, leased by Ford to other operators, are much less complete in the Ford Archives files. The Oliver was in Iron Mountain and was leased to the Oliver Mining Company, who operated it. The Oliver was directly under the city, and its blasting during the night is said to have often aroused the townspeople and occasionally led to damage claims. Enough water was pumped from the lower levels of the Oliver to form the sizeable Crystal Lake on the edge of town. Other mines, the Millie and Walpole, also at Iron Mountain, were owned by Ford but not operated until later. Several mines in this vicinity had been worked to a point where ore was too deep or was too lean.

The Richards mine, about twenty miles northwest of Iron Mountain at Crystal River, was owned by Ford but under lease to McKinney Steel Company, who operated it. This mine was the only one in operation on Ford land when it was bought in 1920. It produced hematite of standard grade with slightly high phosphorus content.[5]

The Millie mine, at the edge of Iron Mountain, was leased to the North Range Mining Company about 1930 when Ford became aware that automobiles would require more steel and less wood. He saw reasons for a blast furnace near Iron Mountain and had already bought dock facilities at Gladstone on Lake Michigan to ship castings to the Rouge. The Depression, however, discouraged plans to make Iron Mountain a foundry town.

In 1926 the leasing of twenty-two hundred acres near Ishpeming provided Ford Motor Company a source of rich, forty-nine to fifty percent hematite ore. This location, seven miles northeast of Ishpeming, was named Blueberry because of the large patch of the berries found when Henry Ford first visited the site.[6] The company had taken an option on the site in July 1925, followed by a year of test drilling revealing about a mile or more of the rich iron formation. The Blueberry mine was developed from scratch by Ford. The necessary service buildings were of steel and brick construction rather than the usual wood construction. Next, a vertical shaft was dug to about eleven hundred feet—all construction

Electric trolley engine pulls ore-filled cars toward outlet of Imperial mine. (833-37025)

was exceptionally durable and safe for workers. Not until 1929 was the Blueberry ready for operation. But when it did operate it was a beauty—a model of cleanliness, efficiency, and safety.[7] It was close to the ore docks at Marquette, served by the Lake Superior and Ishpeming ore-carrying railroad. This railroad, incidentally, was remarkably low on mileage but high on tonnage; its uniformly rust-red gondola cars opened from the bottom to dump their loads from high on the ore docks directly into the holds of giant ore carriers.

But the Blueberry also succumbed to the Depression in 1933. Ford then subleased it to the North Range Mining Company, which paid lower wages, and by skimping on maintenance (which

Henry Ford would never do) kept it running. Other and larger mines, operated at Cleveland Cliffs Iron Company at Ishpeming and neighboring Negaunee, continued to operate to some extent, but visitors to that area were most often told of the unusual elegance of the Blueberry as operated by Ford.

Ford bought ore from the Blueberry operators for many years because it was of high grade, of good structure, and with low silica. But most ore bought by Ford was from the Steel Corporation and from the Oliver Mining Company (large Mesabi mine operators) at reasonable prices. In 1937 Ford was contemplating a third blast furnace at the Rouge plant and took leases on Mesabi Range ore properties containing about 12 million tons.[8] These properties do not seem to have been developed by Ford. Although most ore now used by the Ford Motor Company comes from Duluth and the Mesabi Range, it is doubtful whether Ford-owned deposits are involved. Again, it seems that Henry Ford was dabbling in iron-ore mining to force suppliers into line.

DOLOMITE

Properties on the eastern tip of Michigan's Upper Peninsula in Mackinac and Chippewa counties between Cedarville and DeTour were acquired by Ford in 1931 as a source of dolomite, which is used for the production of magnesium metal. A total of twelve thousand acres was bought for about seventy-five thousand dollars. About three thousand acres were near DeTour, and the remaining nine thousand acres near Cedarville. Some of these properties were bought from individuals, and some were obtained by trades of Ford forestlands for state-owned dolomite lands.[9] Shipments of dolomite were made from Port Dolomite, a commercial harbor on upper Lake Huron.

Magnesium is expensive to produce but is useful in aircraft because of its high strength with little weight. Ford, who exploited vanadium steels because of their high strength with less weight in his

Model T, would be expected also to have an interest in magnesium. Of the two commercial processes for making magnesium metal, the one most prevalent is the electrolysis of brine, but the second—the reduction of dolomite by ferrosilicon—was used extensively during World War II by the aircraft industry. The magnesium smelter that operated at the Rouge plant from 1942 to 1945 made use of dolomite. Near the end of World War II (August 1945) the Cedarville acreage was sold to Michigan Limestone and Chemical Company for $180,000. The smaller acreage near DeTour was retained by the Ford Motor Company as ample reserves.

LIMESTONE

Also to feed blast furnaces at the Rouge, Ford bought limestone deposits near Alpena and Rogers City in Michigan's Lower Peninsula. Limestone is an impure calcium carbonate used as a flux to help in the reduction of iron ore to iron metal. These deposits were bought in 1924 and were near Port Calcite on Lake Huron where Ford ships could load and quickly transfer the material to the Rouge plant. The limestone, a fossiliferous rock, was easily quarried from the extensive surface deposits in that part of the state. Ford Motor Company still gets its limestone from that area.

Blueberry mine shaft house and maintenance building. Power plant to the right of these buildings is out of the picture. This vertical-shaft iron mine was a model of safety and neatness. (Photo from the John W. Bennett collection.)

LEAD

Ford Motor Company prospected for lead deposits on land near Bonne Terra, Missouri, in 1922 and 1923. Four or five drill teams worked for more than a year to find commercial quantities of galena. This venture failed to find good ore. Then in 1924 the company leased and operated the Red Bird mine in a lead-ore zone in Custer County, Idaho, until 1927.[10] Although the ore in Idaho was of good quality, the wages insisted on by Henry Ford prevented the operation from being truly competitive. But Ford costs were not made public, and suppliers were therefore wary of overcharging Ford for battery lead. Ford was planning to build ten thousand batteries per day, each requiring thirty pounds of pure lead. His Highland Park plant was already assembling thirty-five hundred batteries a day. Red Bird was sold by Ford to a small operator.

GOLD

During the summer of 1936 there was a flurry of excitement over reports that gold was being found in Michigan's Upper Peninsula. On May 29 the Fordson Land Company was officially established in Dearborn for "taking title to certain lands in Northern Michigan which lands were to be developed for gold and other minerals." The company was capitalized at ten thousand dollars and in its charter given authority to

search for ores, minerals, petroleum and other products of the land, and to grant licenses to bore, drill, prospect and mine land for gold, silver, copper, lead, zinc, iron, antimony, tin, asbestos, and all kinds of ores, metals, minerals and precious stones, oils, gas and gold; to hypothecate and deal in minerals and mineral land. . . .

Negotiations were started involving a Mr. Knox and the exploration firm of Hollinger Consolidated Gold Mines, who were to do prospecting and mining with Ford receiving royalties under a complex and questionable agreement. The arrangements were never made final before the gold fever in Michigan had died. In March 1942 the Fordson Land Company was declared dissolved.[11]

Ford may have given up too easily, because west of Ishpeming, not far from Ford's iron mine properties, is the only operating gold mine east of the Mississippi. It is the Ropes mine, discovered in 1882, abandoned in 1897, and reopened in 1986 by the Callahan Mining Company. Once again, pulling ore from fifteen hundred feet below the surface has become profitable.[12]

KENTUCKY AND WEST VIRGINIA COAL MINES

At his Highland Park plant, Henry Ford fully realized he was entirely dependent on outside suppliers for his coal, and was vulnerable to work stop-

Directly below the Ford Twin Cities glass plant these men drilled holes to loosen pure silica sand to be melted into automotive glass in September 1942. (833-77057)

pages by either the miners or the railroads. In November 1917 he must have been thinking of ways of avoiding possible shutdowns because he was gathering samples of coal from twenty or more regions of the United Kingdom. These samples his Highland Park laboratories were analyzing.[13] He likely visualized the advantage of having an alternate source outside the United States.

To be independent of labor strife and government interference with transportation, Ford really needed his own coal mines, his own railroad, and his own railroad cars.[14] By 1920 he owned these essentials, not enough to supply all his needs but enough to relieve emergency situations. In a letter to James J. Davis, secretary of labor, Ford later stated: "We bought the mines not because we wanted to go into coal mining but because we had to be assured of an uninterrupted supply of coal at a fair price. That assurance we could not have without ownership. A large business cannot permit itself to be at the mercy of an industry with frequent strikes, car shortages, and general instability."

The Banner Fork properties in Kentucky and the Nuttalburg mine in West Virginia were the first coal properties to be bought. Banner Fork, at Kentenia contained some 12 million tons of high volatile by-product coking coal, producing 3,000 tons per day with four hundred employees. Typical production of Banner Fork coal sent to Ford Motor Company during 1922 was largely classed as "run of mine" and "nut and slack" with much less "egg," "lump," and "block." Average unit cost that year was about $2.50 per ton. In the meantime, Banner Fork was becoming one of the finest mining communities in the country.[15]

The Nuttalburg mine had a reserve of 6 million tons with a daily production of 1,000 tons employing 250 men. Nuttalburg produced "low volatile" (anthracite) coal, shipping typically about 20,000 tons per month to the Rouge plant.

An event took place in September 1922 that spurred Ford into making much larger coal investments. Mining and railroad disturbances had caused the Interstate Commerce Commission to order shipments of coal restricted to "essential" uses such as public utilities, food processing, and home heating.[16] The Highland Park plant and other Ford facilities were shut down for lack of coal. Ford objected vigorously, and after one week coal cars were again allowed to deliver coal to automotive plants.

To safeguard the Ford coal supply, the Fordson Coal Company was incorporated early in 1923 with a capital of $15 million.[17] This organization was to include the Banner Fork and Nuttalburg mines and also the Dexcar, West Virginia, mines purchased in November 1922 and later named Twin Branch. Almost immediately (April 1923) the Pond Creek mines near Williamson, Kentucky, were added to Fordson Coal Company. The largest acquisition of all in the spring of 1923, however, was the Peabody tract of 120,000

Working in the Pond Creek coal mine no. 3 at Stone, Kentucky, in October 1923. For safety reasons, men worked in pairs. (833-35789)

acres estimated to have 20 million tons of coal and 500 million feet of lumber at a cost to Ford of $2,783,000.[18] These Peabody purchases were in the Kentucky counties of Leslie, Clay, Perry, Bell, Harlan, and Letcher. Fordson Coal Company at this time also bought a thousand more coal cars, each of 55-ton capacity.

The central office of Fordson Coal Company was in Stone, Kentucky. Major coal operating centers were designated Kentenia, Stone, Nuttalburg, and Twin Branch. This combination of mines brought available coal supply to 600 million tons. There were sixteen separate mine sites involved. Ford was soon capable of more than supplying his own needs. For March 1927 total shipments to Ford Motor Company were 149,513 tons. Almost one-quarter of his coal became available for commercial sale, and Ford employees in the Greater Detroit area were delivered coal and coke in Ford trucks at cost.

Ford's D. T. & I. Railroad hauled this Ford coal to Detroit from its terminus at Ironton on the Ohio River. To service the coal mines more completely, there were plans to extend the D. T. & I. to Deepwater, West Virginia, (near Nuttalburg). At Deepwater it would connect with the Virginian Railway, which Henry Ford wanted to buy to ship coal to the Atlantic Coast for transhipment abroad.

By 1927 employees working in these mines totaled nearly 3,000. Kentenia employed 473, Stone, 1,713; Nuttalburg, 228; Twin Branch, 507. Wages paid by Ford were said to be about 25 percent higher than average, and Ford opened eleven low-priced commissaries (four in Stone, two in Kentenia, and one each in Hardy, Pond Creek, MacVeigh, Nuttalburg, and Twin Branch locations). Hard-surfaced roads were built to the Ford mines primarily for the benefit of employees. Schools were built and teachers paid at housing locations; recreational facilities were provided for children and adults. Medical help was also needed because a high incidence of trachoma, a serious eye disease, revealed eight percent of the school population infected. Hookworm and typhoid were also prevalent. The people of the region were said to be proud and independent. One is quoted as saying, "We ain't asked nothing from no one."[19] But most people accepted Ford housing, patronized the commissaries, and used the medical and recreation centers. "YMCA expenses" were conspicuous items on Ford budgets.

Although mining employed workers steadily in

A "trip" of coal leaving Banner Fork (Kentonia) mine no. 1 about 1925. (0-10052)

the winter months when heating coal was in demand, the mines were often closed completely during summer. Ford tried to provide employment year-round. His manufacturing plants operated all year, there was no long slack season. And by providing bins at the Rouge plant large enough to hold some four hundred thousand tons of coal, there was space for added coal all year. Daily production from all sixteen Ford coal mines averaged about thirteen thousand tons per day. The average miner in 1920 loaded about fifteen tons per day. With better equipment this output increased considerably. For example, the availability of tramcars at the "workings" was a limiting factor with live mules hauling the trams. The use of "electric mules" increased the supply.[20] Undercutting the "work face" by machine allowed coal to be loosened much faster.

One cannot say coal mining was at all easy or safe. Reports of lost-time accidents in 1924 showed the coal mines to be the worst of fifty-nine Ford plants. Kentenia with 445 employees had had 83 accidents that year, Stone's 1,104 employees had 205 accidents, and the Twin Branch 412 employees had 67 accidents. These coal mines were averaging twenty-five eight-hour days of lost work because of accidents for every one thousand hours worked.[21] That was one-fifth of the working time. Nattalburg was not listed. The Michigamme Iron Mine reported fewer than two days lost per one thousand hours worked, and the Rouge plant slightly more than one day lost per one thousand hours. One could say coal mining was an extremely hazardous occupation.

Besides building roads and improving schools, the Fordson Coal Company was concerned with the general appearance and prosperity of the area.[22] Many old, unsightly, and unsanitary buildings were torn down and replaced where necessary. Land that was poor and grown to brush was cleared and the hillsides planted to orchards. Old Ben Davis apple trees were replaced with better varieties. Peach trees were added between young apple trees. Grapes and berry bushes were planted toward the bottom of hillsides. On the bottom lands garden farming was em-phasized with tracts of onions, lettuce, radishes, potatoes, and other vegetables. These were demonstration areas worked by Ford employees; produce was sold at Ford commissaries in the mining towns. Local farmers were encouraged to follow suit. These were costly ventures by Fordson Coal Company, but as Henry Ford had said, he did not go into coal mining to make a profit from coal. By 1935, after Ford had sold the coal mines, these Fordson Farms had again been neglected and were returning largely to brush dotted with yellow poplar trees.

Beginning as early as 1932 the Fordson Coal Company began leasing and selling its coal properties. Accounting records, however, continued at least

Camp Maher at Twin Branch no. 4 mine in October 1923. (833-35773)

Hardy Mine Camp in 1923. Housing appears structurally sound but aesthetically monotonous. (833-35799)

A long conveyor brought coal down the mountainside from Nuttalburg mine to the "tipple"—a coal-screening and car-loading plant. This photo was taken in December 1925. (833-44727)

until 1942. There are reminiscences indicating that Ford was having trouble with unions, which he had been trying to avoid at that time. Coal mining also being more and more closely regulated by federal agencies was not to Ford's liking. At the end of World War II the Ford Motor Company was disposing of any and all property not paying its way, and the Fordson Coal Company operations, with their multitude of fringe benefits, had not really been profitable financially.

OIL AND GAS

While the Ford Motor Company was organizing to find solid gold in Michigan's Upper Peninsula, black gold was found on company property in California.[23] This was at the Ford assembly plant at Long Beach on San Pedro Bay. Oil was under the plant. Early in 1937 the Union Pacific Railroad had begun drilling on its property next door. In a frenzy, Ford Motor Company leased forty acres surrounding its plant to General Petroleum Corporation (February 15, 1937) for immediate drilling—Ford to obtain royalties. Fifty drillers began work. They were tapping the same oil pool as Union Pacific at about thirty-five hundred feet.

Henry Ford's first oil well came in April 10, 1937, flowing at the rate of about two thousand barrels a day.[24] Four other Ford wells were being drilled at that same time. In all, twenty-three wells were eventually sunk on Ford property—No. 23 reported as producing three thousand barrels a day. There were some gas producers, and Ford used this gas for boiler fuel and industrial purposes. There are records of Ford oil wells operating at least until 1941, if not later.

These wells in California were not the first deep wells Ford had drilled. In 1912 a test well 2,500 feet deep at Highland Park had produced nothing of value. The same results had been obtained from two test wells of about 4,000 feet at Dearborn in 1915–16.[25] In 1924, however, Ford found gas at 1,925 feet in Jackson, Ohio, on his D. T. & I. Railroad property. Later he is said to have found gas on his Canton, Ohio, manufacturing site.

Well no. 1 at Long Beach, California, on March 2, 1937. Drilling had advanced to 1,335 feet, and the rig was encased in steel sheeting to protect the Ford assembly plant from any sudden gush of oil that might deface the building.

NOTES

1. M. E. Willmott, *History of Michigan Iron, Land and Lumber Company*, Acc. 654, Archives, HFM&GV.

2. "Ford Iron Mine at Michigamme Shows Progress," *Ford News* 2 (February 1, 1922): 1.

3. "Company Takes First Iron Ore from U.P. Mine," *Ford News* 1 (November 1, 1921): 4.

4. Lewis, *Public Image*, pp. 160, 163–64.

5. R. S. Archbald, *Reminiscences*, Acc. 65–21, p. 2, Archives, HFM&GV.

6. David L. Lewis, "Henry Ford in the U.P.," *Motor News* 57 (July 1975): 16.

7. "New Blueberry Mine Will Supply Ford Motor Company Iron Ore," *Ford News* 7 (December 15, 1927): 6.

8. Archbald, *Reminiscences*, Acc. 65, p. 7, Archives, HFM&GV.

9. Raymond Turner, *Reminiscences*, Acc. 65–49, pp. 7, 9, Archives, HFM&GV.

10. Archbald, *Reminiscences*, Acc. 65, pp. 11–12.

11. Acc. 323, Box 1, Fordson Land Company, Archives, HFM&GV.

12. "Gold Mine Digs Up U.P. Riches, Memories," *Detroit Free Press*, February 24, 1988.

13. See Acc. 1, Box 122, Raw Materials, Archives, HFM&GV.

14. Lewis, *Public Image*, pp. 164–65.

15. "Coal Mining in Kentucky: A Story of Great Interest," *Ford News* 1 (November 1, 1920): 4.

16. Nevins and Hill, *Expansion and Challenge*, p. 220.

17. See Acc. 444, Fordson Coal Company, Archives, HFM&GV.

18. See Acc. 33, Box 54, Auditing Records—Fordson Coal Company, Archives, HFM&GV.

19. "More Mines Are Bought," *Ford Times* 16 (April 1, 1923): 1, 4.

20. A few mules were in use as late as 1926. Records show three Kentenia mules (Bill, Kate, and John) bought in January 1926 and disposed of in April 1927. Bill was listed as "killed," Kate sold for twenty dollars, and John for ten dollars.

21. "Comparative Report of Lost-Time Accidents in Ford Plants in 1924," *Ford News* 5 (March 1, 1925): 3.

22. "Clean Farming Demonstrated in Kentucky," *Ford News* 4 (September 15, 1924): 1.

23. Acc. 779, Oil Well Operations, 1934–40, Archives, HFM&GV.

24. "Well Puts Ford in Oil Business," *Los Angeles Times*, April 11, 1937.

25. See Acc. 23, Box 2, D. T. & I. Railroad Properties—Deep Test Wells, Archives, HFM&GV.

15

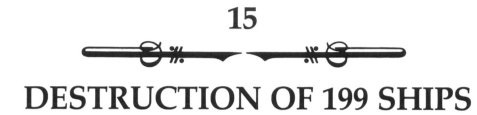

DESTRUCTION OF 199 SHIPS

The city of Fordson, Michigan, was a most brutal host to many an unloved and neglected merchant ship entering its port during 1926–27. The big Rouge plant was gobbling them up as soon as they were reluctantly dragged into its fiery trap. The wide, hungry mouths of the monster open-hearth furnaces voraciously satisfied their insatiable appetite for more and more of these big but innocent and docile creatures.

This sad report illustrates the natural result of overpopulation of a species of ships. During World War I the Emergency Fleet Corporation directed shipbuilding yards on the Great Lakes to build as many merchant ships as possible for the "bridge to France." During 1918 and 1919 shipyards at Ecorse, Wyandotte, Toledo, Ashtabula, Saginaw, Buffalo, Cleveland, Chicago, Manatowac, and Superior built hundreds of cargo vessels of a size permitting them to squeeze through the Canadian canals and locks to the ocean and beyond. These ships, called lakers, saw only two or at the most three years of service before the government-sponsored merchant marine experienced hard times during the depression of 1921, being priced out of the postwar cargo business largely because of lower officer pay rates on foreign ships.[1]

During 1922–25 the United States Shipping Board owned more than a thousand such merchant ships of which about 800 were inactive in a laid-up fleet moored in various rivers and harbors tethered together as large rusting flotillas. In April 1924 the Shipping Board reported it would hold 400 of these ships in reserve and scrap about 400. Most of the ships scheduled for scrap were lakers—coal-fired steamers each averaging about four thousand tons deadweight.[2]

In early 1925 a group of 200 vessels consisting of 150 lakers and 50 larger "subs" (built by the Submarine Boat Corporation of Newark, New Jersey) were offered for sale. The Ford Motor Company, through William B. Mayo and Charles E. Sorenson, immediately studied this offer, and on a second bid involving 199 of the 200 ships, won the right to buy all for $1,697,470. That averaged $8,530 each. The contract, issued by the United States Shipping Board Emergency Fleet Corporation, was signed on August 18, 1925, by Edsel B. Ford, president of Ford Motor Company. Thus the Ford Motor Company, for a time, became possibly the world's largest junk collector.[3]

This contract stipulated that the ships were to be dismantled to a point where they would never again be used in navigation, and that the items removed from the ships could be used solely by the Ford Motor Company. Dismantling was to be com-

An air view of Hog Island on the Delaware River near Philadelphia in 1925. Ford bought twenty-one ships at this location—about the number anchored at lower right. Hog Island was near the Ford Chester, Pennsylvania, plant. (0-7597)

pleted by February 4, 1927. Any one of the lakers, however, could be restored for use in navigation upon payment of an additional $16,470 to the government, the buyer bearing the expense of restoration—about $22,000. The ships were sold by the government in an as-is and where-is condition at the following locations:

109—Norfolk (James River)
21—Hog Island (Delaware River)
30—Jones Point (Hudson River)
10—Staten Island, New York
18—New Orleans, Louisiana
9—Orange, Texas
2—Mobile, Alabama

Intense planning was under way at the Rouge to determine how best to get the vessels to Fordson and conduct the salvage work. None of the ships could operate under its own power without expensive reconditioning. To assist in the movement, seven

A small portion of the 108 ships lying in the James River near Norfolk, Virginia, and the Ford Norfolk plant in January 1926. "Unit 27" in the foreground consists of fifteen ships, mostly of the submarine type. (0-7598)

seagoing steel tugboats were also bought from the government at $42,500 each, plus about $12,000 each for repairs. These were the *Ballcamp, Barlow, Baymead, Barrallton, Bathalum, Buttercup,* and *Humerick.* And three of the lakers (*Lake Bennow, Lake Ormoc,* and *Lake Gorin*) were reconditioned at New Orleans to be used as towboats.[4]

The sub vessels, of 324-foot length and 46-foot beam, were too large to be brought to Michigan through the St. Lawrence canal system. These ships were dismembered at shipyards near the purchase location and their parts loaded into the smaller lakers to be towed to Fordson. The lakers (251 feet long, 43.5-foot beam) would be towed up the Atlantic Coast, across the Gulf of St. Lawrence, up the St. Lawrence river, through the eight canals and forty-seven locks operated by the Canadian government, across Lakes Ontario and Erie into the Detroit River. The Welland Canal alone was twenty-six miles long with twenty-five locks and rise of 326 feet. Fordson is more than 600 feet above sea level. This was before our present, enlarged St. Lawrence Seaway was constructed.[5]

It was imperative that at least one ship be brought to the Rouge that fall of 1925 so that the techniques of ship movement and dismantling could be developed during the winter and before the opening of navigation in the spring. The first laker to be brought to Fordson was the *Lake Fondulac,* towed empty by the tug *Ballcamp.*

Starting from Kearny, New Jersey, on November 14 and heading into the North Atlantic, the tug carried a crew of twenty-one; the *Lake Fondulac,* as a barge, carried nine. As might be expected at that time of year, they were battered for days by gale-force

The tug *Barlow* tows the empty *Lake Fondulac* into the Detroit River on December 17, 1925, after its adventurous voyage through North Atlantic storms and icy Canadian waters. The *Lake Fondulac* was the first of the 199 ships to reach Fordson. (833-45020)

winds and heavy seas. Entering the St. Lawrence at near zero temperature, ice was forming and canals and locks were freezing solid, requiring Canadian officials to provide special ice-breaking services—much to their resentment. And to further challenge the captain, three crew members of the *Fondulac* became mutinous, drinking, stealing goods, skipping ship at Canadian ports, only to be chased back on board by police. After thirty-three days the *Lake Fondulac* was finally pulled into the Rouge (minus the three culprits) on December 17, 1925.

More conventional trips, starting in April 1926, were made up of units consisting of two lakers (as barges) towed by either a tug or by one of the three

A tug with a strong hawser tows four lakers in a line on calm waters during August 1926. Each laker could supply its own steam for steering and auxiliary equipment, but not for propulsion. (833-47446)

The *Lake Grogan* squeezes into one of the Welland locks. Shortly after leaving the canal and entering Lake Erie, the *Lake Grogan* was caught in a gale and floundered on the shore near Port Colborne, Ontario. It was refloated, however, and towed on to Fordson. (833-48160)

Marked ready for shears and cutting torches, the *Lake Copley* from Norfolk
floats dejectedly at the Rouge dismantling docks in October 1926. (833-50088)

reconditioned lakers. Distances varied from 4,332 miles (Orange, Texas, to Fordson) to 2,329 miles (Jones Point to Fordson). Total ship miles necessary to bring in all the ships were estimated to be 500,000. Although the speed of tugs in good weather was twelve knots when free, speed was reduced to six knots when under load. Trips were scheduled to allow about thirty-five days each; scrap lakers were delivered and carefully taken apart at the rate of three per week. During the winter of 1926–27, lakers loaded and ready to be brought to Fordson were held waiting in flotillas at Jamaica Bay, Long Island, until spring when they could be towed to the Great Lakes. During summer, when more ships were being brought to Fordson than could be dismantled, lakers were anchored nearby on the Detroit River until room was available on the disassembly line.[6]

Most of the lakers arrived at the Rouge filled with a cargo of broken up subs that had been dismantled at either Norfolk (19), Hog Island (12), Jones Point (16), or Staten Island (3). Each of these commercial ship-breaking yards was near a Ford plant, thus allowing close supervision of work and scheduling of shipments. The parts of one dismantled sub provided full cargo for 2.5 lakers. So quite typically, one dainty little tug such as the *Buttercup* hauled two large lakers on each trip, the lakers filled with nearly a complete chopped up, five thousand-ton sub. Because of the requirement that Canadian officers guide the ships through Canadian canals and locks, three separate sets of towing vessels were used. One group, including the three lakers reconditioned at New Orleans, hauled their two tows from Atlantic ports to Montreal. Another group consisting of tugs pulled the lifeless barges across Lake Ontario, and a third group of tugs brought these floating scrap heaps across Lake Erie and into the Rouge—perhaps at that time the nation's largest dump. But at Ford Motor Company there was never a mess. Henry Ford saw to that.[7]

Giant shears used to cut through half-inch thick steel plates. Vertical cuts were quickly made as the crane pulled upward on the shears. Oxyacetylene torches were used to make horizontal cuts. (833-45789)

An eighty-ton ship's engine is lifted from a ship onto a heavy-duty flatcar. These engines had had little wear and were again put to use with little reconditioning necessary. (833-46922)

Once at the Rouge, each derelict ship was first stripped of hardware, wood, and other light objects, then started down a half-mile, ten-position disassembly dock. At the first position the superstructures such as masts, deck cabins, and life boats were removed. The ship was then floated to the next position where the cargo of sub scrap was taken out. At subsequent positions down the line, deck sections were cut and lifted out, boilers and engine were hoisted onto railroad flatcars, and hulls above the waterline cut into sections and removed. The last of the stations was a floating dry dock, finally allowing the keel to be cut into pieces and lifted away.

In less than a week all that was left of a ship, it was said, was a bit of oil and rust on the water. What an ignominious ending! It had required five to six months to build a laker.

During 1926 ten ships underwent scrapping at one time at the Rouge dock. Railroad tracks along the dock allowed the use of several traveling gantry

cranes; a mammoth two hundred-ton locomotive wrecking crane lifted the heaviest objects. Ship boilers weighed forty to fifty tons each, and the ship's reciprocating steam engine, capable of twelve to fourteen hundred horsepower, was a load of eighty tons in itself. To keep the dock area clear as work progressed, railroad tracks ran directly to the open hearth building where steel scrap cut to appropriate size could be put into charging boxes for immediate melting, pouring, rolling, and reshaping into Model T or Fordson tractor parts. Still larger pieces were hauled by rail to the pig-cast building where the piece was slowly dunked into a vast ladle of fresh molten blastfurnace iron; when melted the mixture was poured into pigs headed for the foundry.[8]

Sizeable portions of the ships were considered "clean steel." These included girders, sheet, channel, angle, flat bar, and round stock. This could all be used without remelting. Rail lines took these items to storage yards where they were sorted and from

With superstructures gone, boilers and engine removed, this laker will next have its deck plates salvaged. Photo taken in July 1926. (833-47071)

which they were requisitioned for general plant use. Steel pipe and conduit (eight hundred miles of piping) were taken to shops where it was cleaned, straightened, and used for plant construction and maintenance. Tons and tons of plumbing fittings such as elbows, tees, nipples, flanges, couplings, and unions were reconditioned for use. More than twenty-five thousand small brass valves and ten thousand steam gauges, for example, were eventually put to use. For years the ship stocks supplied much of Rouge stock requirements. All stock requisitions were first delivered to ship stocks before being allowed to be filled elsewhere.

Deck cabins removed from the ships were lined up in a field for future use as tool cribs or stockrooms. Boilers and engines were also stored in the open and reconditioned as needed for use in appropriate locations. Besides several Rouge installations, many boilers and engines were sent to outlying plants such as Pequaming and Iron Mountain. Some were sent immediately to France and Belgium to be used in Ford plant construction. Hundreds of small fittings found their way to Ford installations in Brazil and Japan.

During 1926 fifteen hundred men were employed in the Rouge scrapping operation, and 78 vessels were dismantled. However, because it was obvious that the contract deadline of February 4, 1927, could not be met, a one-year extension of time was obtained from the U.S. Shipping Board, justified primarily by the seasonal closing of the Lachine and Welland canals. During 1927 about one thousand employees continued working at the docks, and 60 more vessels had either been dismantled or converted to barges. The last of the ships to arrive at Fordson was the *Lake Annette* in August 1927. In the entire operation 189 ships were dismantled and 216,532 tons of steel recovered, 144,532 tons at the Rouge and 72,000 tons at East Coast yards where 50 subs and one laker had met their demise.[9]

Of the several lakers not scrapped, three had been restored to original condition for overseas shipping of auto and tractor parts. Seven lakers were gut-

ted of engines and superstructures to pass as barges under bridges on the New York State Barge Canal, and deliver materials from the Rouge to Ford plants principally at Chester, Pennsylvania; Kearny, New Jersey; and Norfolk, Virginia. These same barges were used even more extensively in later years to bring coal, limestone, and lumber to the Rouge from Great Lake's ports. The ocean tugs such as the *Ballcamp, Barrellton,* and *Buttercup,* bought in 1925, pulled these barges until 1942 when the tugs were needed by the United States Navy.

Although the lakers had all been built to negotiate the Canadian locks going out toward the Atlantic, these ships had not been especially designed to

A once proud laker, hardly recognizable stripped almost to its keel, rests on the floating dry dock ready for final disposition. Looming in the background, the huge Hulett unloaders and Mead-Morrison transfer bridges attest to the Rouge being devoted primarily to the feeding and nurture of furnaces. (833-46748)

A ship girder being dipped into a ladle of molten iron, the end of the girder being melted off to provide more steel for auto and tractor manufacture. (833-46906)

travel back to the Great Lakes. The gates of the locks swung open in such a way that they would clear the ship when headed downstream but would catch the fantail of the same ship if headed upstream. Thus in returning upstream, the scrap lakers were indelicately shortened by cutting off part of the ship's fantail at Montreal, thus arriving at Fordson in disgrace with their tails crudely clipped. However, when the newly reconditioned *Lake Ormoc* was brought to Fordson to be fitted for Brazilian service in 1928, it was slowly, carefully, and expensively backed upstream through the many locks to preserve its dignity upon arrival. The other two lakers that had been reconditioned as steamers in New Orleans remained in ocean service.[10]

Lakers were vital to the establishment of Henry Ford's 2.5 million-acre rubber plantation at Fordlandia on the Tapajos River, a tributary of the Amazon River of Brazil. To establish an independent settlement in the dense jungle more than seven hundred

miles up the river system from the ocean, water transportation of supplies of every description was necessary. The *Lake Farge,* then reduced to a barge filled with machinery and building materials—steam shovel, pile driver, stump pullers, portable electric generators, huge ice-making machinery, prefabricated building sections, and a portable sawmill—became the freight carrier. On the deck of the *Lake Farge,* among other things a small river tugboat was transported. The ocean tug *Ballcamp* was chosen to tow the loaded *Lake Farge* to its remote Brazilian destination.

The reconditioned *Lake Ormoc* was fitted out at Fordson as a "base ship" with a new diesel power plant, a machine shop, hospital, chemistry laboratory, immense refrigerators, laundry, library-lounge, and comfortable guest rooms. The *Lake Ormoc* served as plantation headquarters until shore facilities could be established. These boats maintained constant radio contact with Fordson, making many round-trips until eventually they carried crude rubber from Brazil to the Rouge to be fabricated into automobile tires. And the very dock, the site where so many lakers had succumbed to the cutting torch, now became the site of the new tire plant.

Being but a small integrated portion of the huge Ford operations at that time, the ship-scrapping project may or may not have made a profit. Henry Ford did not hire many "bean counters." Opinions are that Ford may possibly have made a little profit, but the consensus is that this immense amount of work was done primarily because Henry Ford abhorred waste, and these ships lying idle year after year were conspicuously wasting away. Putting the ships to use was a challenge to Ford's ingenuity—an ingenuity that recognized no confines.

NOTES

1. Edward J. Dowling, *The "Lakers" of World War I* (Detroit: University of Detroit Press, 1967), 107 pp.
2. Special Report No. 744, "Summary of Activities of Certain Shipping Board Vessels Sold to Ford Motor Company," Statistical Department, Fleet Corporation, Washington, D.C. (copy in Acc. 37, Box 3, HFM&GV).
3. 199 Ships, Acc. 37, Boxes 1–7, Archives, HFM&GV.
4. "Ford Launches Another Industry," *New York Times,* August 9, 1925.

5. *Canals of the Dominion of Canada,* Department of Railways and Canals, Ottawa, Canada (1926).

6. "The Story of 199 Ships," *Ford News,* twenty-nine bimonthly installments (August 1, 1928-October 1, 1929).

7. "A Cycle in Transportation," *Iron Trade Review,* five weekly installments (August 9, 1928–September 20, 1928).

8. Pierce Cummings, "From Keels to Wheels," *Dearborn Independent,* March 26, 1929.

9. "Ford Barge Leaves for Brazil Rubber Project," *Ford News* 8 (August 1, 1928): 159.

10. 199 Ships, Acc. 37, Boxes 1–2, Archives, HFM&GV.

During the peak of scrapping—the summer of 1926—excess scrap was stored and used as later needed. All was used by 1929, it is said. (833-46991)

A mixture of sub and laker boilers in outdoor storage at the Rouge plant in July 1926. Most of these were cleaned and repaired, being installed in Ford automotive plants. (833-47404)

16

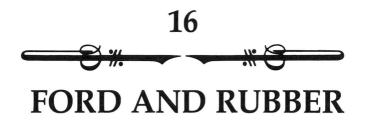

FORD AND RUBBER

Henry Ford, in his younger days, rode a bicycle equipped with pneumatic tires. When he built his first automobile, the 500-pound "quadricycle" in 1896, it was equipped with bicycle wheels with 28-by-1.75-inch bicycle tires. About that same time he first met Harvey S. Firestone, a twenty-eight-year-old carriage salesman from Chicago who raced his expensive hard-rubber-tired carriage on Detroit's boulevard and won several sulky races on local tracks with his fast horses. Firestone was selling carriages in competition with Durant, Dort, Nash, and other carriage makers for the Columbus Buggy Company, owned by his cousin Clinton D. Firestone.[1] Firestone had come to Detroit in 1885 as bookkeeper, and by 1891 was state sales manager for the Chicago-based firm.[2] But the carriages his cousin was building and selling at $110 were overpriced, and the Columbus Buggy Company went out of business in 1897. Harvey Firestone then realized that the best feature of the carriages he had been selling was the set of rubber-tired wheels for which an extra forty dollars was asked. So he decided to manufacture and sell just the rubber tires. It is said that Henry Ford's second vehicle (motorwagon) of 875 pounds was too heavy for the use of standard bicycle wheels, and he bought a stronger set of rubber-tired wire wheels from the Firestone shop on Jefferson Avenue.[3]

About ten years later, Henry Ford was building automobiles in Detroit, and Firestone had built a tire-manufacturing plant in Akron, Ohio. Ford was at that time having trouble with the Selden patent on which he refused to pay a royalty to the Association of Licensed Automobile Manufacturers. Ford was fighting that monopolistic organization in court. Firestone was likewise being stopped from building the popular 'clincher' type tire by the Clincher Tire Association, which refused his entry into their group. Neither Ford nor Firestone wanted to be hampered by these cartels.

The Clincher Tire Association, controlled by the United States Rubber Company (now Uniroyal), had set a price of seventy-seven dollars for a set of four pneumatic tires of the twenty-eight-by-three-inch size Ford wanted. Firestone would sell the same size to Ford for fifty-five dollars a set, but they would be mechanically fastened and not be clinchers. Ford liked Firestone's price and found the tires to be durable. A tire lasting five hundred miles was a good tire in those days. (The same is true today at Indianapolis.)

In March 1906 Ford placed an order with Firestone for two thousand tire sets for his Model N, and was to later increase the order by six thousand sets. Ford soon found, however, that his customers preferred the popular clincher tire because replacements were more readily available. Ford then persuaded

Firestone to build the clinchers and fight the Clincher Tire Association in court if necessary, just as he (Ford) was fighting the Association of Licensed Automobile Manufacturers' Selden patent claim. Ford won the Selden patent suit in 1911, and Firestone's patent lawyers found the Clincher Tire Association's case so weak that it was never taken to court. Thus Ford's tires became clinchers and Firestone became Ford's largest supplier of tires for years to come. Ford's orders to Firestone grew until, with the Model T in 1911, they amounted to $880,000, in 1912, $1.2 million, and in 1913, $2 million.[4]

In 1915 Ford, Firestone, and Edison, all close friends, met at the San Francisco World's Fair to celebrate "the electric dinner" at which an all-electric kitchen was demonstrated. This meeting resulted in their plans to take a vacation trip together the following summer. These camping trips in eastern United States became an annual event for the following nine years, until they became subject to too much notoriety. Fellow travelers, at times, included John Burroughs, Luther Burbank, Warren G. Harding, other Ford and Firestone family members, and finally the wives.[5]

Firestone's early source of rubber had been latex from the wild *Hevea basiliensis* tree in Brazil. Brazil had been exporting rubber since 1827 and had supplied rubber for nearly all tire manufacturers since the discovery of vulcanization by Charles Goodyear in 1844. The quality of the wild rubber was not uniform and neither were the tires. In 1872 the British government had sent Sir Henry A. Wickham on a trip to Brazil to investigate the possibility of cultivating the wild Hevea tree by plantation methods as a commercial crop. He returned to London enthusiastic about the "tree of elastic magic," bringing with him almost seventy thousand seeds for planting in Kew Gardens. He had robbed Brazil of some of its most valuable possessions; next to coffee and Brazil nuts, rubber was Brazil's chief export. As a tree-growing site, the British had in mind British Malaya, and the Dutch had similar plans for their Dutch East Indies. In 1905 the first Far Eastern plantation rubber reached London, and by 1913 Brazil could not compete by selling its wild rubber. By 1920 there had been planted 3 million acres of high-yielding Hevea in the Far East (Malaya, Ceylon, and Java), supplying two-thirds of the world's rubber. Singapore became the rubber capital of the world.[6]

But Britain and the Netherlands were not satisfied with being the primary producers. In 1922 the British Stevenson Plan sought to establish a world price far above the cost of production. This situation was of vital importance to the American automobile industry, which used three-fourths of the rubber imported into the United States. A letter from Firestone to Ford, dated February 17, 1923, called Ford's attention to the British Rubber Restriction Act, which had become effective November 1, 1922, and had raised crude rubber prices from fifteen to thirty-seven cents a pound. For the next several years whenever prices tended to slump, the British-Dutch cartel, through its International Regulations Agreement, would artificially raise rubber prices to unreasonable heights.[7]

To establish independent sources of supply, the United States government in 1923 sponsored an exploration program to find suitable tropical sites in the Western Hemisphere for growing rubber commercially. Sites in Brazil, Venezuela, and Central American states were seriously considered. Privately interested parties also secretly explored these same sites with a view toward establishing plantations. One of the favorable locations was the region along the Rio Tapajos, a tributary of the Amazon River in Brazil—the very region where Sir Henry Wickham had filched his wild Hevea seed in 1872. This region, over seven hundred miles upstream from the ocean, had been highly praised by the government explorers in 1923. And in April 1923 a high Brazilian official had

United States Department of Agriculture rubber survey team in Pará, Brazil, August 1923. Left to right: M. K. Jessup (photographer), Dr. Carl D. LaRue (University of Michigan botany professor), and Dr. James R. Weir (plant pathologist). In 1927 LaRue influenced Henry Ford to invest in Brazilian rubber production. After experiencing difficulties raising rubber trees at Fordlandia, Ford hired Weir as research director in 1933. (1514-24972)

Native clearing crew in front of temporary barracks. Each is wearing a Ford
badge at his waist. (0-3785-A)

invited Henry Ford to visit and invest in Brazil, offering tax concessions. In this Amazon region, Ford Motor Company took an interest; Firestone began to develop a large plantation in Liberia, West Africa, and
Goodyear established small plantations in Costa Rica
and Panama. Ford's choice of the Amazon region was
influenced considerably by a report by Dr. Carl
LaRue, a University of Michigan botanist who had
participated in the 1923 government survey and together with Dr. James Weir, plant pathologist, had
made an independent study of the Amazon region
for Ford in 1926.[8]

Negotiations between Ford Motor Company officials and the Brazilian state of Pará began in late
1926. Ford's legal representatives, Detroit attorneys

O. Z. Ide and W. L. Reeves Blakely, led negotiations
resulting in a free land concession on July 21, 1927,
of one million hectares (2.5 million acres) along the
Tapajos River. His agents paying $125,000 in bribes to
Brazilian officials, however, was upsetting to Ford.[9]

In return for the land concession, after twelve
years of operation the Ford Motor Company was to
pay annually seven percent of profits to the Brazilian
government and another two percent each to the two
municipalities in which the property was located.
Public announcement of the transaction was on October 11, 1927, naming the new organization 'Companhia Industrial Do Brazil.'[10] An enthusiastic Henry
Ford announced that he would fly to South America
with Charles Lindbergh on a South American tour,

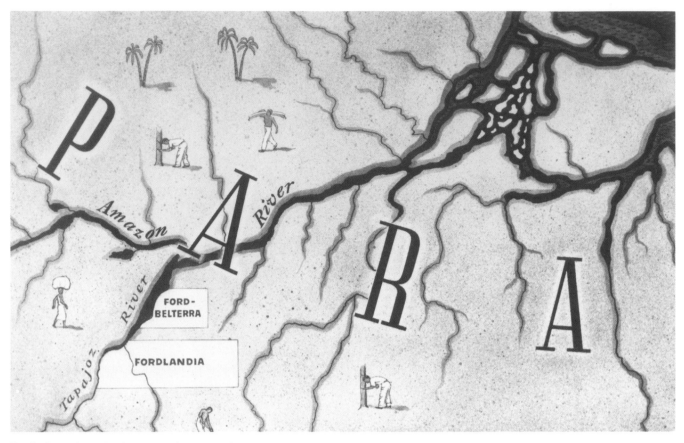

Ford plantations in the state of Pará on the Tapajos River south of the Amazon in northeastern Brazil. At the upper right corner is the Atlantic Ocean, about 750 miles from Fordlandia (Boa Vista), the first of the two settlements to be developed.

and on that trip visit his Amazon Valley property. His trip never materialized. (Also in 1927 Ford joined with Edison and Firestone to form the Edison Botanic Research Corporation, which started testing twenty-three hundred plants for rubber, eventually finding Mexican guayule and American goldenrod probably best for producing domestic rubber.)[11]

Ford men guarded the Brazilian property during the winter of 1927–28, and in August 1928 two ships, the steamer *Lake Ormoc* pulling the barge *Lake Farge*, left the Rouge with matériel to establish a settlement on the banks of the Tapajos. Included in the shipment were a steam shovel, pile driver, tractors, stump pullers, prefabricated buildings, a complete powerhouse, a sawmill, a locomotive and other railroad equipment, ice-making machinery, much food, hospital equipment, a Diesel tug, and motor launches. Einard Oxholm, a respected Danish sea

captain, but with no agricultural background, became manager of the plantation.[12]

Headquarters for the 2.5 million-acre expanse was to be the small settlement of Boa Vista, 110 miles up the Tapajos from the Amazon. At first, the *Lake Ormoc* housed the Ford staff. Buildings were erected on shore as soon as the work of clearing a bit of nearby jungle was under way. Scores of Portuguese Indians were recruited to help cut and burn the dense jungle growth and help with installation of facilities.

According to a statement by Edsel Ford, president of the Ford Motor Company, the immediate development was to involve placing settlements and conducting a widespread campaign of sanitation against jungle diseases. Captain Oxholm was to survey the riverbanks for housing sites, and Dr. L. S. Fallis and assistants from Henry Ford Hospital in Detroit were to start eradicating malaria and hookworm among the natives. A Brazilian, Raymundo Montiero da Costa, was hired to deal directly with the Indians, many of whom lived on plantation property but did not necessarily choose to work for Ford.[13]

Ford offered workers about double the hourly wage to which they were accustomed. They were also given housing, food, and medical services free of charge. Native lumber cut at the Ford sawmill furnished material for homes, food was supplied from the Ford commissary, and the staff of doctors supervised the near elimination of epidemic diseases through the liberal dispensation of quinine and improvements in sanitation—including the issuance of shoes.

The agricultural plan was to completely clear the land and plant an orderly number of small, well-selected wild Hevea trees in the rich jungle soil. By spacing the trees well apart and using cover crops such as soybeans between the young trees, the yield was expected to be much better than the yield from the widely scattered wild trees in their jungle setting. This is what the British and Dutch had learned in the Far East.

The British and Dutch, however, owed much of their success to the manner in which they had propagated their trees. Instead of from seed, they found a single, exceptionally high-yielding tree could be reproduced vegetatively by grafting buds from this tree to a root system of a vigorous and disease-resistant tree. This was called 'cloning,' a technique learned much too late by workers on the Ford plantation. Most of the early Ford plantings were simply the transplantation of young wild trees or cuttings from inferior stock. And more that would have to be learned the hard way was that the cleared, rolling land at the Boa Vista site—now named Fordlandia—would need extensive terracing to prevent the heavy rains from washing the rich soil from the now nearly naked hillsides.[14] A disillusioned Captain Oxholm left in 1930 and Victor Perini, a lumberman from Michigan's Upper Peninsula, for a short while became plantation manager, quickly followed by John Rogge, another Ford lumberman. In 1931 Archibald Johnston took charge.[15]

About eighty-three hundred acres of seedlings had been planted at Fordlandia between 1929 and 1934. But these plantings would require eight to ten

A view of workers' cottages in a subdivision at Fordlandia. The school is seen at a distant corner. It is the dry season and the Tapajos is low. At this early stage (1931) each homesite displays an outdoor toilet because the water system has not yet been installed. (833-56350)

The sawmill on the Tapajos at Fordlandia in 1932. Logs were delivered from the jungle by river, railroad, and truck. Hardwood lumber was shipped by ocean steamer to the United States. (833-57582)

years before producing commercial quantities of rubber, if they did not die from drought during the dry season or from diseases that plagued the growers from the start. South American leaf fungus, leaf caterpillar, lace bug, sauva ants, black crust, red spider, and yellow scale all threatened the foliage of otherwise healthy trees. In short, the trees were not doing at all well compared with those on Far Eastern plantations. The lack of success at Fordlandia is said to have been primarily because of supervision by Ford factory-trained men rather than horticultural specialists.

And Fordlandia had its social problems. The population of the jungle being sparse, sickly, and seasonally mobile restricted the labor force available for the kind of employment offered by Ford. Many who were hired did not become attuned to the Dearborn life-style expected of them. Working by the hour throughout the day was not acceptable to many. They preferred working before sunrise and after sunset, getting daily pay for piecework. Many did not appreciate the wholesome but 'strange' food offered at the company cafeteria and started a serious riot when they found they would have to serve themselves rather than be served by waiters.

The squat, little, screened-in, two-family houses built on the ground were unattractive to people who for generations had lived in homes of palm-thatched construction built high off the ground on stilts so that a small, smoky fire underneath would keep predatory animals and insects away. And why was a bathroom necessary when the swift-flowing river offered the same facilities? The eighteen-hole golf course was not the answer. Neither the square dancing on the village green nor the piped-in Ford Sunday Evening Hour was especially to their liking.[16] With such high wages many preferred to work a short time and leave, rather than stay in that unnatural environment and work steadily. Employee turnover was ridiculously high. However, the high wages, free food, and medical care were so attractive to the lame and the halt that the medical staff and hospital were taxed to the limit. Ford often paid these sickly people for their transportation back down the river to Santarem, a city of about twenty thousand which was said not to have one well-trained doctor or dentist—not even a city water system. Ford plantation medical care was unique in the region, but it could not accommodate all of northeastern Brazil.

In late 1933, with the situation at Fordlandia not at all successful from a rubber-production standpoint, Ford Motor Company hired Dr. James R. Weir,[17] a plant pathologist who had explored the Amazon region with LaRue in 1923. Weir, in studying the situation, recommended that property eighty miles farther downstream on the Tapajos offered a better site for growing rubber. He suggested an exchange of seven hundred thousand remote, undeveloped Fordlandia property for an equivalent acreage in the preferred location. This new location was called Belterra. Weir also immediately traveled to Malaya and Sumatra where he had been many times before, and in December 1933 mailed from Singapore an illicit shipment of 2,046 buddings from fifty-three of the best Far Eastern clones he could find. These had been scientifically developed over almost sixty years from the Hevea expropriated from Brazil by Wickham in 1872. Fordlandia was then relegated to a lesser status as an experimental plantation; the main rubber tracts were now to be developed at Belterra.

Although Fordlandia was as yet nonproductive of rubber,[18] it continued to operate its large sawmill and remained a viable community with its 1.4 million rubber trees, about 340 employees, 229 homes for families, a single-men's dormitory, which could accommodate 900 if necessary, a 125-bed hospital, and three schools. With more than one million acres than Belterra, it was not abandoned by any means.

At Belterra, Weir organized a large research laboratory and nursery where improved budding techniques produced high-yielding rubber strains, which were also more resistant to plant diseases. The technique of double grafting was instituted by which the tree consisted of three separate strains—root, stem, and crown—each selected for optimum qualities. The Belterra experimental laboratory also studied the possibilities of commercial sale of subsidiary products such as teak, balsa, mahogany, eucalyptus, kapok, tamarind, sisal, hemp, jute, cinnamon, ginger, coconut oil, palm, cacao, tea, and coffee. Letters from Weir to McCarroll and Roberge in Dearborn spoke favorably of cotton and tung as Brazilian crops. A field of 180 acres of castor plants was harvested for oil.

Rolling terrain at Fordlandia required terracing to retain topsoil. Here, in 1933, Archie Johnson stands among spindly rubber trees planted in 1929. (833-56508)

An air view of Fordlandia in 1934. Sawmill complex is at right foreground and dock at left. Workers' subdivisions appear at top. (833-62731)

There were 100 acres of mandioca, a base for farina, a favorite Brazilian food. The mandioca was leached of its naturally poisonous cyanide; the farina portion was sold as food and the leachings were used as insecticide. Local groves were already producing oranges, tangerines, grapefruit, pineapple, bananas, and cashew. Weir worked for Ford at Belterra from 1933 to December 1938 for a salary of twelve thousand dollars per year.

Belterra,[19] a community only 150 miles south of the equator, by 1940 had about 7,000 inhabitants and more than 2,000 workers including 261 women and 60 boys. There were 844 houses of which more than half were of palm-thatch construction as preferred by the Indians. Wooden barracks could accommodate 950 single men. Housing, feeding, and health were responsibilities of the company. And a hospital-chapel-mortuary complex was not too distant from the company-supervised cemetery. Archie Johnston, plantation manager and Curtis Pringle, an ex-sheriff from Kalamazoo, Michigan, were able to suppress the Dearborn-like environment and accommodate native customs to a more acceptable extent than had been the practice at Fordlandia.

A diesel-driven powerhouse of 180-kilovolt capacity and a sawmill producing 45,000 board feet per month, together with the carpenter shop and machine shop, supplied materials for Belterra houses and furniture. The first boatload of 160,000 board feet of kiln-dried cabinet-grade lumber had been shipped to Dearborn in 1932 to be sold by the Ford by-products department, and these exotic woods were now being distributed by Cooney, Eckstein & Company of New York.[20] Some of these striking cabinet woods were used as Lincoln automotive interior trim. Some woods were found to be very difficult to cut because of their extreme hardness.

Three major and two outlying schools at Belterra had an enrollment of more than a thousand students, who were taught in Portuguese. A night school taught English to 105 pupils. Major schools were named Henry Ford, Edsel Ford, and Benson Ford.[21] All major schools had a football field and standard playground equipment. Pupils were provided with school uniforms at company expense. Churches, stores, and a recreation building served the workers, as did the Belterra Club with its fine library and golf course. Belterra became the showplace of Ford's Brazilian plantations. In favorable aspects it far surpassed Fordlandia. It became a model community to the extent that the president of Brazil visited the site in 1940 and offered much praise.

In 1941 the two Ford plantations contained 3,651,500 rubber trees, most of them at Belterra. Test tapping had begun, and commercial tapping followed in 1942; 750 tons of latex were produced. By 1950 it was expected that the 38,000-ton annual requirements of the Ford Motor Company would be met. At the Dearborn Rouge plant a tire-manufacturing building had been started in 1937 and began operating in 1939. It could build 5000 tires a day—but not half of Ford's requirements. Tires with the Ford name were manufactured during 1939–40, but not yet from Ford raw rubber. Edgar F. Wait,[22] superintendent of the Rouge tire plant, states in his reminiscences that the amount of rubber from Brazil during 1939–40 would not have kept his plant running one day.

Ford had invested $7 million in his tire factory and had obtained the help of Firestone employees in its construction and initial operation. That Ford was starting to build his own tires brought much lower prices from suppliers, to the extent, according to Wait, the cost of the factory was saved over and over.

When the United States entered World War II, rubber from the Far East became unavailable and

The land at Belterra was flat and more suitable than at Fordlandia for growing rubber trees. This photo, taken in April 1935, shows a portion of a 121-acre nursery containing more than 4.5 million seedlings planted under the direction of James R. Weir. In the photo are Archie Johnson, at left, and his assistant. (0-7672)

A typical outlying school on the Belterra plantation. Girls are playing an organized game while the boys watch. (833-73227-A)

Ford's rubber from Brazil was not yet being produced in quantity. For the amount of rubber available to the United States there was a surplus of tire manufacturing plants. On the other hand, the Soviet Union at that time had a supply of 50,000 tons of rubber annually, much of it synthetic, and needed additional tire-building equipment. The United States government then saw fit to acquisition the Rouge tire manufacturing equipment so that it could be sent to the Soviet Union. Soviet workers helped dismantle the equipment, and it was shipped across the Pacific never to be properly assembled it is said.

The Ford plantations continued to produce despite a serious epidemic of leaf disease, despite labor problems caused by new Brazilian labor laws during the war, and despite restrictions on exportation of lumber. But by the end of the war in 1945 the return of the Japanese-held Far Eastern estates to friendly hands and the development of superior synthetic rubber made the operation of the Brazilian plantations even less favorable.[23] In December 1945 the Ford Motor Company disposed of its rubber interests in Brazil, returning the plantations with an estimated $20 million invested to the Brazilian government for the pittance of $250,000.[24] At that time Ford Motor Company's financial condition could not stand further investments.

Henry Ford never visited South America. His knowledge of the rubber plantations came from his employees—their memos and their hundreds of photographs[25] depicting day-to-day progress. Ford nearly always had at least two investment goals in mind. One was to support his automobile business and the other was to provide a better life for people of the region. This dual objective was apparent in Brazil. If he failed in either goal, it was more likely to be the one relating to the automobile business. This was true in Brazil.

When Ford supervision left the Amazon Valley, the areas were put under control of the Brazilian Northern Agronomical Institute. In 1975, the Brazilian government set up an Inter-Ministerial Commission to study the local problems. An official of the agricultural ministry[26] states that "visitors to Fordlandia and Belterra marvel at the typically American villages that grew in the heart of the Amazon jungle. The houses are well preserved and equipped with crockery, home appliances, books and all sorts of objects imported from the United States. Even the old hand cranked record players still work. It's just like being in a live museum." The agricultural counselor at the American embassy in Brasilia states that a company called Latex Pastore is now using the facilities to produce rubber, though not at commercially viable levels. There is some subsidy by the Brazilian government. Thus the rubber trees planted by Ford more than sixty years ago are again creating employment in that area where subsistence would otherwise be derived primarily from hunting and fishing. And, barring disease, those rubber trees can live three hundred years.[27]

NOTES

1. Harvey S. Firestone with Samuel Crowther, *Men and Rubber* (New York: Doubleday, Page & Co., 1926).
2. *Detroit Directory* (Detroit: R. L. Polk & Co., 1890–98).
3. Alfred Lief, *Harvey Firestone: Free Man of Enterprise* (New York: McGraw-Hill, 1951), pp. 48–53.
4. Alfred Lief, *The Firestone Story* (New York: McGraw-Hill, 1951), pp. 166–67.
5. Nevins and Hill, *Expansion and Challenge*, pp. 485–87.
6. Charles M. Wilson, "Mr. Ford in the Jungle," *Harpers Magazine* (July 1941): 181.
7. Lewis, *Public Image*, p. 165.
8. Carl LaRue, *Reminiscences*, Acc. 65, p. 11, Archives, HFM&GV.
9. LaRue, *Reminiscences*, pp. 11–14.
10. "Ford Acquires Concession of Rubber Land in Brazil," *Rubber Age* 22 (October 25, 1927): 65–66.
11. Nevins and Hill, *Expansion and Challenge*, p. 233.
12. "Industrialist in the Wilderness: Henry Ford's Amazon Venture," *Journal of Interamerican Studies and World Affairs* 21 (May, 1979): 261–87.
13. 'The Ford Brazil Project,' Vertical File, Archives, HFM&GV (23 pages, author and date unknown).
14. Wilson, "Mr. Ford in the Jungle," p. 186.
15. Mrs. Victor Pirini, *Reminiscences*, Acc. 65, pp. 12–18, Archives, HFM&GV.
16. Wilson, "Mr. Ford in the Jungle," pp. 185–86.
17. James R. Weir Collection, Acc. 1514, Archives, HFM&GV. Weir has been characterized as a "conceited crank" and is seldom credited with his important contributions.
18. Acc. 38, Boxes 61, 64, 68, Production Records; see also Acc. 390, Box 86, Wibel's Fordlandia Papers, Archives, HFM&GV.

A good stand of seven-year-old rubber trees at Fordlandia in 1936. (0-3785-A)

Tire molding line at the Rouge tire plant in 1939. (833-70303)

19. Acc. 301, Boxes 1, 2, Companhia Industrial do Brazil Corporate Papers; also Acc. 74, Boxes 1–12.
20. *Distinctive Brazilian Hardwoods from the Ford Plantation in the Amazon Jungle* (New York: Cooney, Eckstein & Co., 1933).
21. "The Ford Rubber Plantations in Brazil" (1941), Acc. 241, Box 7, Archives, HFM&GV.
22. E. F. Wait, *Reminiscences*, Acc. 65, pp. 30–35, Archives, HFM&GV.
23. Joseph A. Russell, "Alternative Sources of Rubber," *Economic Geography* (October 1941): 399–408.
24. "Ford Motor Company Disposes of Natural Rubber Holdings in Brazil," *Rubber Age* (December 1945): 357.
25. Accs. 1660 and 1514, Archives, HFM&GV (photographs of Fordlandia and Belterra showing day-by-day progress on the plantations).
26. Communication from L. C. Secco, Press Department, Ford International Public Affairs, July 13, 1987. Vertical File, HFM&GV.
27. Correspondence with Robert J. Wicks, agricultural counselor, the American embassy, Brasilia, November 9, 1987. Vertical File, HFM&GV.

17

AIRCRAFT

Just wait 'til rainy Saturday comes,
When I shall gather my earthly sums;
I'll build a great big flying machine
And make Tom Edison look pea green.
                    Anon., ca. 1890

Once upon a time, Detroit threatened to be the center of aircraft manufacturing just as it was for automobile production. During the 1920s and early 1930s aircraft leaders in Detroit were Ford, Stinson, Buhl, Packard, Towle, Verville, Stout, Driggs, Hammond, Continental Motors, Aircraft Development Company, Detroit Aircraft Corporation, and others. The Aircraft Development Corporation helped the Loughead brothers develop their prototypes until the Lougheads were offered twenty-five thousand dollars by the Grof brothers, who moved the business to California where the company name was changed to Lockheed for easier pronunciation. And James McDonnell, an engineer for Ford, was to form his own McDonnell Aircraft Company before joining Douglas to create the present McDonnell-Douglas Corporation. Of the Detroit manufacturers, Henry and Edsel Ford not only had plenty of enthusiasm but also had the money to push forward.

THE FIRST FORD AIRPLANE

Edsel Ford, from the time he was fifteen years old in 1909, was active in aviation. His father had rented a small barn at 1302 Woodward Avenue in Detroit where he was building experimental tractors from Model T parts. Henry gave Edsel and three of his shop employees permission to build an airplane using the Model T motor. Charles Van Auken, a boyhood friend of Edsel, was designer and test pilot; Edsel aided in research work and helped build the machine. The finished unit was a single place, high-wing monoplane with direct drive from the twenty-eight-horsepower Model T engine. Controls were conventional except aileron action, which was obtained by warping the wings, a yoke being attached to the pilot's shoulders so that if he leaned to the right the right wing went down, and vice versa.

The first flights, in 1910, were made from a Dearborn farm that had been recently bought by Henry Ford. (This land is now the Dearborn Country

Club.) Finding that they needed a little more power to lift the plane out of the long grass, a revamped Model T engine was installed and the plane flown from the neatly mowed parade grounds at Detroit's Fort Wayne. Although the parade grounds were not too large, they were smooth and bordered the half-mile-wide Detroit River. Flights were successful until the last one when Van Auken crashed into a tree leaving the plane smashed beyond repair. Van Auken, the only one to have flown the plane, was not a casualty.[1]

THE "BUG"

In utmost secrecy during 1917, aircraft and engine specialists gathered at a farmhouse in an isolated section of Ohio to develop an unusually odd vehicle to win the war in Europe. Involved were Henry Ford with his chief engineer C. H. Wills; Charles F. Kettering, head of research at Dayton Metal Products Company; Harold Morehouse, draftsman with Dayton-Wright Aircraft Company; Wilbur Wright, and Elmer Sperry. Kettering led the project under Col. H. H. Arnold of the U.S. Signal Corps. Details of the project were not publicly revealed until almost twenty years after World War II.

The vehicle was to be a pilotless guided missile requiring the talents of the best aeronautical, propulsion, and guidance system minds available in the country. Wright provided aeronautical advice, Ford took responsibility for the engine, and Sperry for guidance systems. Kettering was overall administrator reporting to Colonel Arnold.

The robot was to deliver a warhead of two hundred pounds for any distance from fifty to two hundred miles to reach its target. It was to be a low-cost, long-range, self-guided, self-propelled aerial torpedo. In principle it was simple; in practice it was complex. A gasoline engine was simply to be supplied with only enough fuel to carry a plane and bomb the selected distance in the right direction.

The engine, developed by Wills, was an air-cooled V-4 generating forty horsepower—advanced for the period. It had no carburetor, the air-fuel mixture being set before takeoff. Henry Ford said the engine could be mass-produced for about forty dollars. (The entire vehicle was to cost no more than two hundred dollars.) The engine developed no troubles whatsoever.

First Ford airplane with Van Auken (right) and friend (not Edsel Ford) ready to fly from Fort Wayne parade grounds in 1910. Note the tricycle landing wheels and the Model T engine with radiator mounted parallel to engine rather than perpendicular. (0-335)

Aiming of the "bug" was more of a problem. Sperry, with Kettering, worked on the complications of head winds, crosswinds, updrafts, and down drafts. An ultrasensitive aneroid barometer was designed to correct for updrafts and down drafts. A subtracing anemometer provided a means of stopping the motor after an exact number of engine revolutions for more perfect distance control.

The plane had a wingspan of 17 feet, a length of 12.5 feet, and a weight of 350 pounds without payload. Its speed was fifty-five miles per hour, and it was designed to release its wings to let the fuselage fall to earth as a bomb.

When the device was ready and had passed its tests, "Hap" Arnold went to Europe to prepare launching sites. But by the time Arnold's preparations had begun, a serious defect in the plan had developed—they had run out of war; peace had broken out.

In 1941 the "bug," still a secret weapon, was proposed again to fight the Germans, but its range was not long enough to fly from England to Germany. It would have dropped its bomb on friendly soil. The B-17 bomber was chosen in place of the "bug," but not without some added expense and loss of life.[2]

DIRIGIBLES

In June 1919 Henry Ford witnessed arrival, landing, and departure of the British R-34 at Mineola, Long Island. In July of that year he had rid himself of minor Ford Motor Company stockholders and was

Assembling robot planes in secret factory during 1918. (189-63701)

Experimental robots at secret takeoff site in Ohio. Robot at left on rail
runway ready for flight. (189-63700)

free to take off businesswise in all directions. And
this he did. Ford sent his chief engineer, William B.
Mayo, to Washington to present plans to the navy
department regarding dirigibles. Mayo was to become Ford's chief aircraft engineer as well as chief
steam engineer as well as chief waterpower engineer.

By early 1920 Ford had offered to build for the
U.S. government a $1 million factory to produce zep-
pelins in Detroit. Zeppelin officials had visited Ford

asking for financial aid and offering to provide zeppelin patents in return. Ford was evidently ready to
build airships for the government. Then there seems
to have been a four-year lapse in his dirigible activity.
Perhaps he did not want to deal with the Germans so
soon after the war.

But Edsel Ford, William B. Mayo, William B.
Stout, and C. Harold Wills, all Ford Motor Company
employees, had been for years members and direc-

tors of the Detroit Aviation Society. This organization sponsored such events as airspeed races, aircraft reliability tours, and aerial polar expeditions; all of these events were of national prominence. Secretary of the society was Carl B. Fritschie, a promoter; in 1920 he was instrumental in organizing the Aircraft Development Corporation to make Detroit the manufacturing center of the lighter-than-air aircraft industry. Harold H. Emmons became president of the organization and Fritschie became general manager. More than one hundred subscribers—a veritable "who's who" of Detroit industrialists—bought stock. Among them again were Edsel Ford, Mayo, Stout, and Wills. Henry Ford seems not to have been a stockholder, although otherwise supportive.

The Aircraft Development Corporation was "organized to develop through sound engineering methods a safe and practical Metalclad Airship for commercial and military use," and in 1921 began an engineering investigation of such a ship. Ralph H. Upson, a professor of aviation engineering at the University of Michigan, and the nation's leading balloonist, became chief engineer of the corporation. Under Upson were Lt. Raffe Emerson, who had been in charge of the construction of the USS *Shenandoah*; shop superintendent was Edward J. Hill from the naval aircraft factory at Philadelphia. Several technical consultants including Orville Wright, William Stout, George Holley, with Mayo as chairman, were all advisers to Upson.

In June 1922 the Aircraft Development Corporation was capitalized at five hundred thousand dollars in stock. Some of this was Edsel Ford's money. With an airport and hangar on Grosse Ile (an island in the Detroit River about twenty miles south of Dearborn), the Ford engineering laboratories in Dearborn at their service, and assistance from the navy Lakehurst facilities and the U.S. Bureau of Standards, by 1923 the practicality of a metalclad ship was established. During 1924, letterheads of the Corporation featured "Upson Airships," with offices in the General Motors Building, Detroit. A detailed proposal of a "demonstration" metal-clad ship was presented to the U.S. Navy September 24, 1925. The navy accepted the proposal in August 1926.

The airship to be built for the navy was designated the ZMC-2, a designation referring to a zeppelin-type metal-clad ship of 200,000 cubic feet capacity. The craft was to be 150 feet long and 52 feet maximum diameter, supporting a control cabin of 16-by-6 feet. This low length-to-diameter ratio was a

The metal-clad airship ZMC-2 in September 1929. (Courtesy of the EAA Aviation Foundation Library, Oshkosh, Wisconsin.)

unique feature at that time, as was the use of eight tail surfaces. Supporting structure was of alloy aluminum. An aluminum skin only .008 of an inch thick covered the entire airship and contained the helium lifting gas. Inside the ship were two large air cells (balloonets) of rubber-coated fabric to maintain interior pressure. The thin skin sections with riveted and tarred gas-tight joints required the ship to be kept under pressure at all times to avoid buckling of the hull. Two Wright Whirlwind outrigger engines acting as pullers generated two hundred horsepower each. Top speed of the airship was sixty-two miles per hour; range was seven hundred miles with ascent and descent capabilities of one thousand feet per minute.

The ZMC-2 was successfully flight tested on August 19, 1929, and delivered to the navy at Lakehurst, New Jersey, on September 12, 1929. It had no major accidents during its twelve-year lifetime as a training ship at the naval aircraft station and was finally dismantled because of old age. It had logged 2,250 hours and traveled about one hundred thousand nautical miles.

With the completion of development work on the ZMC-2, the organization branched into other products and became Detroit Aircraft Corporation, with Edward S. Evans as president; it became involved in the manufacture of automotive-hauling equipment. The corporation grew to become the Evans Products Company of today.

The Ford name was never closely associated with the ZMC-2 because of the insistence of Henry and Edsel Ford. But Ford laboratories conducted tests on ZMC-2 materials and the Fords paid five hundred

The dirigible *Los Angeles* tied to the Ford Air Port mooring tower on October 15, 1926. (833-47693)

thousand dollars for a 225-foot dirigible mooring tower at Ford Air Port in 1924 so that the Aircraft Development Corporation would better qualify for government contracts. Aircraft Development Corporation designed and constructed the tower, which could accommodate any airship up to 10 million cubic feet capacity.

In September 1926 the U.S. Army semirigid S-R-1 was the first lighter-than-air airship to tie up at Ford Air Port. On October 15 the giant *Los Angeles* moored at Dearborn at 5:15 A.M. and cast off at 3:35 P.M. with Lieutenant Commander Rosenthal in charge. From all southeastern Michigan, people gathered around Ford Air Port, parking their automobiles a mile or more away, to behold this lumbering giant— the zeppelin LZ-126—given to the United States as a war reparation and renamed *Los Angeles* in 1924. Henry Ford had once intimated he might be willing to buy the *Los Angeles* from the government for use in Detroit-to-London service.

Dirigibles for a short time had become the transportation of the elite, reaching their height of success in the mid-1930s with the *Hindenburg*, which could carry 1,002 passengers to and from Europe at eighty miles an hour. But after our *Macon*, *Akron*, and *Shenandoah* had crashed, and the hydrogen-filled *Hindenburg* had exploded in 1937, the giant rigid airships vanished from the skies. Only the much smaller helium-filled "blimps," which fly mainly on short trips in good weather, have survived.[3]

THE FORD TRI-MOTOR

The introduction of commercial planes made of metal instead of wood and fabric can be attributed to a large extent to Ford pioneering. The sponsorship first of Stout all-metal planes in 1923 is evidence of Ford forward planning. Some of the zeppelin metals—aluminum alloyed with copper and zinc, with small amounts of iron, manganese, and silicon— showed great promise. In this country a trade name for such a metal was Duraluminum.

After William B. Stout had demonstrated products of his Stout Metal Airplane Company, the Fords and Mayo enticed Stout to use buildings at the new 260-acre Ford Air Port. Stout was developing single-engined monoplanes in anticipation of operating an airline. But Ford wanted to run the show and he had the money; he bought the Stout Metal Airplane Company in July 1925. Edsel Ford became president, Stout and Mayo vice presidents, and B. J. Craig secretary and treasurer. Ford had already bought two of Stout's single-engine planes to inaugurate his Detroit-to-Chicago flying service on April 8, 1925.

In discussions at Washington about airmail contracts, it became clear what was needed was a trimotor plane that could carry larger loads, operate at higher speeds, and sustain flight on two engines or prolong it on one. If the Fords could develop such a product, it would surely dominate aircraft manufacturing. Stout and Mayo were to design such a plane.

The Ford trimotor closely resembled Stout's previous models. Henry Ford, however, did not like the appearance of the very first trimotor, and when performance tests were disappointing, he ordered Harold Hicks (a Ford engineer) to take charge of engineering in place of Stout. A "mysterious" fire soon destroyed this first trimotor in its hangar together with three other Stout-designed planes then under construction. This event augured the beginning of a new, larger (sixty thousand square feet) "progressive production" airplane factory.

The second trimotor, all Ford, was ready for testing and demonstration on June 11, 1926, before representatives of National Air Transport, Colonial Airways, Western Air Express, and Florida Airways. The first sale of a Ford trimotor to an airline was to National Air Transport. And Ford was now beginning to use some of his own planes on his Detroit-Chicago-Cleveland Airlines.

These successful trimotors had a wingspread of seventy feet, carried eight passengers, and provided separate space for freight. With powerful Pratt-Whitney radial engines, cruising was raised to 122 miles per hour; maximum speed was above 160 miles per hour. With the Ford-developed radio beacon and the proliferation of well-equipped airports, the Ford trimotor became the darling of the airways. Customers included Pan American, Northwest, Transcontinental Air Transport (now TWA), besides the U.S. Army and Navy.

In 1927 the Ford trimotor and the Ford Air Port attracted Charles Lindbergh, who came with his *Spirit of St. Louis* and gave Ford his first ride in an airplane. On this same occasion, Lindbergh flew a trimotor and invited Henry and Edsel to fly in it with him. Lindbergh was planning a tour of South America and Henry implied he might go with Lindbergh on the tour.

Sales of the trimotor increased to thirty-six during 1928—priced fifty thousand dollars "stripped" to seventy-five thousand dollars with luxury options. Production peaked in 1929 when eighty-six planes were sold. But sales diminished during the early Depression years: twenty-six in 1930, twenty-one in 1931, and only three in 1932. Used trimotors became available at prices ranging from ten thousand dollars to forty thousand dollars. The sales staff blamed much of the business failure on Ford's reluctance to streamline the plane further and install more powerful engines for a higher cruising speed. By November 1932 Stout, Mayo, and Hicks had all left the scene, and Ford's former employee, James McDonnell, was busy developing the successor to the Ford trimotor, the McDonnell-Douglas DC-3.[4]

THE FLIVVER PLANE

The Flivver was a midget plane in which Henry Ford took a particular interest. The plane was designed and built as a project of Henry Ford and his chief test pilot, Harry Brooks. The designer was Otto Coppen, who was brought in purposely for the Flivver. It was built in a nearby museum building out of sight of Mayo and Stout, who wanted nothing to do with it.

There were only two Flivver planes built. The first was a tiny, low-winged, single-place monoplane with a twenty-three-foot wingspan and a fuselage sixteen feet long. Height was five feet, and its weight empty 550 pounds. A three-cylinder, radial, air-cooled, thirty-five-horsepower Anzani engine provided a cruising speed of eighty five miles per hour. The plane had a convenient landing speed of thirty-five miles per hour.

Several advanced construction features included a fuselage framed of metal tubing instead of

The Ford trimotor plane of which 198 were built by the Ford Aircraft Division. This particular plane is no. 31 of Model 4-AT, photographed August 17, 1928. (833-5854)

Interior of Ford trimotor, facing cockpit. (833-51622)

wood, wide-spaced landing wheels to prevent ground looping, and live-rubber shock absorbers. As soon as this first plane was operational in July 1926, Harry Brooks used it as a personal plane to commute daily from his home north of Detroit to the Ford Air Port in Dearborn. In this first Flivver plane Charles Lindbergh flew during his visit to Ford Air Port in 1927. This plane is now on display in the Henry Ford Museum.

Two years later, a second Flivver was built with some improvements in structure, notably a slight dihedral in its wing to increase lateral stability. Greatest changes, however, were in the power plant and fuel tank installations. A Ford-designed, lightweight, two-cylinder, horizontally opposed air-cooled engine of thirty-six horsepower was installed, along with a much larger (fifty-gallon) fuel tank. This plane was

A Ford trimotor takes off from Ford Air Port in July 1931. This photograph, taken from the roof of the Dearborn Inn, America's first airport hotel, shows the air terminal, airport runways, and to the far right, the dirigible tower. Trimotor factory buildings and hangars are to the left out of the picture. (833-56370-8)

designed to break the light-plane long-distance record held by a French flier. Because the Ford plane consumed only 2.4 gallons of gasoline an hour at an airspeed of eighty-five miles per hour, theoretically it could fly about seventeen hundred miles on 50 gallons of fuel.

A flight from Dearborn to Miami, Florida, was planned, a distance of 1,400 miles. On January 24, 1928, Brooks flew the second Flivver toward Miami, but after 471 miles was forced down at Asheville, North Carolina, by bad weather. His second attempt began in Dearborn at 3:00 A.M. on February 21. That day he flew nonstop to Titusville, Florida, before darkness forced him to land. He had flown nearly 1,200 miles and had established a new world distance record for light planes. Brooks's good fortune, however, did not last. A few days later, he crashed into the ocean off Melbourne, Florida, and was lost. The reason for the crash has never been determined for

Harry Brooks with flivver plane no. 2 at the Ford Air Port in 1927. This was the plane in which Brooks experienced the fatal crash off the coast of Florida. (189-5105)

certain. At this point Henry Ford seems to have lost interest in single-engine planes for a while.[5]

But in November 1935 Henry and Edsel were experimenting with the Ford Model 15-P. This was a two-passenger monoplane powered by a Ford V-8 engine to produce 115 horsepower at 4,000 RPM, providing a speed of 100 miles per hour and a range of 500 miles on 30 gallons of gasoline. Soon after Ford obtained an experimental license in January 1936, the plane was sold to the U.S. Bureau of Air Commerce. This plane was never reproduced. It is thought that the automotive engine was too heavy to be really practical. Rotary piston engines provided needed power from less weight.

THE MODEL 14-AT

This unique Ford-built plane was never given a name. It never really flew. Its development and testing were done in relative secrecy. In 1932, at the depth of the Great Depression, trimotor business was poor and the automobile business was poor, which meant that Ford engineering was under great pressure to create something that would sell. The Ford automobile quickly leaped from one with a four-cylinder engine to one with an eight-cylinder engine. What could be done for the Ford Airplane Division? It was to be a giant passenger airplane having features never before tried in American design practice.

According to *Aero Digest* in the April 1932 issue,

> The new Tri-Motor Ford 14-AT transport airplane represents a distinct advance in the design of large passenger craft. Its novel aerodynamic, mechanical and passenger accommodation features make it outstanding in its class. Developed by the Airplane Division of Ford Motor Co. to fulfill the needs of airlines for deluxe operation on trunk airways and cross-continental routes, its comfortable accommodations rival the most luxurious forms of surface transportation. Anticipating the requirements of night operations, sleeping accommodations comparable to those of Pullman cars are provided.

But the plane did not make its appearance at the April International Air Show at Detroit City Airport as predicted by the press. A news release by Ford Motor Company indicated the plane was still undergoing tests.

But the plane did exist. Its wingspan of 110 feet, length of 80 feet, and wing area of 1,600 square feet were surprisingly like the much later B-24 bomber of World War II. Its power and top speed were considerably less, however, because it had only three engines rather than the four on the B-24.

The three 14-A Hispano-Suiza engines produced twenty-five hundred horsepower, the center engine of eleven hundred horsepower being mounted high over the wing—an awkward-appearing position. The landing gear was partly retractable, and the wheels were equipped with "pants." The landing gear arrangement was that of a "camel squat." While loading, the forward part of the fuselage was squatting low to the ground so that passengers could enter the plane in one step off the ground. In a takeoff position the doorway was four feet off the ground. Possibly in an emergency this plane could have landed with retracted wheels. (With modern planes it is said there are two kinds of pilots—those who *have* landed with wheels up, and those who *will* land with wheels up.)

The interior of the plane was plush to say the least. There was a smoking room, two lavatories, a steward's galley, and a baggage compartment. The length of the cabin was forty-one feet; ceiling height was six feet, ten inches. As on a Pullman train, seats were made into beds, and upper berths used when needed. There were reading lights, and stewards were on push-button call.

It is said the 14-AT taxied up and down the runways of Ford Air Port for some time with Harry Russell as test pilot, but problems with vibration and structural weaknesses kept the plane on the ground. Its heavy, water-cooled engines, a choice of Henry Ford, were a distinct disadvantage. The 14-AT was considered Mayo's project, but Harold Hicks, Ford's engine expert, was disgusted with it. Edsel Ford ordered the plane scrapped before it ever flew.[6]

THE B-24 LIBERATOR

Henry and Edsel Ford again became involved in aircraft production in 1940 when another war with Germany was imminent. This time, however, the U.S. government offered financing—use of profits

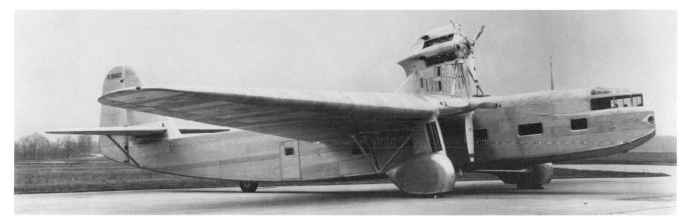

The 14-A trimotor in 1932. This experimental Ford plane—the most luxurious of them all—never really flew. It was scrapped by order of Edsel Ford. (833-56854-6)

from the Model T was not necessary. Aircraft projects of considerable magnitude included bombers, aircraft engines, and motorless gliders.

The largest of all the many war production contracts given to Ford Motor Company was that of the Consolidated B-24 Liberator. This contract called for spending nearly $200 million, and resulted in the manufacture of 8,685 of these four-engine, thirty-ton planes at the Ford bomber plant at Willow Run (Ypsilanti, Michigan). The plane was designed by Consolidated Aircraft, and was capable of high-altitude precision bombing at heights beyond the range of antiaircraft fire. Its service ceiling was thirty thousand feet and range twenty-five hundred to three thousand miles at speeds reaching three hundred miles per hour. These planes served in all major theaters of war, hundreds also being flown by the Allies.

The B-24 Liberator was undoubtedly an excellent bomber by design. The greatest contribution by Ford Motor Company, however, was the concept and realization of mass production of aircraft. Charles E. Sorenson, innovator of the Model T moving assembly line in 1913, insisted and demonstrated that a mechanism as large and complex as a heavy bomber of 1.5 million parts, held together largely by seven hundred thousand rivets, could be assembled in Model T fashion. Despite labor and material shortages during the war, the bomber plant at Willow Run reached production of a completely assembled plane every hour. Sorenson announced in 1944 a capacity of 650 planes per month. This rate was an order of magnitude greater than prewar production standards, And, to boot, cost to the government had been lowered from

$379,000 to $216,000 per plane during that period of wartime inflation.

In August 1940 Ford Motor Company was offered a contract to build eight thousand Pratt-Whitney eighteen-cylinder air-cooled aircraft engines to be used on B-46 bombers—not the B-24 being built at Willow Run; $14 million was allocated by the government. Work was immediately started on a factory building within the Rouge complex. This steel, brick, and glass building was constructed under a wood and tar paper box during the winter of 1940–41, and the building alone, without equipment, cost Ford Motor Company $39 million. The first engine was completed in August 1941, just one year after the signing of the contract. During four years of production, 57,851 engines were manufactured. During this time man-hours required per engine were reduced from 2,330 to 905. This Rouge "aircraft building" is now used to manufacture automobile engines.[7]

COMBAT GLIDERS

Another World War II contract given to Ford Motor Company in May 1942 called for the building of one thousand gliders. These had been designed by Waco Aircraft Company of Troy, Ohio, and designated CG-4A. This was a motorless aircraft with a wingspread of eighty-four feet, a length of fifty-two feet, and a weight empty of three thousand pounds. The plane was designed to carry fifteen soldiers or a reconnaissance car or a 75mm howitzer.

The B-24 Liberator bomber of which Ford Motor Company assembled 8,685 during World War II. With four Pratt-Whitney engines, this plane had a ceiling of thirty thousand feet and a range of three thousand miles. (0-222)

Until Pearl Harbor, Ford had been operating a large sawmill and woodworking plant at Iron Mountain, Michigan, where wooden station wagon bodies had been produced. This closed plant together with its available skilled woodworkers was ideal for manufacturing these wooden gliders. The planes were not entirely of wood. The fuselage had a tubular metal framework covered with fabric, but the balance of the plane, except hardware, was constructed of laminated wood glued together under high pressure and heat. Some four thousand special fixtures were needed to process glider parts rather than station wagon parts.

Within four months after receiving the blueprints from Waco, the first Ford-made glider was produced. Walter Nelson and his Iron Mountain workers had adapted automotive production procedures to glider manufacturing. The Ford method used waste steam to speed the drying of the thousands of parts and assemblies required for the glider. Methods that at other plants had required twenty-four hours for complete drying of parts now required only ten min-

The CG-13 glider designed to carry forty troops or two Jeeps with their crews. One hundred of these were built at Iron Mountain, Michigan, during the latter part of World War II. (Photo from the John W. Bennett collection.)

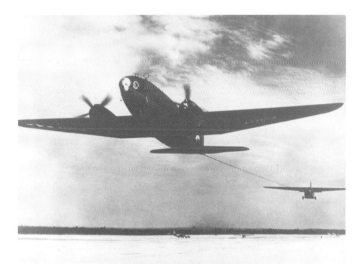

A Curtis Commando C-46 lifts a Ford-built glider from the snow-covered airfield at Iron Mountain. The long nylon connecting cord had enough elasticity to allow the glider to snap to the Commando's eighty miles per hour flying speed without damage to planes or personnel. (Photo from the John W. Bennett collection.)

utes at the Iron Mountain plant. Time to build the CG-4A was reduced to one-half, and the cost was reduced from twenty-five thousand dollars to about ten thousand dollars each.

More than four thousand of the CG-4A model were built, most of them in 1943. In January 1944 a larger CG-13A Waco was ordered by the government. This model differed only slightly in appearance, but was capable of carrying either forty fully equipped soldiers or two Jeeps and their crews. With the heav-

ier cargo, hydraulically operated landing flaps were required to reduce landing speeds to a reasonable rate. Only a hundred of the larger gliders were built.

These gliders might land at sixty miles per hour on rough terrain, and often ended up against fences, walls, or trees. A damaged nose opening sometimes prevented combat cargo from being unloaded. Men could usually manage another means of exit. These gliders, after being towed in a "glider train" to the front, could be released at perhaps eight thousand feet altitude to glide almost an hour if necessary to reach the proper landing site. In 1943 General "Hap" Arnold (the man who had praised the "bug" in 1918) stated that "glider pilots and airborne troops will be the forefront of the attack." Arnold spoke the truth.[8]

NOTES

1. News releases, Acc. 3–1, NR 102–1, Archives, HFM&GV.
2. "Reveal U.S. Perfected Guided Missile in 1917," *Detroit News*, November 24, 1961; Eugene Farkus, *Reminiscences*, Acc. 65, pp. 97–100, Archives, HFM&GV; J. L. McCloud, *Reminiscences*, Acc. 65, pp. 257–58, Archives, HFM&GV.
3. Acc. 6, Boxes 252, 257, Archives, HFM&GV; Walker Morrow, Small Acc. No. 1365, Archives, HFM&GV; Ralph H. Upson, "Metalclad Rigid Airship Development," *Journal of the Society of Automotive Engineers* (February 1926).
4. *Instruction Manual for Ford Trimotor* (Dearborn: Ford Motor Company, 1929); Douglas J. Ingalls, *Tin Goose: The Fabulous Ford Trimotor* (Fallbrook, Calif., Aero Publishers, 1968); William B. Stout, *So Away I Went* (New York: Bobbs-Merrill, 1951).
5. Nevins and Hill, *Expansion and Challenge*, p. 246; Lewis, *Public Image*, p. 177; Al Esper, *Reminiscences*, Acc. 65, pp. 43–48, Archives, HFM&GV.

6. Richard L. Hagelthorn, "Dearborn's Spruce Goose," *Dearborn Historian* (summer 1982): 71–82.

7. Nevins and Hill, *Decline and Rebirth*, pp. 182–214; *Flight Manual for B-24 Liberator* (Washington: Aviation Publications, 1977);

Charles E. Sorenson, *My Forty Years with Ford* (New York: W. W. Norton, 1956), p. 343.

8. Nevins and Hill, *Decline and Rebirth*, pp. 205–8.

18

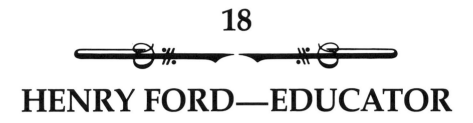

HENRY FORD—EDUCATOR

With but a sixth-grade formal education, Henry Ford was nevertheless destined to be recognized as an educational pioneer. As noted an academician as Dr. George Washington Carver proclaimed Henry Ford in terms such as "Prince of Educators" and "Greatest of all my inspiring friends, Educational Demonstrator, Mr. Ford." And the prominent criminal attorney, Clarence Darrow, said of Ford's experimental schools, "If schools of this type could reach all of the youth of America, in time it would result in the abolition of crime and poverty, both of which are a disgrace to civilization."

Henry Ford preserved in Greenfield Village the two one-room school buildings that he attended. His first serious educational experiment involved ten homeless boys who were invited in 1911 to live on a farm in Dearborn at Ford's expense, attend public school, and learn to help support themselves by doing simple farm tasks. This trial with the ten boys encouraged him to start the Henry Ford Trade School adjacent to his factory at Highland Park in 1916. The Trade School flourished until Ford's death, ultimately graduating eight thousand students, many of whom were to hold responsible positions with Ford Motor Company.

Ford visualized an educational system that would offer cultural and vocational training. In early 1930 he announced that he would be spending $100 million in promoting his educational ideas, and this, no doubt, he did. His schools may have received more of his attention than did his automobile business for the rest of his life.

In the rural areas where Ford owned farmland and located his Village Industries, the local school was usually refurbished and teachers paid by Ford. Large donations were given by Ford and his wife to institutions such as the Berry Schools in Georgia, Tuskegee Institute, Fair Hope School in Alabama, and the Lincoln Memorial University in Tennessee.

The Edison Institute School system in Greenfield Village, a $10 million investment in education, provided instruction from the first grade through the second year of college. These schools accommodated as many as three hundred students and charged no tuition whatsoever. This was perhaps Henry's greatest single educational adventure. The Greenfield Village grounds, now open to the public, were originally the institute's private campus.[1]

EDISON INSTITUTE SCHOOLS

From its very beginning, the Edison Institute was predominantly a system of schools using museum-type buildings as learning laboratories. Among the first buildings brought to Greenfield Village was the Scotch Settlement School, which Henry Ford first attended in 1871 and from which he dropped out in 1879. The Scotch Settlement School was put to use for classroom instruction in September 1929 just before the incorporation of the Edison Institute and the dedication of Greenfield Village and Henry Ford Museum in October 1929. During the 1930s the Greenfield Village School System expanded to consist of kindergarten and several grade schools, the Edison Institute High School, and the Edison Institute of Technology.

Also within supervisory range of the Edison Institute were at least fifteen district schools located within one hundred miles of Dearborn in rural areas of southeastern Michigan where Henry Ford owned considerable land and was paying most school expenses either directly or indirectly. In more distant locations were several more schools, less directly supervised from Dearborn, but benefiting from Edison Institute leadership and guidance. These schools in northern Michigan and in Bryan County, Georgia, were heavily subsidized in one way or another by Henry Ford.

Although the number and quality of Edison Institute–directed schools had expanded rapidly in the 1930s, the influence of Henry Ford and the Edison Institute were to diminish in the late 1940s and nearly disappear in the 1950s. Most of the outlying schools reverted to purely public operation, and the last of the Greenfield Village schools to survive was the Scotch Settlement School, which ceased formal operation in 1969.

The Edison Institute and Related Schools
Greenfield Village School Buildings
  Ann Arbor House (kindergarten)
  McGuffey School (early elementary)
  Scotch Settlement (late elementary)
  Town Hall (late elementary)
  Miller (elementary)
  Edison Institute High School
  Edison Institute of Technology
  Clinton Inn (cafeteria, now called the Eagle
    Tavern)
  Webster House (home economics)
  Secretary House (home economics)
  Armington Sims (industrial arts)
Henry Ford Hospital
  Convalescent School

Henry Ford (right) with Joseph Rycraft in the summer of 1906 recalling their school days at the Scotch Settlement School. At least thirty Fords attended Scotch Settlement, including Henry Ford's mother, Mary Litogot. This building was moved to and restored at Greenfield Village in 1929. (0-411)

Southeastern Michigan Rural District Schools
  Wayne County
  Cherry Hill (elementary)
  Nankin Mills (elementary)
  Willow Run (elementary)
    Lenawee County
  Brownville (elementary)
  Centennial (elementary)
  Comfort (elementary)
  Green Lane Academy (elementary)
  Waring (elementary)
  Macon High School
  Macon Town School (elementary)
  Pennington (elementary)
  Mills (elementary)
    Washtenaw County
  Rawsonville (elementary)
  Saline
Michigan Upper Peninsula Schools
  Pequaming (high school and elementary)
  Alberta (elementary)
Sudbury, Massachusetts, Wayside Inn Schools
  Boys School (agricultural trade school)
  Southwest School (elementary)
  Redstone—Mary's Little Lamb (elementary)

Bryan County, Georgia, Schools
  Community High School, Ways, Georgia
  George Washington Carver Institute
  Cherry Hill (elementary)
  Strathy Hill (elementary)
  Rabbit Hill (elementary)
  Port Royal (elementary)
  Oak Level (elementary)
  Fancy Hall (elementary)
  Park Hill (elementary)
  Dixie-Daniel (elementary)

SCOTCH SETTLEMENT AND MILLER SCHOOLS

The Scotch Settlement and Miller schools deserve special mention because Henry Ford attended them both as a boy. These two buildings are now in Greenfield village. They are furnished as Henry Ford remembered them. Henry's father was at one time or another on the school board of each of these schools.

Both schools were put to use as grade schools in the Greenfield Village school system during the time the Edison Institute schools were flourishing.

The Edison Institute teaching museum and classroom building as it appeared October 6, 1934. A separate structure housed the ballroom, gymnasium, and swimming pool. (188-11301-D)

Now each of the buildings is used as a Greenfield Village demonstration school. Scotch Settlement is provided with an instructor to conduct brief, old-fashioned classes to tourists. Miller School is available by appointment to elementary school teachers who bring their classes to experience an entire day in a one-room school—in period costume preferably.

THE McGUFFEYS

Although Henry Ford never met the McGuffeys, the concepts the two men expressed in their nineteenth-century textbooks made a profound impression on young Henry as a student. This Eclectic Educational Series, more commonly known as the McGuffey Readers, of which 125 million copies were sold, provided training in spelling, phonetics, grammar, and classic English literature along with a dash of conservative political philosophy. And perhaps even more important, the books presented instruction in character attributes such as aspiration, responsibility, honesty, fairness, and charity.[2]

Henry Ford desired to pass these fundamental values he had learned on to younger generations. He ordered thousands of reprints of the 1867 edition of the readers, gave them to young people, and distributed them to schools and libraries. The Greenfield Village schools used the primer and readers in their classes through the sixth year.

In 1934 Henry Ford moved the circa-1780 log birthplace of William Holmes McGuffey (1800–1873) from its original Washington County, Pennsylvania, location to Greenfield Village. And with logs from the McGuffey farm, a one-room school building was constructed, now known as the McGuffey School.

The brothers, William Holmes McGuffey and Alexander Hamilton McGuffey, (1816–96), had collaborated in writing the Eclectic Series. Alexander, the younger brother, with the help of two wives (in succession) fathered fifteen children. The youngest of the children, Kingsley Rich MacGuffey [sic] (1880–1859), was induced by Ford to move to Dearborn in 1935. Kingsley MacGuffey and his wife Sarah had one son, Henry (1929–50), who attended the Greenfield Village schools at Ford's invitation.

Lower elementary classes were held in the replica McGuffey School from 1934 until regular schooling in the village was ended after Ford's death. Visit-ing classes now occasionally use the school building, and there is a brisk sale of McGuffey Readers in the Village and Museum gift shops.

WORKERS ENGLISH SCHOOL

At Highland Park, where Model T production was breaking records during 1914, Henry Ford was hiring new men in droves. More than one-third of these men were recent arrivals to the United States from countries such as Hungary, Italy, Poland, and Russia. They could not read or write English, and could barely understand spoken English. They thus could not carry out instructions presented in English, and were therefore inefficient in their work. To improve these men, Henry Ford organized classes in English, which would not only help them in their work but would help them and their families adjust to life in the United States.[3]

Classes in reading, writing, and speaking English were held at the factory; instruction was by plant employees who had had teaching experience. These sessions were outside working hours; instructors worked without extra pay. Lessons included training in United States naturalization requirements; classes often culminated in massive citizenship ceremonies conducted especially for Ford English School graduates.

Enrollment reached more than 2,200 with 150 instructors involved. Students representing fifty-five nationalities attended lessons for an average of six to eight months to complete the course. Upon graduation, students were presented with diplomas, which were accepted by the United States district officials at Detroit entitling the holder to his first papers without further examination. As many as six thousand foreign-born Ford employees celebrated Americanization Day at Detroit's City Hall at one time. These classes continued through 1915, providing Ford Motor Company with a relatively stable and appreciative workforce.[4]

OUGHTRINGTON HALL

The Fords, Henry, Clara and Edsel, visited England during the summer of 1912 and located the

Workers at classes in front of the Ford Motor Company plant in Highland
Park in 1914. This English Language School prepared men for better jobs and
for U.S. citizenship. (0-4547)

birthplace of Martha Bench, Clara's mother, at War-
wick. Two years later, while war was raging in Europe, the Fords became aware of the plight of Belgian
refugees who had fled their country and were homeless in England.

With the help of Percival L. D. Perry, head of
the Ford plant at Manchester, the Fords leased Oughtrington Hall and its thirty acres of land. This estate
was near Warrington, between Liverpool and Manchester, not a great distance from Clara's mother's
birthplace. The mansion was renovated, furnished,
and opened in fall 1914 to accommodate ninety refugees including families with children. Among the refugees was a Catholic priest, a doctor, a chemist
(pharmacist), a tailor, dressmaker, and shoemaker.
Farm acreage with implements and livestock supplied by Henry Ford allowed production of considerable food for the group.

For the children, a teacher, schoolroom, and
playground equipment were provided. Trades were
taught to adult refugees. Many of the refugees were
eventually able to find work and living quarters with
relatives and friends in Britain. The Fords gave about

ten thousand dollars a year to Oughtrington Hall for
operating expenses, spending a total of more than
one hundred thousand dollars for rent of the estate,
food, shelter, clothing, and schooling for nearly four
years before the home was closed near the end of the
war in 1918. Final assets of the Ford Belgian Refugee
Home, amounting to several thousand dollars, were
turned over to the Manchester Belgian Refugee Committee. In May 1920 most of this money was accred-
ited to "societies in Belgium for the relief of distress."[5]

TRADE SCHOOLS

In Henry Ford's mind, a working knowledge of
industrial arts was the most practical knowledge a
city boy could have. To this end Ford established several schools where he could offer boys a technical
education fitting them for responsible work in industry. His first and major trade school was begun at

Highland Park in 1916; the trade school boys became the envy of many a Detroit high school student as well as most adult workers in the Ford Highland Park plant. The training the boys received qualified them for the most demanding of industrial responsibilities.

Classes not only emphasized the mechanical arts leading to tool-and-die making but also included English, history, drafting, chemistry, physics, metallurgy, and bookkeeping. Class work alternated biweekly with shop practice.[6] Wages, less than adult wages, were paid for the shop work done. Graduating students were offered positions with Ford Motor Company, but some graduates chose to work for other firms where wages might have been higher. Ford did not seem to resent some of his students leaving his company. He had helped the young man, and that was his prime consideration.[7]

Ford trade schools like that in Highland Park were later established at the Rouge plant in Dearborn and at the Dagenham plant of Ford of Britain. And in all the many schools Ford sponsored, he insisted there be facilities and instructors for training young men in shop practice. This was true from Richmond Hill, Georgia, to Borehan, England, to Fordlandia and Belterra in Brazil.

THE SUNDAY LADY OF POSSUM TROT[8]

About fifty miles north and west of Atlanta, Georgia, are seven hills to which in 1834 the name Rome was logically applied. In the area just beyond Rome a large and prosperous plantation named Oak Hill was developed by a Capt. Thomas Berry, who fought and lost with the Confederates but whose credit reputation was such that he was able to reestablish himself in Southern splendor.

One of the six daughters of Thomas Berry was Martha, who attended the local one-room school; after completing an additional year of finishing school in Baltimore, she returned to the plantation where her interest solidly remained. One Sunday while Martha was playing the piano in the one-room log school (Possum Trot), three small boys stopped to listen. She was so shocked by their poverty and their extreme ignorance that she decided then and there to start a Sunday Bible school, offering as an inducement a warm meal. This was the beginning of a forty-five-year effort by her in educating rural youth.

Miss Berry's objective was to offer poor farm boys a chance to attend school regardless of their

Trade School boys leaving the Highland Park school in May 1927. The school (fitted with awnings) was adjacent to the Ford factory buildings at right. (833-49096)

means—if they were willing to work for their tuition and board. Her goal was "to teach education to wear overalls." A good education should be available to these poor farm boys who could not afford to go away to school.[9]

In 1901 her father died, leaving the plantation house and five hundred acres of land as her share. In 1902 the Berry School was formally opened, and Martha built a small dormitory and a few cabins for instructors. There being few rural public schools in Georgia then meant education was not a recognized necessity, and Miss Berry was on her own.

Everyone, including instructors, helped work the farmland. Farm crops were to provide the income necessary for operating the school. Miss Berry soon realized the crops alone would not provide enough, and began her lifelong career of soliciting donations to make the unusual concept succeed. Among the early large contributors was Andrew Carnegie. It was in 1921 that Miss Berry met the Fords unexpectedly at the home of the Thomas Edisons in West Orange, New Jersey. Miss Berry invited Ford's wife to visit. By that time Berry Schools had schools for both boys and girls, each having separate facilities. Clara Ford wanted to visit the girls' facilities.[10]

On their first visit, the Fords were served their noon meal in the school dining room by the girls. After the meal, Clara Ford saw the clean but austere kitchen and remarked that they deserved a better stove. That was the beginning. For the next twenty years the Fords were major benefactors of Berry Schools. Clara Ford not only upgraded the kitchen but also donated money for an entire girls' dormitory costing more than $1 million. It was named Clara Hall. Plans for an impressive dining hall were considered at this same time. The two buildings were completed in 1927, when Berry School became Berry College.

Henry Ford was no less impressed by the schools. The principles "earn while you learn" and "learn by doing" were dear to Henry's heart. His factory trade schools operated on those principles. He immediately asked the school to sell its twenty teams of mules, offering to replace the mules with twenty Fordson tractors. He provided a brick factory, gave them several new trucks, and equipped an automotive shop.

Within another few years Ford paid for a large Ford classroom building with adjoining library and auditorium. The Henry Ford Chapel was also built,

as were a gymnasium and recreation hall. In 1938 Mary Hall, another dormitory, this one named for Henry Ford's mother and equivalent to Clara Hall, was the last of the major buildings in the Ford group. Clara had given more than $1 million and Henry at least $3 million.[11]

The Fords visited Berry College many times on the way from Dearborn to and from Richmond Hill, Georgia. Food, charcoal briquettes, fertilizer, and other supplies were ordered by Ford to be shipped by the carload to Berry College at Mount Berry. Ford on occasion brought his old-time orchestra and dancing instructor, Benjamin Lovett, to Berry College to demonstrate and teach dancing to the students.

The Fords visited Berry College in the spring of 1947, just weeks before Henry died at Dearborn on April 7. As a token of appreciation, Clara Ford, in May 1947 was granted the degree of Doctor of Humanities. Only Martha Berry, then deceased, had ever been granted this distinguished degree by the college. Berry College now accommodates more than fifteen hundred students and offers graduate degrees in liberal arts, science, and business administration.[12]

WAYSIDE INN SCHOOLS

There were three schools on Ford property in the South Sudbury district of Massachusetts. Henry Ford had purchased the Wayside Inn in September 1923, and soon after 2,667 acres of surrounding land. On this property he not only restored the 1686 Wayside Inn made famous by Longfellow's *Tales of a Wayside Inn* but also a gristmill, a sawmill and a blacksmith shop, all near the inn.[13]

To provide schooling for the children of his Wayside Inn employees, Ford in 1926 resurrected the old Redstone Schoolhouse built in 1798, which once had been painted red. Legend supported the contention that Mary and her little lamb had attended this school. The school, originally District 2 of Sterling, Massachusetts, was moved to the Wayside Inn location, rebuilt, and renamed the Little Red Schoolhouse. Whether Mary and her lamb had really attended the school is still not certain, but Henry Ford presumed she had, and oversaw reenactment of the scene with a 1927 Mary and live, fleecy lamb. The ceremony was attended with much ado and many photographers. The school was small even for a one-

An aerial view of the Ford buildings at Martha Berry Schools, Mount Berry, Georgia. (0-9232)

room school. In it one teacher taught about a dozen pupils.[14]

The next school to be opened by Ford on Wayside property was a boys' boarding school. It started in 1928 with thirty boys from Boston. The main goal of the school was the "development of character and the preparation of boys for their future careers." The school started with a one-year curriculum, advancing to a four-year agricultural program in 1933. Called the Wayside Inn Boys' School, enrollment reached forty to fifty, with at least five instructors employed.

The third school, the Southwest School, had been built about 1800, and had been used as a school for about one hundred years before being destroyed by fire. The foundation was on the newly acquired Ford property. From detailed sketches provided by former students, the fairly large one-room frame school was rebuilt on the original site in 1930 to serve pupils from the town of Sudbury. One teacher, paid by Henry Ford, handled the fifth, sixth, seventh, and eighth grades. Graduating classes of about six students went into Sudbury for their eighth-grade examinations. It is understood they passed with high honors.

The Wayside Inn properties are reported to have cost Ford $2,848,177 during 1923 to 1945. The cost of his three schools was a large part of this cost.[15]

LINCOLN MEMORIAL UNIVERSITY

Henry Ford had had considerable difficulty obtaining a steady coal supply for his automobile plant at Highland Park. To free himself of this dependence on other people's railroads and coal mines, he bought in 1920 the Detroit, Toledo and Ironton Railroad through Ohio, and coal mines in Ohio, Kentucky, and West Virginia. One of these mines in southeastern Kentucky, the Banner Fork, was near the Cumberland Gap in the Appalachian chain. Just through the gap near Harrogate, Tennessee, was Lincoln Memorial University, a school for mountain children operating on a basis like that of Berry Schools.

Assistance to this school began in 1926 when Ford contributed implement repair shop equipment amounting to $1272.26. In January 1927 Stanley Rud-diman, then president of the D. T. & I. and his wife visited the school and arranged to give them $4,326.53 worth of materials consisting of tractors, an automobile, and Estey organ, farm equipment, fertilizer, a Radiola, and Victrola. In February of the same year, Ford bought for the school's use the Lon Overton Farm of two hundred acres, the consideration being $40,000 plus $451.98 expenses. This property was conveyed to the university in 1933.

Lincoln Memorial University was involved to some extent in the program of the Edison Botanic Research Corporation to investigate goldenrod as a domestic source of commercial rubber. The program, we now know, was unsuccessful. The university, in 1936, received a new school bus from Ford, who by then had disbursed about $50,000 in their behalf. No more gifts are recorded in Ford records.

Henry Ford with pupils of the "little red schoolhouse" where "Mary and her little lamb" had presumably gone to school. The lamb in the picture had taken part in the January 1927 reenactment directed by Henry Ford. (188-7955)

The Ford Naval School for the training of machinist mates during World War II. Their workshop was the Rouge plant, a portion of which is in the background. A similar school for aircraft trainees was operated by Ford at the Willow Run plant in Ypsilanti, Michigan. (833-74681-329)

NAVAL SERVICE SCHOOL

The largest of the many Ford instructional programs during World War II was the United States Navy Service School at the Rouge plant in Dearborn. A year before Pearl Harbor, on December 6, 1940, ground was broken for the training of navy men to become machinist's mates. Within forty days of the start of construction the first contingent of 150 students took up quarters in the first barracks building. There would soon be eight barracks, each with 250 bunks, to accommodate two thousand men. Related facilities included an administration building, mess hall, galley, recreation building, canteen, reading room, and a power plant for steam and electricity. A sixty-bed hospital was soon added.[16]

The land was owned by Ford Motor Company, which built and equipped the buildings at its own expense. The school was then leased to the navy for one dollar per year. Rear Adm. C. W. Nimitz, chief of the Bureau of Navigation, accepted the facility for the navy, and Comdr. William E. Miller was put in charge of the school.

After six to eight weeks of recruit training at a naval station and another month of basic training at the Service School Training Station at Great Lakes,

Illinois, the students were enrolled at the Ford facility. Students had been assigned by competitive selection. The training at the Rouge—a twelve hundred-acre workshop—was normally for ninety days. During this time the students would be taught the mechanical arts by Ford instructors, but under the disciplinary command of navy officers.

Training consisted of eight hours lecture per week and thirty-two hours of shop work. Experience was obtained in the operation of machines such as lathes, drill presses, milling machines, and shapers. After one month of experience on a machine, a student would help a beginner on the same machine, thus acting as instructor. One Ford instructor could oversee ten such combinations. Training was also offered in carpentry, pattern making and foundry practice. Many trainees were prepared for Pratt-Whitney aircraft engine maintenance at the Ford engine plant, and an advanced course of three months was provided machinist's and electrical mates in diesel engine principles.

Back at the barracks, orders were given by loudspeakers—there were no general assemblies. There was, however, a recreation building where eleven hundred men could be seated for biweekly movies and Sunday chapel services. Navy cooks and bakers prepared food for two thousand. Facilities for football, baseball, volleyball, and soccer were provided. Every two weeks a thirty-six-hour leave was enjoyed. Before Pearl Harbor, 2,450 had graduated. The school continued throughout the war.

OTHER SCHOOLS

The schools described in this chapter are merely representative of the great variety sponsored by the Fords. More examples have been omitted than have been included. Practically every Ford manufacturing plant has had its apprentice school, and nothing has been said of the Ford schools for veterans of World War I and World War II.

Besides the schools Henry Ford operated on his own property, there were at least thirty-two other educational institutions to which Henry and Clara Ford donated sizeable gifts. These gifts included several foreign contributions such as to the China Mass Education Movement, the Beirut College Patriarchal, Royal Hungarian Universities, and Pekin University. The millions of dollars and thousands of hours contributed by the Fords to education are inestimable.[17]

NOTES

1. *A Home for Our Heritage* (Dearborn: Henry Ford Museum Press, 1979), 180 pp.
2. Harvey C. Minnich, *William Holmes McGuffey and His Readers* (New York and Cincinnati: American Book Company, 1936), 180 pp.
3. "Assimilation through Education," *Ford Times* (June 1915): 406–11.
4. "The Making of Americans," *Ford Times* (November 1915): 150–52.
5. "Oughtrington Hall," Vertical File, Archives, HFM&GV.
6. *Henry Ford Trade School* (Dearborn: Henry Ford Trade School, 1950).
7. "Henry Ford Trade School," 44 pages, 1948, Vertical File, Archives, HFM&GV.
8. Tracy Byers, *Martha Berry: The Sunday Lady of Possum Trot* (New York: G. P. Putnam's Sons, 1932).
9. Margaret Jean Hindman, "The Berry Schools," *Herald* 3 (January 22, 1937): 8.
10. "Berry Schools," Acc. 1, Box 44, Archives, HFM&GV.
11. L. J. Thompson Records, Acc. 884, Archives, HFM&GV.
12. John L. Sibley, address, presentation of Doctor of Humanities, Berry College, Rome, Georgia, 1947.
13. Nevins and Hill, *Expansion and Challenge*, pp. 498–99; Lewis, *Public Image*, p. 225–26.
14. "The Wayside Inn Schools," *Herald* 1 (May 18, 1934): 8.
15. Nevins and Hill, *Expansion and Challenge*, p. 499.
16. "The Navy Goes to School," *Ford News* 20 (November 1941): 283–87.
17. See Thompson, Acc. 884, Archives, HFM&GV.

19

THE RICHMOND HILL EXPERIMENT

The town of Richmond Hill is seventeen miles south of Savannah, Georgia, just off I-95 after crossing the Ogeechee River. It may seem of little consequence now, but fifty years ago this area was the scene of dramatic social and economic revolution under the guidance of mentor Henry Ford.[1]

It is said the Fords, in 1925, were tiring of their winter home in Fort Myers, Florida, because of the heat, dampness, and lack of privacy. Years earlier (1917) Ford had explored the Georgia coast by yacht with his close friend and traveling companion, John Burroughs, who had remarked that Georgia's Ogeechee country was less damp, the timber magnificent, and there was excellent birding. In 1925 the Fords again docked at Savannah and were induced to visit an old plantation site on the Ogeechee River, where, in a setting of giant live oaks, Ford's wife decided she would like a southern-style winter home.

Records show that in March 1925 agents for Ford bought one hundred acres and had obtained options to buy more land in that section of Bryan County known as Bryan Neck. This is a peninsula bounded by the Great Ogeechee, Florida Passage, and Belfast rivers with more than fifty miles of riverfront. This section of Georgia had once consisted of prosperous rice and cotton plantations on land granted by King James of England in the early eighteenth century. The early prosperity was not only be-cause of the rich, moist soil and warm sun but also because of the labor of hundreds of slaves.

During the Civil War the Bryan Neck territory was known as the "bread basket of the confederacy" and became a principal target of Sherman's March to the Sea. After the war, the plantations were ne-glected and some were abandoned.

When Ford started to buy the Georgia property, his agents tried to disguise the name of the buyer, but this was not possible for long. As soon as news-papers discovered his identity, they wanted to know the purpose of his buying the land. Ford interests de-cided that the newspapers should be told that Ford was buying land at several locations in the United States to test his tractors.

When one of Ford's agents (R. L. Cooper of Sa-vannah) suggested that a piece of property would be a good investment, Ford told him that he was not trying to make money—that he was already making more than he could use in the automobile business. A clue to Ford's intentions was evident in another conversation with the same agent when Ford asked what most of the residents did for a living. The agent replied that they "make moonshine liquor," to which Ford responded that he did not blame them much, but that it was his intention to give them a better op-portunity. During these early land acquisitions more than fifty stills were confiscated, and it became Ford's

Aerial view of business section of Richmond Hill, about 1940. Lumber mill and Atlantic Coast Line Railway are in foreground. Upper left are garage, commissary, and office buildings. Upper center is the Consolidated School. Upper right are chapel and community building. (0-6716)

objective to give these deposed men honest work with which to support their families.

For almost ten years land was acquired until about seventy-five thousand acres were owned and known as Ford Farms. This tract included most of the town of Ways Station, Georgia, where both the Seaboard and Atlantic Coast Line railroads had stations and where there was a school, a general store, and a post office. The tract also included several smaller settlements and nearly twenty old plantations, one being Chisholm (twenty-three hundred acres), which included Fort McAllister of Civil War fame. There were also many small plots totaling about 530 parcels. Ford intended to buy St. Catherine's Island, which was for sale for $750,000. But when the owner found that it was Henry Ford who was interested, the price was raised to $1 million. This disgusted Ford and there was no deal.

Not until 1935 did Henry and Clara Ford decide exactly where and how to build their winter home. The location was to be the Richmond Plantation site on a bluff overlooking the Great Ogeechee River. The building was to resemble Savannah's famous Hermitage, using the Savannah gray bricks taken from the abandoned mansion on the Savannah River just a few miles north of the city. (Two of the slave huts from the Hermitage Plantation were moved to Greenfield Village where they are on display.)

In anticipating the view from his new homesite, Henry envisioned the possibility of shoddy boat sheds being erected on the opposite bank of the river. He asked his agent to buy 150 acres directly across the river from Richmond to protect his view. The owner of the property would sell no fewer than 4,023 acres—the entire plantation of Vallambrosia in Chatham County. Thus it too became part of Ford Farms.

While overseeing the building of their home, the Fords were accommodated at Ways in their private railroad car, the Fair Lane. Clara, in particular, enjoyed planning the house. When not in Georgia she worked with a wooden model of the proposed building, having scale-model furnishings made to help her choose the most appropriate full-scale pieces. Much of the furniture for the new home was then selected from the Henry Ford Museum in Dearborn and shipped to Ways. (The fully furnished wooden model is now displayed in the Henry Ford Museum.) After the Georgia home was completed, the entire Georgia property was given the name Richmond Hill Plantation, and development of the area began in earnest.

View of the Ogeechee River from the veranda of the Richmond residence. By buying the 4,023-acre Vallambrosia Plantation across the river, Ford assured himself of a pleasant scene on the opposite bank. (0-6568)

Although the Fords stayed in Georgia but a month or so each spring, their annual visit, plus almost daily contact through their personal secretary, Frank Campsall, kept the plantation operating vigorously all year. Under a general manager, John (Jack) Gregory, a hardfisted native Georgian, the operations of lumbering, farming, housing, health, education, and even oystering were implemented.

Beginning in 1936 Ford was to build 292 buildings on his Richmond Hill property. The most costly would be his personal residence valued at $362,736. The sawmill was next most expensive, costing more than $100,000. Other sizeable investments were the community house ($47,000), maintenance garage ($31,000), powerhouse ($29,000), Carver School ($37,000), chapel ($28,000), ice plant ($28,000), commissary ($18,000), trade school and kindergarten

($13,000 each). Other community buildings included a post office, fire station, bakery, and health clinic. Eighty-five buildings were on his property at the time of his death in 1947—the total expense $933,642.

As Henry Ford observed the plight of the people living in that section of Georgia, he was convinced that education was the key to their future. Georgia law required segregation of blacks and whites. Equal but separate educational facilities were the rule but not necessarily the practice. Henry soon began to provide support to small outlying schools such as Port Royal, Oak Level, Cherry Hill, Brisborn, Park Hill, Fancy Hall, and Tucker Place. A school census counted 211 boys and 172 girls in the district of school age.

At Ways, a trade school building was one of the first construction projects. It had a power plant, a small sawmill, and a well-equipped machine shop for training boys in wood- and metal-working. The consolidated white school at Ways, completed in 1928 and drawing pupils by bus, provided a standard high school education. Ford next built a large community house housing kitchens, dining hall, and living quarters to provide live-in training in domestic arts for the girls. A school paper, dramatics, photography, music, and sports were added to the curriculum.

There had been seven small disorganized, ungraded schools for black children on the 120 square miles of Ford property. In these dilapidated buildings were offered seven to eight months of schooling per year providing a maximum attainment of perhaps sixth-grade level. Of these pupils, Ford stated, "They are all right. All they need is a chance, and we are going to give them a chance." In September 1939 a black principal (H. G. Cooper) was hired, and pupils were taken by bus to the chapel in Richmond Hill where the fall term was used to classify pupils into appropriate grades.

In the meantime a new school building for kindergarten through seventh grade was readied, and in March 1940 Dr. George Washington Carver, the noted agricultural scientist, was invited to dedicate the George Washington Carver School for Blacks. The Carver School started with 150 pupils and grew to nearly 300. This school was equivalent in size and equipment to the white Consolidated School, and each year a grade was added to allow students to proceed with their education. Here again, emphasis was on industrial arts and agriculture for the boys, and domestic arts for the girls. A hundred-acre garden plot behind the school was operated by the boys, who were paid for their work. Training in the social graces and hygiene were not overlooked. An adult education program emphasizing crafts also flourished at the Carver School during the early 1940s.

The schools were under the jurisdiction of the Bryan County Board of Education, but Ford was footing a good portion of the bill. As the schools began to exhibit a clean and efficient effect, so too did the children begin to take pride in their own appearance and skills. Ford built six small chapels like the one at Richmond Hill. They were close to his schools and were primarily for use by the students. Weekday morning prayer and musical services were planned and conducted by the pupils, under teacher guid-

Lawn dancing at the Richmond residence in the late 1930s. Ford's dancing instructor and musicians from Dearborn organized these events, which included some of the pupils who had been taught dancing at the Consolidated School. (0-4893)

The boys Trade School with its powerhouse on the left. The school was equipped with tools for making useful articles from either wood or metal. Students took home the items they made. (0-6558)

ance. Services were nondenominational and parents were welcome. There was seldom any preaching, but Sunday choral programs and frequent weddings often taxed the capacity of the building.

Perhaps the greatest contribution of Ford to this area of Georgia was his generous support of the Ways Station Health Clinic. Beginning in May of 1935 Ford assumed financial responsibility for the clinic, and provided for its expansion to accommodate three times as many patients. The population was suffering from abnormally high incidences of typhoid fever, syphilis, smallpox, diphtheria, hookworm, and malaria.

The fall of 1936 witnessed a serious epidemic of malaria. A November 1936 letter from the State of Georgia, Department of Health, started, "On the basis of information provided by the Ways Station Health Clinic, it is estimated that between 50 and 75 percent of the total population of the district suffered from malaria during the current 1936 malaria season, including a high proportion of estivo-autumnal (Black-Water) malaria." Nurses contracted the disease, as did Ford's chauffeur who was bedridden for weeks.

In January 1937 seventeen nurses were employed in a campaign to test and treat the entire population of the district. Of 682 whites, only .3 percent

The community house accommodated groups of girls who lived by the week in the dormitories and, besides going to regular school, made their own clothing, cooked and served their own meals, and learned table etiquette and ballroom dancing. (0-6557)

were found still infected and requiring treatment, but of 1,162 blacks, 11.6 percent needed treatment with the expensive Atabrine tablets. Two weeks later, tests were again taken with few found positive and needing treatment. In successive years treatment was continued, and by 1940 only one case was reported, the patient working for Ford Farms but living outside the district.

Dr. Holton, the clinic doctor, had told Ford that an estimated 90% of the people—adults and children—had hookworm. The program of eradication included medication, but depended primarily on improvements in sanitation. The main thrust was toward obtaining acceptance of the cement-enclosed privy specified by the county, and provided at no expense by Ford. Besides supporting the Ways Station Clinic, Ford hired nurses to teach sanitation to children in both black and white schools, and inaugurated a program of mosquito control by draining the old marshes and rice fields on his plantation.

Lumbering became the chief industry at Richmond Hill. Plantation acreage classified as timber amounted to forty-six thousand, of which most was pine and pulp-sized hardwood. There were also considerable gum and cypress. The volume of merchantable pine on the plantation was estimated to be 41 million cubic feet. Of this, about half was sawlog size,

and the rest mostly pulpwood. Some saw cuts were classified as piling and some as railroad ties. The timber operations were the only operations at Richmond Hill that consistently showed a profit.

Operation of the large Richmond Hill sawmill in 1939 allowed the beginning of a house-building program that would provide 207 new tenant houses within the next few years. Most of these buildings were in the residential developments of Richmond Hill and Blueberry Village. Several house designs were used, and sections of each design were preassembled at the mill so that complete houses could be erected on site in minimum time. Total time per house thus required but a few days rather than several weeks. Costs of houses averaged about thirty-five hundred dollars. Rent payments for these homes

The chapel and student body of the Consolidated School. There was a separate and similar chapel for pupils of the George Washington Carver School. (0-6566)

George Washington Carver School built to consolidate seven outlying black school districts from which pupils were brought by bus. (0-6559)

were ten to fifteen dollars per month for employees in 1941, but rose to thirty dollars for nonemployees in 1951. Some of the homes, however, were provided as part of an employee's salary, and some were offered to poor families for a token rent of one dollar. Older houses in poor condition were used by families rent free.

The sawmill also produced lumber for construction of the community house, the new schools, the chapel, and for several small black churches—"praise houses" they were called. Henry Ford's chapel erected near the Wayside Inn near Sudbury, Massachusetts, was prefabricated at Richmond Hill and shipped north. The sawmill eventually became heavily engaged in the manufacture of commercial door and window frames to be sold to building contractors.

The carpenter shop associated with the sawmill was first devoted primarily to the making of lettuce and tomato crates, wooden forms for hundreds of concrete fence posts, and occasionally a casket. *Little Lulu*, a twenty-eight-foot cabin cruiser powered by two V-8 automobile engines, was another carpenter shop product. Home furniture, school furniture, kindergarten toys, and church pews became popular specialties of the Richmond Hill carpenters.

Agricultural research was prominent at the plantation. In 1937 H. K. Ukkelberg, one of Thomas Edison's chemists who had worked at Fort Myers on rubber experiments, was hired by Ford to supervise the farm crops and direct the research laboratory. "We won't carry on the goldenrod work any more," he told Ukkelberg. "Just plant a little for sentimental reasons." Of ten thousand experimental plants tested by Edison, goldenrod had been found most promising as a source of domestic rubber. Edison had died in 1931. Ukkelberg's instructions were "to find new crops or better varieties of old crops grown in this section, and to develop new uses for these crops and for available waste materials."

Georgia's marshland soils were found to be too acid and lime additions were needed. Of the many crop experiments started, some of the more immediate included the extraction of starch from sweet potatoes and water chestnuts. Alcohol, made from sweet potatoes and from rice, was blended with gasoline for use as a motor fuel. About 350 varieties of soybeans (Henry's favorite crop) were grown and tested for oil content, resulting in selection of a variety yielding 22 percent oil, to which the name Seminole was given. Experiments with the spacing of soybeans in rows showed how to increase yields. Use of basic slag as a soil conditioner was found to increase yields of soybeans by 30 to 40 percent. More than 200 young tung trees were selected from which tung nuts were tested for oil content. Oil content ranged from forty to seventy percent; the high-yielding trees were then chosen for further propagation.

Perilla, an oil-producing plant, was grown for several years under various experimental conditions, none of which proved commercially successful. Other oil-producing crops were chia, castor beans, and abutilon. Crotolaria, a legume, was grown as green manure and as a possible source of cellulose for rayon and plastics. Other crops tried on the Georgia soils were buckwheat, sugarcane, ramie, dashcens (tavo), goldenrod, and tephrosia (a source of rotenone). Cotton varieties were compared for yield. Those mentioned included "stoneville," the Chinese "million dollar cotton," and "sea island."

On the reclaimed marshlands there were also experimental acreages of English peas, carrots, mustard, turnips, beets, broccoli, rutabagas, onions, cabbage, Irish potatoes, okra, cucumbers, and perilla as well as the cotton. Iceberg lettuce was raised on about 120 acres with fair results. In one season eighty-four hundred crates were sold at a profit of $12,122. A

Second and third grades at the George Washington Carver School. Henry Ford with the teacher (upper left) and Fred Gregory (upper right). (0-6717)

crop of gladiolus, consisting of 664 ½ dozen flowers, was reported as producing a profit of only $6.05 after calculating all costs. A shipment of 3,359 bags of Red Bliss potatoes brought $3,874. Although Ford did not anticipate profits, he wanted to prove that the plantation could be self-supporting.

A major effort was put forth in the use of forest wastes: bark, sawdust, and treetops. One goal was to produce a heavy denier, multitwisted type of rayon that would be suitable for tire fabric, belting, upholstery, and so on. A viscose rayon department was equipped in 1939; by 1940 it could produce small quantities of 150-denier, 40-filament thread from sweet gum wood pulp by using an alkaline cooking process. By sending the thread to a northern knitting mill, two dozen or so pairs of socks were knitted and samples sent to Ford. It was never determined whether the cost of mass-producing socks from wood pulp by this method would have met the then prevailing market price of $1.50 per dozen pairs. Another research project resulted in pilot-scale production of lignocellulose plastic tile made mainly from corncobs and sawdust. Samples of the dark-colored four-by-four-inch tile were sent to Ford for inspection. These projects were not carried to completion because the research laboratory burned in September 1941 and was not rebuilt. The war situation was to require that the emphasis be exclusively on food crops.

Lumbering and farming accounted for most of the workers. An examination of a typical 1939 payroll at Richmond Hill shows 351 white employees working four to eighty-four hours per week for an average weekly wage of $14.18. Rates ranged from 12.5¢ an hour for laborers, librarians, and cooks to $1 per hour for each of three brick masons and a Trade School instructor. Wages for 320 black employees, recorded on a separate payroll, ranged from 12.5¢ per hour to a maximum of 30¢ for black teachers. The average weekly wage for blacks was only $6.36. At this time, at the Dearborn Rouge plant, the standard wage for blacks and whites was 75¢ an hour, or $30 per week. Thus Richmond Hill was hardly a financial panacea for the working population of the region. It is said that Ford wanted to pay higher wages but was advised against it because of the ill will it might create among other employers.

Nevertheless, to quote Dr. Holton, the community physician in 1940, "Henry Ford, by means of his health clinic, his schools, and employment, has changed the population from a sickly, suspicious, il-

Ukkelberg, Ford, and Gregory examining plastic tile made from wood wastes. (0-4447)

literate and undernourished group into one of the healthiest communities in Georgia." And as one employee commented, "Contentment with your surroundings means more than a few extra dollars."

Motor trucks rolled back and forth between Richmond Hill and Dearborn throughout the year. Flowers, fresh fruits, and vegetables, together with Mrs. Bell's canned figs, were regularly forwarded to the Fords' home, Fair Lane. At Christmas time, mistletoe, holly, pecans, sweet potatoes, and specially cured hams enhanced festivities in the North. Going in the opposite direction, Ford often loaded his trucks with Ford-Portland cement for construction work and concrete fence posts at Ways. Before Ford visitations to Georgia, favorite breads, cakes, dairy products, books, phonograph records, sheet music, and other niceties were trucked south. The recipe for Scuppernong grape wine had been furnished far in advance.

There was much excitement at the plantation when the Fords and their party were to arrive. Fifty additional people were hired by Gregory to handle the extra work of cleaning, cooking, serving, arranging flowers, and keeping the grounds neat and trimmed. Old-fashioned dances would be performed on the mansion lawn. And every nook and cranny of every building had to be ready for a glance from Ford, who was fast of foot and sharp of eye, known to shown up at unexpected times and places, ready to talk to whomever was about.

One of the many charitable deeds of Clara Ford concerned an elderly black lady known as Old Aunt

Jane. Janie Lewis, who had once been a slave, lived in a hovel with no income. Clara Ford provided a small, modernly furnished home for her alongside her old home, and arranged for food, clothing, and medical care for the rest of her life. Henry Ford was likewise sensitive to the needs of the deserving of the community. In particular, physically handicapped men were given employment. Ford believed that any man could earn a living if given an opportunity. Crippled people, young and old, who he thought could benefit from treatment in the Ford Hospital in Detroit, were sent there for stays as long as a year, if necessary, with expenses paid.

To show their appreciation for what the Fords had done for the community, the residents launched a campaign to have the name Ways Station changed to Richmond Hill. This required considerable negotiation with the two railroads and the U.S. Postal Department. But it was finally accomplished, and celebrated with great fanfare on May 1, 1941.

Progress on the plantation was just nicely under way when World War II began to affect operations seriously. Several hundred acres were taken by the army for Camp Stewart. A location and easement were provided for an aircraft guidance cross beam. *Little Lulu*, the all-purpose cabin cruiser, was requisi-

The Fords built a new home beside Aunt Jane's old home. They supplied new furnishings, food, and medical care for the rest of Aunt Jane's life. (0-6609)

tioned by the coast guard for patrol duty. The steady flow of new cars, trucks, and tractors from Dearborn was interrupted. Government regulations about materials, manpower, wages, rents, and new taxes made life much more difficult for Gregory and the Dearborn accountants. Priorities were needed to obtain required maintenance materials. And Henry, now seventy-eight years old, was almost completely occupied elsewhere with production of bombers, tanks, gliders, Jeeps, and so on.

In the spring of 1945, Ford suffered a stroke. This situation was not publicized. However, control of Richmond Hill then became largely Clara Ford's responsibility, and things were never again the same. In late 1945 a lengthy financial appraisal of the Richmond Hill operations called for drastic reduction in expenses. The sawmill workweek was reduced to forty hours; cost of upkeep of Fort McAllister and several small private cemeteries was questioned. *Little Lulu* was sold to save upkeep expense, and school graduation classes no longer made their annual pilgrimage to Dearborn.

The year 1946 saw more severe changes. There was serious questioning whether operation of the plantation would continue. In March, while at Richmond Hill, Frank Campsall died. And Clara Ford dismissed John Gregory, naming Ray Newman from the Dearborn Ford Farms as superintendent. Clara Ford had not liked Gregory, and when he indicated to her that Henry Ford had verbally promised him the property known as Belfast as a gift, she denied there was such a promise although she possessed a copy of the deed signed by Ford. Newman's orders were to show a profit. The Trade School was closed in June, as was the community house schooling for girls. Costs were being drastically reduced, and the entire property might have been sold had Ford not been living.

The next year witnessed Henry Ford's death at Dearborn in April, shortly following his Richmond Hill visit. His will bequeathed the entire property, except the main residence, to the Ford Foundation. A 1948 appraisal of the property was close to $3 million. At the time of Ford's death, he had invested $4,267,000 in Richmond Hill Plantation. According to income tax returns he had lost $3,525,600 on plantation operation, and had contributed $429,235 for school purposes. Clara Ford indicated that she would like to see the farm and forest operations continued for the good of the people in the area. She deplored the suggestion that the community house become a

Conversation between Ford and Will Showers, who had been hired as watchman on the Ford Farms after he had lost his leg in a sawmill accident elsewhere. (0-6556)

public inn. She did not want the property "commercialized," she said.

Ray Newman, as administrator of Henry Ford's estate, handled the business of closing down operations. Farm and lumber work continued, however, until after Clara's death in September 1950 and after the removal of Richmond household furnishings back to Fair Lane in Dearborn. The final blow to operations came when the sawmill burned on May 11, 1951, for a loss of $275,890. Benson Ford announced complete discontinuance of operations in a letter to employees dated September 6, 1951. School properties were deeded to the Bryan County Board of Education by the four grandchildren of Henry and Clara Ford, as heirs. Powerhouse boilers were treated for standby; forty-three cars and trucks and eight tractors were transferred to the Ford Foundation, and Clara Ford's 1940 Lincoln Zephyr Brunn Town Car sold.

Plantation utilities were cancelled, Dr. Holton's bill paid, and the new proprietors, Southern Kraft Timberland Corporation, took possession from the Ford Foundation on November 28, 1951. Accounts were kept through March 30, 1952, when Newman prepared his "final receipt." Newman's pay continued through June 1952. The final files, temporarily stored in the firehouse at Richmond Hill, were shipped to Dearborn in November 1952.

Of the twenty-six years that the Fords owned the Georgia property, the most enjoyable must have been limited to as few as four or five. These would have been the years 1937, when the residence was furnished and first occupied, through 1941 when the war began to curtail vacation time and pleasure.

These years were undoubtedly most productive as well as pleasurable at Richmond Hill. The Fords had delighted in the locality because of the privacy it had provided. Clara Ford said that they were not "locked in" at Richmond Hill as they were elsewhere; that they were free to move about in safety and without the publicity usually entailed. Local residents remarked that Henry Ford had every appearance of being a boy again as he darted from one point of interest to another. Clara Ford loved especially the home and gardens. Henry enjoyed the powerhouse and sawmill in particular. But most significant, together they knew they were materially helping an appreciative community.[1]

Henry Ford relaxing on the steps of the Richmond residence. (0-415)

NOTE

1. The material in this chapter is taken entirely from the archives of the Henry Ford Museum & Greenfield Village where abundant and detailed records of these Georgia operations are preserved. See "Guide to the Records of Richmond Hill Plantation, Richmond Hill, Georgia 1925–1952," compiled by Ford R. Bryan, 1983, 100 pp.

INDEX

Page numbers of illustrations are in italics

Ford R. Bryan is now a historical researcher at the library and archives of the Henry Ford Museum & Greenfield Village. He holds the M.S. degree from the University of Michigan. After working as a spectrochemical analyst in the manufacturing research department of Ford Motor Company, Bryan became supervisor of analytical spectroscopy at the Ford Scientific Laboratory. He has published more than seventy technical papers relating to optical spectroscopy. His other publications include historical articles and a book, *The Fords of Dearborn*.

The manuscript was edited by Thomas B. Seller. The book was designed by Mary Primeau. The typeface for the text and the display face is Palatino.

The book is printed on 70-lb. Meade Moistrite Matte paper and is bound in Roxite B-grade cloth.

Manufactured in the United States of America.